Things I Wish My Mother Had Told Me

Things I Wish My Mother Had Told Me

Lessons in Grace and Elegance

LUCIA VAN DER POST

JOHN MURRAY

First published in Great Britain in 2007 by John Murray (Publishers)
An Hachette Livre UK company

3

A CIP catalogue record for this title is available from the British Library

ISBN 978-0-7195-6668-4

Book Design by Janette Revill
Typeset in Adobe Caslon by Palimpsest Book Production Limited, Grangemouth, Stirlingshire

Printed and bound by Clays Ltd, St Ives plc

John Murray (Publishers)
338 Euston Road
London NW1 3BH

www.johnmurray.co.uk

For my family, who matter more and more as the years go by, and in memory of my own mother, whose grace and dignity in the face of life's adversities taught me much.

Contents

Introduction

To start at the beginning: I'm not young. I've got two grown-up children and five very small, very much loved grandchildren (all boys, since you ask). Whilst I'm not too attached to some of the things that come with being the age I am (problems with the waistline, sagging, wrinkles, finally giving up on the notion that I might one day do a long trek in the Hindu Kush), there are, when I count them, lots of good things that come with having survived more than a decade or two.

Firstly, if you've been lucky enough to have lived my sort of life, which has had an inside ring seat on a fascinating period of womanhood – the arrival of the very first tights, the miniskirt, the power suit, the rise of women up the corporate ladder, at the stock exchange, in the law courts and up into space, right through to the present day – then you have, perforce, picked up a few savvy hints along the way. Since it seems a shame for all of us to have to learn everything from scratch, to make all the discoveries the hard way, to reinvent, so to speak, the wheel, this book is an attempt to pass on some of the things I've learned in life.

In the course of a tremendously full journalistic career, I've been lucky enough to have had easy access to many an eminent expert – beauty gurus, emperors and empresses of the fashion world, surgeons specialising in nips and tucks, masters of the art of cobbling, specialists in nutrition and spiritual healing, fine cooks, top-notch designers and decorating fundis – and I've learned something from them all. I've also got a bit cannier at sifting what seems like good sense from the hot air and downright guff. I hesitate to call it wisdom, which sounds so self-congratulatory and smug, but all of us who are lucky enough to live so long (*so* much better than the alternative) do, out of self-protection, garner a little more nous and insight with the years.

Of all the things I've learned, it is that grace and generosity of spirit are essential ingredients to the well-lived life. They add a certain elegance to the most mundane encounter, let alone to life's more major dramas. I don't mean elegance of the merely superficial kind – though that, too, is not without its charms. I mean the sort of elegance that, if we looked into it, we would discover is rooted in some kind of moral code. Kindness is elegant. Malice and cruelty are not. Warmth and generosity are elegant. Coldness and jealousy are not. Touchiness and being quick to take offence isn't elegant either. (My father always had a motto: 'Darling,' he used to say, 'never, ever be offended. Only small people take offence.') Social snobbery – which is rooted in a belief that material values, such as money and worldly status, are more important than human and moral worth – is not elegant. Nor is the sort of behaviour that finds it acceptable to be rude to those who cannot answer back whilst simultaneously being charming to those from whom favours may be expected.

But, above and beyond the inner things that make a difference, there are lots of practical tips I've picked up as I've coped with the modern woman's lot in life: too little money, too little time, children I love, jobs I've sometimes hated and mostly loved, a busy husband and his career, moving house and trying to keep hold of a sense of oneself as life hurtles by. I've made plenty of mistakes and there are lots of things I'd do differently if only I could. This book is an attempt to help others avoid making the same mistakes while doing things in ways that make them and those around them happier.

I've also learned that small things can make a lot of difference. Having family and friends we love and care about is all that most of us need to wake up with a smile. If we can then add some graceful flourishes to that sound foundation – if we can look good, feel well, enjoy our leisure, create a home that's filled with peace and some well-chosen decorative touches, good food that doesn't break one's back to serve, flowers, books and wine – we're almost there.

This book is mostly about the graceful flourishes, and it covers some of the things I wish I'd understood or known about a little earlier on. I hope it helps and I hope you find it fun.

How to Wear Clothes

How to Dress

Women have only two ages – girlhood and womanhood. Christian Dior

It was Oscar Wilde who said that only a fool doesn't judge people by appearances. He was right. How we look matters. It matters for all sorts of reasons. In the Western world we have to wear something every day and, whatever it is, you may be sure it tells the world something about you. It signals – more quickly than a lightning strike – whether we are fun, clever, elegant, shy, intellectual, dowdy, sloppy, showy . . . You name it, dress can convey all these qualities and more. Psychiatrists say that they can judge the psychological health of a person from how they dress – it can speak of optimism and openness, or despair and utter hopelessness. Those who don't bother can find themselves trapped in a downward cycle of not liking the way they look, and so they take less and less trouble, and therefore they like the way they look less and less. Then they often pretend they don't care, that it's better not to take part in a competition you can't win.

I've met very few people who truly don't mind how they look. In the course of my life as a journalist I've sometimes written about make-overs and I've never known a woman not to be amazed and thrilled when the make-over has been successful. I once took to a make-over specialist (Susie Faux of Wardrobe, 020 7494 1131; www.wardrobe.co.uk) a bolshie, right-on, overweight colleague who wore terrible clothes, no make-up and had some kind of apology for a hairdo. Susie's heart (she told me later) sank when she first saw her, but a few hours later the colleague turned up on my doorstep in a figure-flattering, navy-blue, below-the-knee shirt-dress and good shoes, with her hair and make-up professionally done. She was in tears. Weeping, she handed me a vast bunch of flowers, saying, 'I didn't think I could ever look pretty.' I nearly cried myself. If she could be transformed, so can anybody. It's good for one's self-esteem. It helps one face the world more confidently. It's good for the gaiety of the nation.

And, what's more, it's never too late. Rebecca, in Anne Tyler's *Back When We Were Grownups*, decided at fifty-three that she 'had turned into the wrong person' and that her 'loose and colourful style of dress' edged 'dangerously close to bag lady' and so concluded hopelessly that 'it was too late to make any changes'. I think she was wrong. There was – and always is – plenty of time to change, no matter what your age. And it's worth it. Completely empirically, one observes that those who dress prettily, elegantly or glamorously have a lot more fun than those who don't.

And much of it doesn't depend on the looks that nature gave you. Some of the most famous seducers of powerful men in history were far from classic beauties. They learned instead to behave as if they were. Take the Duchess of Windsor, who was almost forty when she was introduced to the then Prince of Wales. Lady Furness, the Prince's mistress at the time, thought her so plain that she felt it quite safe to ask her new friend 'to look after the little man' whilst she went to New York. *Big* mistake. Mrs Edward Simpson, as she was at the time, was no fool. She lost weight, became a model size 34–24–34, discovered which mode of dress suited her newly skinny figure, learned to hide her unattractive hands, turned her harsh vowels into a soft Southern drawl, polished up her repartee, studied how to present stylish food and how to please her man. It worked. 'I'm nothing to look at,' she told Elsa Maxwell, 'so the only thing I can do is dress better than anyone else.'

But I also believe that dressing at least moderately well is part of proper manners. Turning up in scruffy clothes to a dinner that somebody has taken trouble with is rude. It takes the shine off the evening. Wearing flip-flops to the White House, as some American teenagers famously did, seems to me to show a lack of respect and to speak of an unattractive bolshiness. We've all known women who've turned up at work in entirely inappropriate gear: plunging necklines, skirts that are too short. It is distracting and unprofessional. But neither have I ever understood why you can't combine glamour with brains. The fad of some intellectuals for thinking that their IQ depends upon wearing dreary clothes doesn't seem to me to evince much capacity for rational thought.

I also think that the older you get, the less you can afford to look scruffy or unkempt. The young can get away with it, but as time passes it looks less and less attractive, and in the middle aged and older it can look downright creepy. Older women these days may well be sitting in the High Court and on the boards of City banks (think of Marjorie Scardino in her Armani suits; think of the glamorous Baroness Kingsmill, slim, blonde and beautiful; think of Helen Mirren), or presiding over operating theatres, running countries, writing books, and living full and active lives. They needn't have grey hair any longer, if it doesn't suit them. Skincare and beauty companies, nutritionists and personal trainers, are making sure that these women are honed and toned, pampered and groomed. Glamour is a great life-enhancer and there's no need to surrender it simply because the years are rolling by. Nor does it depend on continually buying loads of new clothes. A great haircut, fabulous shoes, cute bags and jewellery (which does *not* have to be expensive) all can do much to add more than a touch of glamour.

There's no need to copy fashion blindly either. I'm of the view that the older you get, the more quietly you should follow fashion – follow it, of course, but at a distance. Wear diluted versions of the hot looks. And I believe in the dictum of Diana Vreeland, the legendary editor of America's *Harper's Bazaar*: 'The greatest vulgarity is any imitation of youth and beauty.' Which brings me to honesty – an essential element of real style. What is vulgar and inelegant in imitating youth and beauty (which is entirely different from wanting to look your best) is that it is dishonest, it is trying to pretend that things are other than they are.

I don't think there has ever been a better time for women wanting to look their best. It takes a modicum of time and money but then doesn't everything that is worth while? I like to remind myself of the words of Luciana Avedon, wife of the famous photographer Richard Avedon, who said:

> There will always be glamorous women who declare that they do nothing special to maintain their trim, attractive bodies; a zest for living is what keeps you young, they proclaim. I do not envy them; I just don't believe a word they say. Luciana Avedon

I'm with Luciana Avedon. Glamour requires work but the tools are there. And they are to be found in places and at prices within reach of almost all. She was only putting into other words what Helena Rubinstein, the great cosmetician, always said: 'There are no ugly women, only lazy ones.' I believe that too.

Finding Your Own Style

There is no such thing as an ugly woman – there are only the ones who do not know how to make themselves attractive. Christian Dior

I can't believe I'm quoting Paris Hilton, but she is alleged to have said: 'Dress cute wherever you go. Life is too short to blend in.' She's right. What a waste of all the fun that's out there to be had. But finding how to 'dress cute' in a way that suits us isn't easy for everybody. To start with, we're all different. Some of us share the same sub-groups of problems (short legs, large hips, rounded stomaches, no boobs, large boobs: you get the picture), but each of us is a unique package and finding out how to make the most of ourselves generally takes a bit of time. It also takes a bit of ruthless honesty. The first essential is a long, straight look in the mirror, deciding what is good about your body and what isn't. Once you've worked out what needs hiding and what enhancing, you're on your way to finding a wardrobe to suit you. The art of disguise is what it's all about, particularly as one gets older, when crêpey necks and flabby arms are not a pretty sight.

But none of us gets it right all the time. We can all look back and blush at the mistakes we've made in our day. But if we care enough, we can learn by trial and error what suits us and what we should steer well clear of. I know, for instance, that whereas I love dead plain, classy, classic clothes, they do absolutely nothing for me other than make me look like a rather dreary librarian (I'm sure there are some very glamorous librarians, but you know what I mean). I need something a bit quirky or eccentric to look interesting. I need to hide my now not-so-great waist and go for things that hint at the waist but don't show up its deficiencies. I've got decent legs for my size so, even though I'm a grandmother (remember?), I can still get away with shortish skirts if I wear dark tights. I go for curvy jackets that make it seem as if my waist goes in, and dresses that have either a slightly high (empire or princess line) waist or a low one.

* Every wardrobe needs one divine dress (mine is in brilliantly cut black jersey, with long sleeves, a deep V-neck and a curving, long, quirky skirt, by the Turkish designer Ischiko) that always looks good even on days when you don't feel so good.

If we're great beauties we can probably get away with a slightly slapdash approach. I do know (very) few women who are such raving beauties that you never notice the clothes. Most of us aren't so blessed. We have to make the best of what the good Lord has given us. This is where personal style and a touch of élan comes in. If you look carefully at women who have great personal style, it goes on serving them well into late middle and old age (think of the late Diana Vreeland, Coco Chanel, Charlotte Rampling, Judi

Dench, Helen Mirren). What we see is that somehow at some stage they evolved a personal way of dressing and of being. They develop, if you like, a trademark that is all their own. Style, as one of my first editors, the late Ernestine Carter of the *Sunday Times*, once wrote, 'has nothing to do with youth . . . or age . . . or sex . . . It has nothing to do with class or colour . . . or money . . . It shows in small ways as well as big . . . Style is personal. It is what is worn . . . as well as the way it's worn.' And most devastatingly of all, she went on to say, 'Style is like charm . . . you either have it or you don't.' It certainly isn't dependent on beauty or conventional looks. Diana Vreeland was no beauty but, my goodness, she had style. She piled on the bracelets. Wore the high-necked black sweaters. Patted on the pale, almost kabuki-like make-up and slashed her lips red. When she entered a room you noticed it. She was a living example of the fact that if you make a style your own, if you believe in it and wear it with confidence, others will believe in it too. Coco Chanel cropped her hair short, came up with a new liberating uniform of soft jersey trousers, skirts and jackets, and made them glamorous. With them, she always wore huge ropes of pearls (she preferred them to be fake; pearls of such size and in such number would be vulgar if real, but the fact that they were fake removed any pretentiousness) and her trademark jewelled cuffs.

Those who use lack of funds as an excuse might ponder the story of Gloria Guinness, a legendary style icon in her day, who had been poor in her time. When she had very little money she would buy a beautiful piece of jersey, cut a hole in the top, put it over her head and tie an attractive sash around her waist – and everybody would ask her where she'd bought her dress. Now that is serious style.

When I think of my most stylish friends (mostly well past the first flush of youth), I realise that they are not the ones who take refuge in conventionally 'tasteful' attire. They shop at Japanese designers, such as Issey Miyake and Comme des Garçons; they love the Belgians, such as Martin Margiela and Ann Demeulemeester. They go for Shirin Guild, whose loose, slightly arty, ethnic take on fashion is perfect for those whose waist is just a distant memory. If they put on weight they fall in love with Wall (www.wall-london.com), whose easy trousers and roomy shirts and sweaters make them look interesting. They believe in a touch of eccentricity – but not too much. Whilst they always look fashionable, they're not slaves to fashion. Many of them do wear a lot of black. They tend to have evolved a style that includes minimalist Japanese clothes, trousers, flattering sweaters and jackets (some of them acquired over time) and they mostly stick to a chic template that is essentially fairly constant as well as being all their own. They've learned that it is better to buy one really amazing piece – a jacket, say, from Miyake or Yohji Yamamoto, Chloé or Marc Jacobs that can clock up many years of service – than a whole mountain of cheaper numbers that die a quick death.

All these women illustrate an interesting point. The kiss of death when one gets older is to dress in bland good taste.

The older you get the less classic you can afford to be. A brilliantly tailored understated suit may look divine on a slim young thing but once you're over fifty you'll just look mumsy. So unless you're a drop-dead beauty, when you can get away with anything, forget the tasteful understated dinky bits of jewellery, the quiet modesty of the court shoe, the absolutely dead simple dress, and opt for something much more dashing.

For the young, sometimes a really classy pair of premium jeans, a spanking white T-shirt, a cutely cut jacket and some great accessories are all they need. Think Elle Macpherson, Liz Hurley and many others. The key is that white is very flattering, but it must be clean and truly white. Girly shirts and blouses look good with designer jeans too. Footwear matters greatly; in the winter, for going to the supermarket or doing the school run, boots are fabulous. For summer days, loafers, for those who don't mind wearing flatties, look classy. The whole look can be jazzed up with high heels. But you need to start by knowing that you look good in jeans. (For more on jeans, see p. 88.)

At the end of the day, though, style is hard to define, but one thing is certain: most of us know it when we see it. It takes in clothes – an awareness of how to dress and how to give one's way of dressing a certain distinction – but since style is an expression of who we are and it tells the world something of our inner selves, it is also no accident that most of those women deemed stylish by their peers are also dab hands at creating attractive homes and preparing lovely food.

If you have trouble finding your own style – and, after all, some of you may well be doing infinitely more important things than cruising the fashion floors – or if you feel your look or wardrobe is in need of a fillip, it might be a good idea to book an appointment with a personal shopper in a good store near you (see p. 95).

Don't be predictable – be you.

Natalie Massenet of net-a-porter.com

Problem Shapes

BIG BOOBS: Get a proper bra (see p. 58). A shallow V-neck creates the illusion of length. Never wear high round necks, but you can wear high collars.

SMALL BOOBS: Get a proper push-up bra if you're wearing anything with a low neckline. You can wear high necks and, if your boobs are small enough, even go bra-less.

LARGE HIPS: Go for A-line skirts, and skirts and dresses that skim rather than fit tightly. Do not be tempted to wear a tent or you may well end up looking like one. Distraction is the name of the game. Provide interest at the neck – a gorgeous blouse with a fantastic collar, great jewellery. Spandex is a large girl's friend. Jackets that curve in at the waist and out again make the curves look charming instead of bulky.

FLABBY TUMMY: Avoid ruched or pleated skirts. Never wear anything too tight. A low-slung waist for skirts or dresses, or high-waisted, princess-line dresses, flatter and hide the tummy. Keep away from belts tied around the middle. Marks & Spencer sells great stomach-holding underwear, some of which also contains the thighs firmly. As I write, the 'sack' or the 'big easy' is hotly tipped as the fashion item of the moment – perfect for hiding flabby tummies. Keep it as short as your legs and decency allow, clad your legs in great tights and you're away.

LARGE BOTTOM: Choose waisted jackets that flare out and end below the bum, hiding it. Never wear those boxy jackets that make even skinny beans look square. Keep away from high-waisted trousers. Perk up your top half. Curves are nothing to be ashamed of so wear something fitted, provided it is not remotely tight. Indulge in diversionary tactics. Keep the eye of the beholder looking upwards. The 'sack' (see FLABBY TUMMY) is great for you, too.

CURVY: Don't dress in kaftans and tents as they'll only make you look larger. Get jackets and skirts that fit properly but that skim the curves. Take care with grooming. Get a sharp haircut, neither too short, nor too long. Add great earrings or a brilliant scarf or necklace. For evenings, a scintillating taffeta coat in a brilliant colour (emerald green, claret, scarlet) over sleek, well-fitting black (either a skirt or trousers) can look a million dollars – both Suzy Menkes and Zaha Hadid do this look to perfection. You probably shouldn't wear flat shoes; a heel will give greater length to the leg, which is never bad.

SLIM: You should be so lucky. You can indulge in fashion's more extravagant notions – large sleeves, huge belts, tweed skirts. You can also look adorably frail in slightly large clothes. Shirin Guild, for instance, actually looks good on the very slim because it accentuates the delicacy of the skinny frame.

BAD LEGS: Trousers, of course. Dark tights. Careful assessment of the best length for the hem of a skirt or dress. In winter wear boots under dresses and skirts. Choose shoes that have height and lengthen the leg, and never, ever wear an ankle-strap.

How to Dress for Work

The first question has to be: what work? The television industry, for instance, seems terminally scruffy, with jeans and T-shirts being the standard uniform. On the other hand, if you were even the lowliest cupboard girl at Condé Nast, you wouldn't survive long if you didn't know how to put your Topshop or your Primark numbers together with a bit of verve and originality. And you'd better make sure that your hair is shiny, your shoes up to the minute and your make-up spot on if you don't want to be ushered out of the door the minute your work experience is up.

But on the whole the real conundrum is why so many women adopt such a bland uniform for work. Whilst I do understand that wearing an itsy-bitsy miniskirt and vertiginous heels when trying to look like a safe pair of hands for a million-dollar fund isn't a good idea, I can never understand why turning up in dreary clothes is meant to add gravitas to the proceedings. I've lost track of the number of highly paid accountants and lawyers who take refuge in terminally boring uniforms of safe shoes, black, grey or navy suits (and I'm not talking Alexander McQueen here) and unenterprising haircuts. Americans can be some of the worst offenders, though they are admittedly often very well groomed, which makes up for a lot. Look at the women in high political life across the pond. Apart from Condoleezza Rice, who looks splendidly and appropriately chic, they mostly wear middle-of-the-road trouser suits with bland jackets (the better to hide the hips and stomachs), sensible shoes and a string of pearls. Where's the fun and the personality in that? It's perfectly possible these days to dress much more zippily and yet still look like the safe custodian of a tough criminal case or a zillion-dollar trust fund. Ségolène Royal, the former French presidential candidate, showed that it can be done. The polls told us that her penchant for a lot of sharply cut, very feminine white suits was a large part of her appeal.

Great shoes dress up the look of a suit no end and, whilst I concede they're not great for tubes or buses, what's wrong with keeping a couple of pairs in the office drawer or carrying them around in the oversized bags that are the current fashionable tote? Then there's the suit itself. Suits don't have to be boring. Key is the jacket, which should be sexily cut so that it doesn't look bland and boxy. A proper working wardrobe should have lots of different jackets, sharply cut, curvy, with flattering collars and necklines (and, most particularly, not those masculine revers that you get on men's suits), to perk up even classic black trousers or any number of skirts.

For certain roles (investment banking, corporate law) you need to look as if you're one tough cookie when it comes to the negotiating table but a real woman underneath, very efficient yet worldly and sophisticated. Or, as Melanie Griffith put it so memorably in *Working Girl*, with 'a head for business and a body for sin'. For which no better garment was ever devised than the trouser suit. But a great trouser suit, not the safe boring one so beloved of middle America. Remember how Gucci, under the now departed Tom Ford, did the office babe look to perfection? All efficient pinstripes, but sexed up with great shoes and sometimes a very girly camisole with a tiny bit of lace showing at the neckline. The trick is to find one that is beautifully cut, that has some curves so that you look womanly and, for the sake of your own self-esteem, also has an air of authority. The masters of the art are, of course, Jil Sander and M. Armani.

GOOD LABELS TO LOOK FOR

- **At the expensive end**

Alexander McQueen does fabulous suits and jackets – very sexy but appropriate, too, for the workplace.

Chloé – blouses and dresses to take out a mortgage for.

Paul Smith for suits and dresses.

Stella McCartney specialises in brilliant tailoring and she seems to be coming into her rather fabulous prime.

Joseph – not exactly a label but a shop that understands the need to combine proper grown-up clothes with a good dollop of fashionable fizz. Its rocker trousers are a staple in many a working woman's wardrobe.

- **Middle market**

Betty Jackson knows how to cut a jacket so that it's feminine, easy to wear and slots into the working wardrobe.

Diane von Furstenberg's dresses may be a bit ubiquitous, but she keeps ringing the changes with fabrics and colours.

Anna Sui does great dresses, some brilliantly demure in a kind of sexy nanny way.

Phillip Lim is a label stocked by www.net-a-porter.com that I love and that is astonishingly reasonably priced for what he offers.

MaxMara usually has great coats, jackets and dresses.

Sara Berman does brilliantly wearable versions of the hot fashion trends.

Jigsaw

Wallis

Jaeger

- **Cheap end**

Zara – for dresses, jackets and coats.

Marks & Spencer – for good trousers and jackets. Check out the Limited Collection and Autograph.

Primark

Dorothy Perkins

In fact a trouser suit by M. Armani should be in the wardrobe of all who can afford him – it can take you anywhere from the toughest business meeting to the most seductive dinner (you just add some stilettos, possibly a lacy camisole under the jacket and a jewel or two). Neither of these two comes cheap so you have to think of them in terms of investment dressing.

If you're just starting out on the corporate ladder and don't yet have the salary to fund these labels, you could do a lot worse than scour the rails of Marks & Spencer. Its Limited Collection has improved no end and you can usually find well-fitting trousers that capture the mood of the day (i.e. if cropped trousers have been on the catwalk, you can bet your last cent that Marks & Spencer, Topshop, Zara *et al.* will have them in their stores before you can say copycat). Then either search for jackets in Marks & Spencer itself or scour Zara, Topshop, Dorothy Perkins or even Primark for perky numbers that will do the job without looking dull.

Skirts have been big recently and there are lots that manage that tricky manoeuvre of looking both feminine and pretty and yet suitable for work. Teamed with a sexy jacket and underneath a cashmere sweater, a good shirt or blouse (Chloé, Chloé, Chloé, if you can afford it), they make more beguiling workwear than boring trouser suits. A selection of really cute, well-cut jackets (*not* boxy) can go an awfully long way towards giving you a versatile wardrobe.

These days dresses can go happily to work, too. The

days when they only came with shoestring straps and minuscule sleeves are long gone. I think so many of us complained so loudly that the designers actually listened for once and now there are lots of delicious wearable numbers about.

How to be Glam

> Glamour is what makes a man ask for your phone number and a woman for the address of your dressmaker.
>
> Lilly Dache, a French-born designer who worked in the US

Never underestimate the power of glamour. It's life-enhancing and even the plainest woman can be glamorous. Glamour is quite different from beauty. It depends a lot on a sense of personal style and some inner confidence, which isn't always easy to come by but can be cultivated. A great help, though, is a terrific haircut. Do not be tempted to go to cheap colourists or Tracy in the high street (unless she's extraordinarily talented and just about to be poached by Daniel Galvin). A tiny, but I mean tiny (most of us don't want to go too far down the Anna Piaggi route) bit of eccentricity – or perhaps a better word is individuality – helps. Also well-chosen jewellery, but not too much of it, just some stunning earrings, for example, or a fantastic necklace that works with the clothes you're wearing. For instance, I bought some amazing scarlet amber gobstoppers in Oman, which look wonderful with plain black, fizzing it up no end, but I wouldn't dream of wearing them with much else (except possibly with plain white linen in the summer). They'd be too much. But some of this sort of jewellery can be bought very inexpensively in the high street – just remember, don't be timid.

Sexy shoes (I keep coming back to them because dowdy shoes kill anything stone dead; for more, see p. 70) and a good handbag (see p. 75) helps, too.

A fine perfume – but never too much (it's vulgar and bad manners to douse yourself in a smell so strong that nobody can escape it). If you can't afford an expensive scent it's worth looking at natural essential oils, sold in lots of spas and slightly hippie shops and galleries, which don't have that horrid chemical smell of the cheaper scents. (For more on scent, see p. 167.)

How to Wear Black

. . . because no matter what's on the catwalk today, one day you surely will.

'Why is it that whenever a woman wants to feel alluring, she reaches for a little black dress? What makes a simple sheath – devoid of ornamentation, the colour of mourning – so luminous? Why is it that a little black dress seems so familiar while at the same time so mysterious and seductive?' So asks Amy Holman Edelman in her book *The Little Black Dress*, thus blithely ignoring the fact that a black dress can just as easily make a woman look like a menacing crow, a drab Mediterranean widow in mourning or an ageing anorexic. Not good looks, any of them. But remember Audrey Hepburn in *Breakfast at Tiffany's*, I hear you cry, and what about Jackie Onassis, the very picture of poignant, elegant grief at JFK's funeral? True, true, but study the photographs. It's the props that make them. The little black dress is but a chic, anonymous vehicle for drama elsewhere. With Audrey it was the hat, the shades, the long gloves, the earrings, the umbrella, the shoes. Could you honestly describe the dress? With Jackie O it was the vulnerable, little-girl, pared-down look, the pale visage, and the impeccable hair and make-up that formed the unforgettable image.

Mlle Chanel herself, she who is credited with coming up with the very first little black dress, warned us: 'Scheherazade is easy. A little black dress is difficult.' As well she might, given that that first LBD was a simple number that would look divine on anybody blessed with a size 8 figure, no evident stomach and invisible hips, but rather rubbishy on the rest of us.

So what do we learn from that? That if we're going to wear black – and we surely will because black is the new black more often than it isn't and it certainly won't ever be going anywhere for long – we've got to learn how to wear it. It needs drama. It needs to be cut either limpidly in soft seductive chiffon or silky drapes, or skilfully shaped to follow the curves of breast and waist, or sharp and chic the way M. Dior did it in his last few brilliant years and Alexander McQueen does it now. Just because it's black it doesn't mean it's going to make you feel like a million dollars, though it will make you feel thinner, a quality not to be underestimated. So given that some day soon you'll be wearing black, here's how to do it so that the total look is rather more Catherine Deneuve than Edith Piaf.

1. VERY SEXY SHOES. Preferably red but, speaking personally, I often wear some brilliant emerald-green Marc Jacobs open-toed platform shoes. At night you can do glitter.

2. ADROITLY CHOSEN JEWELLERY. You could do the Coco Chanel pearls number. Mlle Chanel, you will not need reminding, was scarcely ever seen without them and, when she wore black, she piled on the strings. They were fake – of course, so much more chic in her view than real. Have a great big socking pendant right in the middle of the neckline or pin on a funky brooch. You should probably wear earrings – preferably to add light and 'lift' the complexion. Just don't do all of it together.

3. GREAT HAIR. Clean, shiny, groomed, beautifully cut and tended to.

4. A CUTE HANDBAG. Jewel-like or glittery for evening.

5. ADD ANOTHER COLOUR in the shape of a shirt or blouse

or scarf. Colours like emeralds, teals and purples work well with black. Also, surprisingly, navy.

6. SOME BARE SKIN near the face is essential. High necklines and long sleeves (especially both at once) look a little too governessy.

7. ADAPT YOUR MAKE-UP. Black drains away light from all but the most luminous complexions. See below for how to make up when wearing black.

Make-up for Wearing Black

Black, we all know, is brilliantly chic and a wonderful default colour for when we're feeling low *but* it can drain the colour from one's face. That is when make-up needs to be applied with greater care. Here is advice from Valentine Alexander, my make-up guru, on how to make up when wearing black. To book a session with her, telephone her in Paris on +33 6 1061 2678.

1. Before a special evening, start off with a mini-facial at home. The main purpose is to exfoliate and all the beauty ranges, including Boots, now sell exfoliators, which remove dead cells and bring radiance back to the skin. If you can afford it, use a high-quality mask – such as Givenchy's Black for Light Mask or Guerlain's Issima Purifying Invigorating Mask – but any good mask will make a difference and once again ranges like Boots do a great job.

2. Apply a brightening moisturiser. When shopping, look for

those two words on products at Boots or even in your local supermarket. If you can afford it, the top of the range is Chanel's Éclat Original cream.

3. Use a light-reflective concealer around eyes, on lines from nose to mouth and around the lips, and on any age spots or imperfections. I prefer Chanel's version but again concealers are made for every budget. If you have purplish-blue circles around your eyes (a hazard, it seems, after facelifts or laser treatment), Clinique's CX Colour Corrector is terrific.

4. Apply a well-blended layer of your favourite foundation, an exact match with your neck and décolletage. Valentine likes Clarins True Comfort Foundation Light Reflecting but always make sure it's a good match with your skin.

5. Fix your foundation with a diaphanous light layer of light-reflective powder.

6. Sculpt cheekbones with light-reflective bronzer, like Becca's Frangipani or Armani Sheer Bronzer.

7. Lipstick – for classic blondes, Chanel's Rouge Noir. For mousey browns, choose a good colour from Lancôme's Rouge Absolu collection.

8. For smokey eyes, use Clinique's Kohl Shaper for Eyes in Black Amethyst and a good mascara.

I told you it wasn't easy but it is worth it.

Occasion Dressing

Remember the old adage: 'Beware of any enterprise that requires new clothing.' I don't believe in buying special outfits just because there's a grand stiffy on the mantelpiece. I've made more mistakes buying in a hurry because I'm going to the races, to a wedding, to the opera or whatever, than at any other time. I often think it's much, much better to spend the money on a terrific haircut and great shoes.

Of course weddings often do need special outfits – if you're the bride, you obviously do, but also the mother, sister or mother-in-law of the bride may all feel it's an occasion to buy something new and special. For those who can afford it I can't do better than recommend Anna Valentine, one half of the duo who, as Robinson Valentine, produced the Duchess of Cornwall's spot-on wedding outfits. Anna Valentine isn't cheap, because her things are made to measure and she uses fine fabrics, but she knows absolutely how to produce beautiful clothes that are elegant and graceful too. She's to be found at 15 Cross Keys Close, London W1U 2DN; 020 7935 2050.

A close friend, who married for the second time in her late fifties, got Vivienne Westwood (44 Conduit Street, London W15 2YT; 020 7439 1109) to make her a made-to-measure dress and it was a dream. In a gorgeous greyish-green taffeta, it had her trademark asymmetrical figure-flattering cut and revealed just the right amount of décolletage: more and it would have been vulgar; a little less and it would have been prim. Again, not cheap, but worth it for the really special occasion.

Browns, of 23–27 South Molton Street, London W1K 5RD; 020 7514 0000, offers a special service for the growing number of brides who aren't teenaged virgins. It takes suitable models (mostly dresses but also some suits and coats) from designers' standard catwalk ranges and then has them made up into slightly more suitable bridal colours.

For sisters, mothers and other female relations of the bride, I think it's hard to beat coat dresses. Burberry's Prorsum range has had some humdingers in the last few collections, particularly its recent gold double-breasted coat with a collar, which could take you to anything from a grand evening 'do' (where I happened to see one) to a wedding, a dinner or the theatre. Most designers have some really pretty coat dresses in their summer collections. Even our old friend Marks & Spencer has had a gold evening dress-cum-coat, whilst Hennes (H&M) has sold a gold brocade coat for just £29.99. I don't know how they do it.

Coats over dresses are another practical solution to the problem of needing some cover-up for outdoors and something a bit more partyish for when everything moves indoors. Sources vary from season to season, but Paddy Campbell does the look well.

Ascot and the races are part of the set-pieces of the British summer season, and cutting-edge design (Yohji

Yamamoto, Commes des Garçons) aren't what they're about. They *are* about looking pretty and feminine (unless you're prepared to go to outrageous lengths to attract the paparazzi's eyes) and here somebody like Laura B Couture of 8 Yeomans Row, London SW3 2AH: 020 7581 4123, understands the sartorial language perfectly, providing exactly the sort of charming suits, coats and dresses that are spot on for these inherently conventional events.

Party Time

This, of course, is part of looking glam. Apart from great make-up and grooming (about which more in the next chapter), here are some aids for adding allure come the evening.

1. A glamorous evening coat is well worth tracking down. You can sometimes find them in ethnic shops. If you find one, buy it, in velvet for winter, or silks and satins for spring, summer and autumn. Jewel colours look fantastic. I have an antique Korean wedding kimono coat in a deep blue that always comes out when I need to be glamorous but want to be warm.

2. For real class it's hard to beat a gorgeous skirt (caramel, orange or pillar-box red) in taffeta or silk, teamed with a plain round-necked cashmere sweater and some great jewellery. Penelope Cruz in a scarlet taffeta skirt and a

black cashmere sweater made everybody else on the red carpet look tarty. If you're thin enough, you can belt the sweater.

3. A black lace skirt is a great all-purpose standby.
4. If you don't think your arms and décolletage can stand being uncovered, find a lacy top that covers the offending parts without looking prudish or heavy.
5. Other good cover-ups that do the job, without looking too obvious whilst they do it, are boleros, shrugs or lace jackets (remember Helen Mirren at the BAFTAs in her crinkled cream silk Jacques Azagury dress, which she topped with a little gold bolero).
6. I like discretion – I think a bit of mystery is much more alluring than too much cleavage or too much leg (as for too much of both, don't even think about it). My 'taste' guru, Amanda Platt, has a sensible piece of advice: 'You can quite often get away with one slightly tarty thing (vertiginous heels, footless tights, slightly revealing cleavage) but more than one is tacky.'
7. If you're in the money and you're in doubt where to look, the two names who do evening wear brilliantly are Giorgio Armani and Valentino. If you're young (her clothes often mean bare arms), Alberta Ferretti has a fabulous range. If you're on a budget, it's worth knowing that lately Zara and even Warehouse have started stocking

evening wear. I have a friend who found a gorgeous evening dress in Monsoon, so it's worth trawling the high street before you lash out on designer names.

8. One beautiful silk shirt with a huge, flattering, stand-up collar is fantastic for the older woman. Think Carolina Herrera – she always teams hers with great-fitting trousers or, for grand evening events, with a flowing taffeta skirt.

9. A really sexy evening look, if you've got the figure, is a well-cut tuxedo trouser suit – Yves St Laurent is the master. To make it work you need to judge very carefully just how many buttons to leave undone on the jacket. It may look better with a lacy or a glittery camisole underneath the jacket. The high street is copying the look – remember Hennes, which for a brief, wonderful moment sold Karl Lagerfeld's take on the black tuxedo suit – so keep your eyes skinned.

Cheap Chic

For years *Vogue* used to have a regular feature titled 'More Cash Than Dash' but I always thought it was a bit of a cop-out because it seemed to assume that only the young were poor – there was never anything for grown-ups who might be having trouble with their cash flow. Now, if you're young and slender, it's really a doddle buying cheap. The best wheeze for getting away with inexpensive clothing is to be a size 10 – everything looks wonderful. It's once you get heavier, and older, that it's harder to get away with spending less.

It is worth saying that if you are short of cash, it is encouraging to note how few garments some really stylish women have – though the few do admittedly tend to be very good. For instance, I once looked into the wardrobe of Amanda Platt, an alarmingly chic personal wardrobe advisor. It was quite a shock. I have scarcely, ever – outside a third world country – seen such a tiny wardrobe. There seemed to be almost nothing in it. For the closet voyeur this is what it held: five skirts, some Brora tops (skinny polo ribs for winter, which it was at the time) and Issey Miyake's Haarts' seamless knits, one pair of trousers, a jacket and skirt, an old black Armani suit ('from his heyday') for funerals, an old Donna Karan black dress, and a new Temperley dress, which she wore to every party that Christmas, teamed with a Gucci cardigan. Her shoes consisted of two pairs of Robert Clergerie boots and an old pair of Chanel shoes for best. That's it, folks.

So you don't need a lot of clothes to be chic but you do need to avoid mistakes (because that's money wasted). So no impulse buying unless you absolutely know that you will get lots of wear out of what you've suddenly lost your heart to. Think what your wardrobe needs before you buy and, if you see a garment that you fancy, think hard about how it will fit into the life and the wardrobe you already have. Just remember: simply because something has a high price, that doesn't mean it's expensive, and just because something doesn't cost much, doesn't mean it's a bargain. If it's £10 wasted, it's still money wasted. If it's hundreds spent well on something that's worn often, it's cheap at the price.

I've sounded off already about how great the high street is but it's worth saying again that you need a good eye and you need to take time and trouble. You can easily buy a couple of tops for £30, which may not be a lot of money but if they're badly chosen and never look good it's £30 down the drain. Do that several times and you've wasted the kind of sum that would have bought a really classy number.

There has never been a better time to buy inexpensively. I cannot do better than recommend the usual suspects: Zara (a dream, really), Marks & Spencer, Hennes, Primark, New Look, even Tesco and George at Asda. Gap is good for more casual wear, for jeans and T-shirts, that sort of thing. It takes a lot of shoe leather to cover them all, but it is astonishing what you can find.

* Learn what you can economise on. Personally, I think chain stores do great plain, classic trousers, but it's probably worth adding a sassier jacket to bring them to life. Try to have one pair of really great shoes and one fabulous handbag, as that'll make everything else look classier. Really cheap shoes and bags are the biggest give-away of all.

I'm not sure about second-hand shops. I have friends who've found wonderful things in them but I haven't had a lot of luck myself, outside costume jewellery (which is often fantastic) and the odd silky blouse. I usually find that the things I really like are not only relatively expensive but they never look quite right once they're home. Obviously, if you come upon a Kelly handbag going for a song, you'd be daft to pass it up, but as a serious strategy for dressing I've never known it really work. It's only fair to say, though, that for some of my friends their favourite garment of all time turns out to be the one-off brilliant find tracked down in an antique market in Northumberland, or in Holt, Norfolk (where there happens to be a terrific shop), but you do need to keep on looking (great for those who find it fun) and to be lucky. Other great finds in vintage shops are handbags (many swear by the handbag corner in Alfie's Market, 13–25 Church Street, London NW8 8DT; 020 7723 6066; in particular there's a fab stand called The Girl Can't Help It, which has wonderful vintage evening bags, costume jewellery, hair combs, etc.) and, as I've mentioned earlier, costume jewellery. Not so well known, though, are cocktail hats – they don't make them now the way they used to.

It's also worth drawing your attention to a website called Yoox (www.yoox.co.uk), which offers a mix of recently off-season discounted clothing from many of the great designers as well as some new niche names. It also has a fantastic vintage site but the prices there tend to be high for this is serious, collectable vintage, not mere second-hand clothing.

Outlet stores are a great place to shop. I still own a couple of garments I bought many years ago in the US at

Woodbury Common (www.premiumoutlets.com), the daddy of them all (in particular a wonderful pair of heavy silk cream summer trousers).

I have a very chic friend who, like her husband, is in the arts field and so they're very short of cash. She always looks a dream, partly because she has innate taste and partly because she buys much of what she wears at Bicester Outlet Village, a very upmarket way of buying last season's still perfectly fashionable clothing at very reduced prices. Check it out: 50 Pringle Drive, Oxon OX26 6WD; 01869 323 200; www.bicester-village.co.uk.

If you're in Italy, particularly Milan or Florence, you will be temptingly close to some terrific outlet stores. There are so many that it's impossible to list them here. Suffice it to say that my daughter is still wearing some fantastic Prada shoes and I am still wearing a lovely Prada evening coat, both bought in the Prada outlet outside Florence for very little some years ago. The Italian outlets obviously require something of a journey to get to if you don't live in Italy, but you can check them all out on www.italianfactoryoutlets.com and it will direct you to where to find the outlets for Gucci, Prada, Dolce & Gabbana – you name it, the directory will have it.

WHAT IS WORTH SPENDING MONEY ON

These tips come from Averyl Oates, the very fashion-forward buying director of Harvey Nichols, and so somebody who absolutely has to know what's what when it comes to looking stylish.

1. A **good coat** is a great investment as winter is long and it's key to the impression you make. If you can't afford an expensive coat, you can find great 'on trend' coats in the high street stores at very reasonable prices but try to personalise them by changing the buttons, or adding a border to the hem, so that you don't meet other people wearing the same coat.

2. Invest in a **good handbag** – it will go on looking good for ever.

3. **Fabulous shoes** can make even a high street dress look fantastic.

4. **Accessories** should be either very cheap or very expensive. Don't waste money on the middle ground.

5. A **classic little black dress** is worth spending money on as it can be worn in any season and updated with key accessories.

6. **Don't follow trends slavishly** if they don't suit you. Look out for key pre-collection pieces that you think you like and then buy the watered-down versions at good prices.

7. **Vintage shops** are great places to find gems. Many designers scour the vintage shops for inspiration for their collections. If you find the right piece you will be able to wear it for ever.

8. A **good blow-dry, manicure and pedicure** are priceless. They will give you the confidence to carry off any outfit.

9. A **pair of Spanks knickers** is essential under those tight-fitting dresses, giving you a flat stomach without the work.

10. **Try to plan your outfit** the night before, if you are a busy working woman, to save last-minute panic and therefore fashion disasters when you're in a hurry in the morning.

Up, Up and Away

– or What to Wear to Travel

First things first: get a tan *before* you go. We all know by now – don't we? – that sun is a big no-no for the skin. As Dr Howard Sobel, one of New York's best-known 'derms' puts it: 'If you don't wear sun protection creams, then almost everything else you do is a waste of time.' But to look your best you do need to look a little sun-kissed. Head to one of the fast-tan booths to be found all over the country. I think Palmer-Cutler tan treatments are amongst the best and they're used in good salons nationwide. For Londoners, Heidi Klein Holiday Shop (174 Westbourne Grove, London W11 2RW; 020 7243 5665; www.heidiklein.co.uk), has a Black Box Tanning treatment that takes just sixty seconds. Otherwise try the Fantasy Tan, which works a treat without strange orange hues or peculiar streaks, but the downside is that you need two treatments in a row for best results. Both last for something like seven to ten days – time enough to do a little gentle topping up with some natural sunlight (0845 129 8431 and at www.fantasytan.co.uk).

Always pack a great notebook. The most chic are tiny ones with very fine paper from Smythson or the moleskin ones, beloved of Ernest Hemingway and Bruce Chatwin, which have little leather ties and which can now be found in most good stationers. Ella Doran, a gifted graphic designer, has done some rather more fun ones for John Lewis. They have little pockets for keeping receipts, plus transparent envelopes for pressed flowers, dropped feathers, seeds or the like, as well as lots of different-coloured paper to make it easy to divide up the notebook into shopping hints, travel notes, recipes, expenses and so forth. They cost just £14.99.

 Always take a fold-up bag for bringing back home the things you won't be able to resist buying. Longchamp make them in delicious colours and you can get them at every duty-free shop.

Sunnies (or Shades)

It's a fine line, when choosing sunglasses, between trying to look fashionable and not seeming to emulate the WAGs. However, sunglasses are essential urban and holiday armour. We need them to protect our retinas from the thinning ozone layer and to shelter behind on the days when we've, er, celebrated a bit too hard and long the night before. They hide the wrinkles and also make us feel better dressed as well as a tad more glamorous.

They should, ideally, have tip-top lenses (according to legendary opticians Cutler & Gross, this means plastic CR39 lenses, which conform to European Standard BS EN 1836:1997) to protect the retina of the eye from harmful rays and to shield them from glare.

But I think most people seem to take the whole label matter much too seriously. It does appear that Victoria, Kate, Gwyneth and all the usual suspects have only to don a certain pair and they sell out in seconds – *even if* they're sporting price tags in the hundreds of pounds. At Heidi Klein, the oh-so-cute store that caters for the holiday needs of the sort of people who mind about these things, they tell me that when Kate Moss donned a pair of Oliver People's sunglasses, they were sold out in forty-eight hours flat. The same thing happened when Victoria Beckham was seen shading her peepers with some shades from Dolce & Gabbana. This is an expensive game to play, though, since these sort of people seem to own too many pairs for anybody sensible to keep up with. After the Dolce & Gabbanas, for instance, both Beckhams were spotted wearing Tsubis, a cult Australian brand costing around £165 a time. And after *them* came the Chanels, the Pradas, the Diors, the Guccis . . .

Just recently the fad has been for huge – as in ridiculously huge – shades. Subtler types have gone in for vintage. A cult name in these circles is Linda Farrow Vintage, which are sold in the Linda Farrow shop in Harrods. These are *not* second-hand but they come from a cache made during the 1960s, 70s and very early 80s and which, for some reason, weren't sold at the time. Some were designed for Emilio Pucci but there are lots of huge, chic Jackie O styles.

Cutler & Gross, which is the fashionable shop for what is called 'eyewear' in the trade, has a branch at

16 Knightsbridge Green, London SW1X 7QL; 020 7581 2250, and is devoted to nothing but mint-condition vintage. This is where you'll find all the iconic shapes worn by movie stars of yesteryear.

Keeping up with trendy fads is best done through those magazines that specialise in photographing whatever it is that Jennifer, Angelina, Posh or whoever is wearing – you can then take your pick, but you can be quite sure they'll be expensive, anything from £100 upwards. At Heidi Klein Holiday Shop (see p. 44), they simplify the matter each year by choosing just a couple of brands and they have a knack of knowing what's the hot brand of the season.

But you don't have to spend the sort of sums that the latest shades command. I trotted round town perfectly happily in a pair that cost £15 from Topshop and was asked several times where they came from.

A new/old name on the scene for those who like something more subtle is Oliver Goldsmith. A great name in the 1960s and 70s, it has been resurrected by Oliver's granddaughter, Claire, who tracked down the old factory where they are now making sunglasses by hand just the way they used to. These are high-quality glasses, so they're not cheap (£230–£250). Find them at Browns of South Molton Street, branches of Matches and from www.retrospecs.co.uk.

For sheer classic elegance, no fuss, no show, let me recommend Persols (if you want great service and are in London, go to Isis, 153C Fulham Road, London SW3 6SN; 020 7823 8080). They have very good lenses, come in simple shapes and they're the kind worn by elegant Italian aristos (the sort who don't want to get into the pages of *Hello*).

How to Pack

I think there's a packing gene and not many of us have it. Proper packing is an awesome art. This is how Sean Davoren, the head butler at the Lanesborough Hotel, who has packed and unpacked more suitcases than you and I could bear to contemplate, does it.

You should start by investing in at least thirty sheets of tissue paper. If that sounds extravagant, his canny butler advice is that you can reuse it many times and, furthermore, you can easily buy it at John Lewis and Paperchase. In an ideal world (not mine, but perhaps yours?) you should compile a list of what you intend to wear each day that you're going to be away and lay all the items out on the bed. You should layer the bottom of the suitcase with tissue paper.

Men should start with their trousers and lay the waist-band inside the suitcase with the trouser legs hanging over the sides. All shirts, undergarments and other folded items should be put neatly on top of the trousers. Shirts should have tissue paper in the centre, the sleeves should be folded inwards and a further layer of tissue paper placed over the shirt, which is then folded in half. Sweaters should have tissue paper rolled into the arms, with another layer of tissue paper placed on the outside before folding them in half. After this, the trouser legs (these are still hanging over the sides of the suitcase, remember?) are folded over the top of the shirts, sweaters, etc.

For business trips, men should put flat tissue paper inside their suit jackets and the jacket should be folded in half by flipping over the sleeves from the top of the shoulder to from an X-shape. Do all this and you won't have to iron a thing at the other end.

At Anderson & Sheppard, very swanky bespoke tailors who take some 200 suits at a time to New York for their annual trunk shows, they use plastic bags to keep their suits looking pristine (John Hitchock, the Managing Director, says they buy them in specially, but old ones from the dry-cleaner's will do). The key is to have a plastic bag that is much longer than the suit. Fold the air-filled empty part of the plastic bag over the bottom edge of the suit, seal this with Sellotape to keep the air in and *then* fold the suit in half. The air provides a layer of protection round the suit, which keeps it from forming creases.

Women should cover dresses from head to toe in tissue paper, inside and out. These should, if possible, be folded at the shoulders and the line of dresses to keep their shape. Again the key to garments arriving crease-free is to create pockets of air. The toes of shoes should be stuffed with tissue paper (which certainly makes sense if you've spent £500 on your Manolos). Shoes should be put in shoe bags to prevent heels marking clothes or ripping delicate silks. Belts should be rolled and placed in the pockets of space around the central pile of clothing.

Women should take care to seal up their cosmetics. Shops such as Muji, Peter Jones and Boots sell empty, small-sized plastic bottles, into which you can decant make-up. Put them all into zipped plastic bags but, if push comes to shove, even an ordinary carrier bag would do. Just make sure there are no holes in it.

The Yacht

Since boat etiquette requires that passengers go barefoot, you'll need to make sure your toes are as pretty as they come. Go for a good pedicure. Yes, of course, you can do all that hard skin removing at home (every beauty counter has a line in do-it-yourself products) but there's nothing like a good professional for making nails look groomed and cared for.

You'll also need some other more tangible props. Think about a delicious floaty kaftan from Allegra Hicks or Ananya for those evenings when you're sipping something white and chilled whilst the sun sinks like a great big orange. And even Marks & Spencer is doing lines in matching bikinis, bathing costumes and kaftans these days. Then you'll need a wrap. Buy a feather-light soft pashmina blanket (use it as a scarf, shawl or blanket) in pretty soft pastel stripes from www.kuljitsidhu.co.uk. Gorgeous sunglasses, it goes without saying, are important. Cutler & Gross do some brilliantly retro ones if you want a change from the big designer names (Gucci, Prada, Chanel, Chloé *et al.*).

Next, a great hat. This can be hard to pack so you will

either have to wear it on the way, buy a fold-up proper panama (which, bizarrely, as I'm sure you know, comes from Ecuador) or look out for one at a local shop when you land. You'll also need some floaty linen – Shirin Guild (at 241 Fulham Road, London SW3 6HY; 020 7351 2766, as well as at Liberty) does this beautifully – and a couple of great accessories. The true luxury holdall has to be Bottega Veneta's Cabat holder in plaited leather. It's beautiful, it's perfect – very Jackie O – and it costs a small fortune (£2,495 in the larger size; £1,995 in the smaller), from 33 Sloane Street, London SW1X 9NR; 020 7838 9394. Get some great shoes for stepping ashore (Tod's loafers look very laid-back Italian if you're wearing trousers) and you're set.

The Plane

Be comfy. Celebrities or the really rich, whose first-class tickets (or, even better, private jets) are secure, like to slob about in Juicy Couture. I like to wear easy trousers, either a pair of quite grown-up-looking cargo pants – which means not too much hardwear or fancy bits on them – or some loose navy-blue silky cropped trousers), teamed with a T-shirt and a cashmere cardigan. Gap's line of 'boyfriend pants' (i.e. loose and easy) are very comfortable for travelling, if not very smart, though if you pair them with a good jacket they can look great. If I'm going from somewhere cold to the tropics, I wear tights underneath and remove them before landing. Over everything I wear a three-quarter-length coat. A trench would be perfect, if they suit you, or a swinging trench without a belt for those who don't like tying things around their middle. I never get on a plane without a pashmina – all that air-conditioning. Debbie Moore of Pineapple Studio fame once told me that she always puts her feet in brown-paper bags, which stops them swelling up. I've never had the nerve to follow her advice and anyway I'm lucky in that my feet don't swell up – but if yours do and you can face it, there's the remedy.

If you find airports stressful, check out Holistic Silk (www.holisticsilk.co.uk). Its silk products are filled with 'aromatic herbs and ancient wisdom' (the better, I assume, to make the hassle seem like nothing in the face of eternity). Kit yourself out with their Japanese brocade slippers with magnetic insoles (£65), which deal with blocked chi; block out frenetic sights with their silk jet-set eye mask; rest your neck on one of their silk neck pillows, and don't forget your silk yoga mat bag for restoring your karma at the other end.

Cash-CA (www.cashca.co.uk) has a Cashmere Flight Kit, comprising an eye mask, lap blanket, knee-length socks and ballet slippers, all carried in a pillow bag that comes in delicious colours (from Harvey Nichols, 109–125 Knightsbridge, London SW1X 7RJ). Some picky people take their own feather-filled cushions and, if you have one of those delicate constitutions and can't sleep on the mundane ones provided by airlines, Ginger Lily (www.gingerlily.co.uk) does little silk travelling pillows. Personally, I've got enough to carry, what with books, toiletries and all the rest.

Now that you can check in online it's really worth doing. It saves all that worry about where you're going to sit and it means you can get to the airport that much later. You can also – if you're organised enough – get your bags sent on ahead through www.firstluggage.com.

With big sunglasses, to hide the jet lag, and a really terrific bag (here it really counts) that is easy to carry, you can emerge looking great.

The Safari

It's got to be khaki, hasn't it? Though you don't want to arrive looking as if you think you're Meryl Streep in *Out of Africa* – too embarrassing. Since I go to Africa a lot I tend to buy good khaki things whenever I see them because you can't always find them when you need them. And however appealing crisp white looks against the khaki, resist the temptation because when you're in the bush hoping not to be seen by anything wild, if you're wearing white you might as well stand up and shout, 'Here I am!'

You'll need good shorts, comfy long trousers (often long is best because, if you tuck them into your socks, it keeps the insects at bay), a fleece or jacket and a sweater (those early-morning drives can be perishingly cold) – all in khaki or beige. A few pretty tops for evening and some costume jewellery for perking the look up and that's it. Don't forget a sunhat and a rucksack to carry things like your bird book, suncream and binoculars. Safari lodges are good at doing laundry – they turn things round the same day – so you won't need to take a lot.

The Beach

Well, of course, it depends which beach. If it's the Caribbean's St Barth's, you'll need to look to your smart togs – jewelled flat sandals and ballet pumps, chic black capri pants, easy white linen, big shirts over skinny pants, floaty tops in pristine white, huge woven bags, great big beads for glamming up. Swimming costumes from Eres and La Perla are expensive, but that's because proper corsetry (which they offer) costs more to make. Lotty B (the wife of Mustique's doctor – find her wares on www.lottyb.com) does beautiful silky sarongs and floaty kaftans, or you could go for one of Bamford & Co's beautiful white silk embroidered kaftans (from Bamford & Co, Draycott Avenue, London SW3 3AJ; 020 7589 8729). Heidi Klein's shop in Notting Hill (see page 44) is filled with very hip beachwear all year long, thus neatly filling a great big gap. Get your swimsuits, bikinis, cover-ups, sunglasses, sunhats and even a quick tan in its tanning booth, all under one roof.

If you are in despair over swimwear, Lands' End, that waspy American brand, will sort you out. It uses Slendertex, a light but fine supporting material, and has swimsuits with tummy control panels, high necks or waist-flattering styles, and even – for those who've had breast cancer – special mastectomy suits. Its amazing website (www.landsend.co.uk) has a marvellous section called 'anxiety zones' where you can click on to your particular problem (big boobs, pear-shape or whatever) and up will come a range of suggestions, such as little skirts to cover the tops of thighs of the heavy-hipped, or panels to hold in lumps and bumps, and it stocks some styles up to size 30. I've had women readers in tears of gratitude for the tip. Get a catalogue by telephoning 0800 61 71 61. You can also shop on the US website at www.landsend.com, which has an even larger selection.

The City Weekend

This assumes a city weekend in what's laughingly known as a 'temperate climate' (i.e. northern Europe – or possibly New York). Unless you're in the private jet set, this means serious discipline, particularly with airlines getting tougher about baggage by the day. I've partly solved the problem by settling on one pair of trousers, which I team with three different jackets to give me three separate looks. I have a brilliant soft feminine navy-blue crêpe jersey jacket and trousers by the dear, late-lamented Jean Muir. It's very chic, but comfortable enough for flying. Under the jacket I wear a soft navy silky top but if it were very cold I could put on a navy cashmere sweater instead. A sassy cropped navy jacket with taffeta cuffs and taffeta revers (instead of the crêpe jersey jacket) turns the outfit into evening wear. I add jewellery, some sexy shoes and I'm ready for dinner, the opera, whatever. To make it look different the next day I wear a sharp lime-green jacket in an identical cropped, sassy shape over the navy trousers and silky top. Now the Jean Muir label has very sadly disappeared, but you can easily replicate the solution by searching for an attractive trouser suit and then buying separate jackets (everybody, but everybody on the high street does them now in very cute shapes and colours). The great thing about this plan for a capsule wardrobe is that it needs just two pairs of shoes (one pair does the day look and another turns on a bit of style come the evening).

Over it, of course, goes a coat, which will vary depending upon the time of year. In winter it's heavier; in summer I choose something more like a raincoat.

To give even greater variety you could pack a couple of other tops, possibly one of Chloé's delicious floaty smocks, if you can afford it, or otherwise one of Topshop's sweet numbers, and a skirt. But for shopping, museum viewing and city touring, comfortable shoes have to be the non-negotiable accessory. Tod's loafers are great. I personally think wearing trainers is pretty naff but you can get away with plimsolls (either Converse plimsolls or the French brand Bensimon, www.bensimon.com, which is terrific).

Snow

Designer skiwear seems to me to come at preposterous prices for those who aren't married to hedge-fund managers (Chanel skis, I ask you, as if the snow can tell), but really cheap options aren't easy to find. Which isn't to say that if you *are* married to a hedge-fund zillionaire, you won't look awfully pretty posing outside your private chalet in Chanel, Ralph Lauren, Armani, Prada *et al.* It's just that for the rest of us there are cheaper options.

If you're really skint (skiing holidays don't come cheap) it's worth checking out Tchibo (www.tchibo.co.uk), which is a German company that started off selling coffee and, for some reason that bears no relation to conventional business school teachings, has branched out into selling whatever its buyers have found to be a bargain that week. It could be cookie cutters or children's slides but during the winter season it often offers skiwear at astonishingly low prices (£39 for a jacket). It's also worth checking out www.outdoormegastore.co.uk, which has some great inexpensive buys, too.

Skiwear has to be functional; it has to keep out the wet and the snow, so you can't afford to compromise. The fancy brands are mostly for those who spend more time promenading around the resort's smartest shops than perfecting their parallels. Marks & Spencer and Topshop both often sell skiwear or, more precisely, anoraks that fit the purpose. Otherwise high street shops such as Ellis Brigham or Snow + Rock are the experts. You could choose an all-in-one ski suit, though fashions in recent years have turned back to the trousers and anorak option. You'll also need proper ski socks, which provide warmth as well as a buffer between your feet and the unyielding surfaces of the ski boot, and proper ski gloves that have linings and real insulation, and are waterproof (no, delicate cashmere won't do). Proper thermal underwear – long johns and a long-sleeved vest – are vital. Get them at Marks & Spencer or www.figleaves.com.

For skiing in really cold places I have a neck-warmer and a warm hat. And when heli-skiing in British Columbia, I found foot- and hand-warmers (little packs with magic contents that warm up when you open them, to be put inside your boots and gloves) miraculous. Don't forget great but efficient sunnies (you must protect your eyes against UV rays, which when reflected off the snow can damage the retina) and goggles for those dodgy days.

Underpinnings

Since delectable underwear doesn't seem to be the British woman's birthright – unlike French and Italian women, whose streets and stores are awash with delicious little bits of nothing – you'll have to make an effort to find it. But things are getting better. We should all genuflect in the direction of Marks & Spencer, which now has divine bits of frippery with matching pairs of pants in gorgeous colours and which do their job (of giving proper support) brilliantly. Its Magic Knickers are fabulous for days when you want to wear a clingy dress and need to hide any incipient rolls of flesh. Underpinnings, as we all learn the hard way, are more essential than we think. The right ones can turn a rather shapeless little number into something surprisingly sexy. The wrong ones, leading to drooping boobs (nothing is more ageing, particularly as one gets older and there somehow seems to be more of them) and floppy tummies, can make the most avant-garde of numbers look like a shapeless tent.

The right bra is more important than anything else, unless you have tiny little boobs, which may not be great for your sex life or for propping up certain sorts of décolletage, but are certainly an asset when it comes to wearing fashionable clothes. The major mistake that most of us make in choosing a bra is to buy one that is too large around the back and too small a cup. I always thought I was a 34D until I got myself measured professionally and found I was really a 32E (i.e. smaller in the back, larger in the cup). Real support comes not from the bra straps but from a good fit around the back. Some 60 per cent of women, say the surveys, are wearing the wrong-sized bra. Playtex recently launched a new idea: bras that go up in half-sizes for all those who are neither exactly one size or the other. Very useful.

 The website www.figleaves.com offers lots of great information on bras, how to choose them, how to measure yourself and how to make sure they fit.

Lacy underwear makes one feel deliciously feminine but it doesn't provide a smooth silhouette. Under T-shirts you need the right size seamless bra in a skin tone (*not* white). If you really feel you've gone to seed around the middle, then all-in-one 'bodies' are great if you want to wear something like a Diane von Furstenberg or an Issa wraparound jersey dress where every little roll shows.

Delicious underwear is good for one's morale and anything that doesn't come in a pack of three has to be good news. These days there are more delightful underwear shops around than ever before and that great Italian underwear chain Intimissimi – the patron saint of those who love glamorous undies but can't afford Agent Provocateur or Myla prices – has opened on Oxford Street in London.

I don't think one needs masses of bras unless one has an extraordinary variety of necklines to cope with. For most of us what we need is: one cotton bra in white, one black in Tactel for wearing under the tightest tops, one nude and one multi-strap (for strange-shaped necklines and yokes). Then you need a divinely pretty one for those days when . . . you never know what may happen. And two pairs of matching knickers in your preferred shape to match each bra (as Nanny always said – you never know when you're going to be run over).

Under see-through or white shirts, wear a nude bra, not a white one. Nude Hanro camisoles are perfect for wearing under lightweight tops to give a better line. Hanro is a brilliant name to look out for if you need very, very fine underwear of the highest quality.

As for thongs, I can't imagine who thought them up but if you like wearing them . . . fine. Me? I think they're about the most uncomfortable and hideous items I've come across in a long time.

When it comes to tights, it goes without saying – doesn't it? – that opaque tights are what you wear if your legs aren't great. Grey with a slight sheen makes a great change from black. In summer, when opaque tights no longer cut it, you need to take care over the precise cut-off point of the hem of your skirt. Wild coloured tights can work if carefully chosen; I've seen purple ones look amazing with black and even red. One great beauty, no longer young, came to dinner recently wearing a black dress and wild tights in red and cream stripes with red shoes. She looked fantastic. Such eccentricity needs a really good eye if it is to work. But a lot of pattern only works on *very* slim legs and even then it needs to be carefully teamed with everything else. The Wolford brand (www.wolfordboutiquelondon.com) may be more expensive than most but in my experience their tights last longer and have a knack of providing just the colour and texture the season requires. Otherwise Marks & Spencer's are terrific.

If you have areas that need to be corralled in, the name to remember is Spanx (even Gwyneth, we are reliably told by those magazines that specialise in such titbits, has worn them on occasion), which has all sorts of shapes for controlling different bits. You can get just knickers, or knickers with long panels to hold in the thighs, or all-in-ones for the big night when you want the whole torso to look taut and firm. The

Spanx Hide & Sleek Hi-Rise Body Smoother, for instance, starts just below the bra line and goes all the way down to mid-thigh, smoothing down the bulging bits and cinching in the waist. A name to conjure with. You can find them at Rigby & Peller (for details, see p. 64) and lots of stores with good underwear departments. Online you can get them from www.figleaves.com. Agent Provocateur has a sexier alternative, a waspie that is made from duchesse satin and is more like an old-fashioned corset, pulling in the waist.

Specialist Shops

AGENT PROVOCATEUR has lots of shops – check them out on www.agentprovocateur.com. You don't go to them for serious support underwear; you go for delicious silky creations, all lacy, frothy and fabulous. They also have lots of wittily naughty-sounding things like Maitresse Body Wash and candles called Strip or Tease.

CARINE GILSON, 12 Lowndes Street, London SW1X 9EX; 020 7823 1177; www.carinegilson.com. Her speciality is making the most divine underwear to order. She uses silk from Lyons and hand-made Chantilly lace from Calais, and she turns out ravishing bras, panties, slips and negligees. But she also does swimwear, using the same corsetry techniques.

COCO DE MER, 23 Monmouth Street, Covent Garden, London WC2H 9DD; www.coco-de-mer.co.uk. Sam Roddick (daughter

LINGERIE WEBSITES

www.bravissimo.com now offers bras in cup sizes that go up to K but also does delicious underwear in all the more usual sizes.

www.figleaves.com has almost every great brand you can think of, as well as Playtex's very new bras that go up in half-sizes. It also has an excellent eight-step guide to finding the right size bra for you.

www.bodas.co.uk does everyday underwear in finest cotton as well as it can be done. It will also revamp your underwear drawer. For £150 (£100 of which is redeemable against the underwear you buy), they'll give you the ultimate underwear make-over. They'll go through your drawers, tell you what to keep, what to throw – and, but of course, what to buy. Then they'll sell it to you. And they tell you not to use fabric conditioner with underwear that contains Lycra – it rots it. Worth knowing, that.

www.mytights.com is a brilliant site for all sorts of fashion brands that otherwise you'd have to track down in specialists shops. Besides control-top, extra-long and petite tights and stockings, there are tights for flying (to help with the circulation), footless tights and those wonder pants – Spanx.

www.myla.com offers tiny confections of delicious silk and satin for those who want something sweet and sexy rather than more serious upholstery.

of Anita) has created a rich, sensual, fun place to buy some lovely – and some extraordinary – underwear. She sells vintage-inspired silk knickers, bras, petticoats and nightwear, but check them all out carefully because sometimes there are some extraordinary erotic surprises lurking amongst the apparently blameless pieces. There are also erotic accessories and some really delicious lotions and potions.

RIGBY & PELLER, 2 Hans Road, London SW3 1RX; www.rigbyandpeller.com. Only lissom young things can get away with itsy-bitsy pieces of underwear. Post childbirth and once the years start to pile up, proper underwear makes all the difference. Rigby & Peller is the place to turn to once things begin to droop. There are fantastic collections that provide support and a touch of allure for the sake of morale. Things aren't cheap, but they will fit you properly – and it's worth getting your bra size checked out professionally every five years or so. They say that some 80 per cent of their customers turn up wearing the wrong-size bra.

INTIMISSIMI, 90–92 Oxford Street, London W10 1DY; 020 7637 49550; www.intimissimi.com, is an Italian brand that specialises in moderately priced but deliciously pretty underwear and it has just arrived in the UK, to the great excitement of those who used to have to go to Italy to buy its wares. It's many a young girl's favourite lingerie store of all time.

Paris

A few great underwear stores not to miss:

SABBIA ROSA, 71–73 rue des Saints-Pères, Paris 75006; +33 1 45 48 88 37, (one of Sofia Coppola's favourite Paris shops), is like a divine boudoir filled with deliciously soft silky bits of underwear. Underwear for honeymoons.

RYKIEL WOMAN, 4 rue de Grenelle, Paris 75006. A special project of Nathalie Rykiel, daughter of Sonia, this is a Parisian take on our very own Coco de Mer, i.e. lots of delicious erotic underwear (anyone for pink silk whips?) as well as some wonderfully useful silk jersey workout pants, cashmere wraps, sweet knickers and the like.

CARINE GILSON, 18 rue de Grenelle, Paris 75007; +33 1 43 26 46 71. She does divinely luxurious couture lingerie but there are always some ready-to-wear numbers that you can take away on the spot.

New York

VICTORIA'S SECRET, www.victoriassecret.com, the working girl's playground. There are branches everywhere and, if it isn't having too vulgar a moment (always a risk), a great place for inexpensive, delightful fripperies. It also stocks some of Intimissimi's ranges.

KIKI DE MONTPARNASSE, 79 Greene Street, New York,

NY 10012; +1 212 965 8150. The latest destination for the downtown set. Described as somewhere between 'lingerie store, high-end sex store and boudoir lounge', it offers luxurious underwear and nightwear and, though distinctly on the naughty side, there's not a hint of seediness.

One's Chapeau

. . . Or all you need to know about hats.

I'm a great believer in the power of the hat. David Shilling (who now only makes hats for special commissions) used to say, 'The whole point of a hat is to make its wearer look beautiful.' My sentiments precisely, though I like Miss Piggy's addition of allure and mystery. Miss Piggy, fans will remember, thought: 'One's *chapeau* provides the perfect opportunity for a profound fashion statement. Your hat should not merely say, "Here is my head," but rather it should convey a sense of allure, mystery, even intrigue. Here *moi's chapeau* [this under a picture of a rather large black sombrero-style felt, tipped at a jaunty angle] is saying, "*Oui*, I have time for one quick chocolate malted in that café with the umbrellas that have tables on their handles, but then I must board the Oriental Express for a rendezvous with the Duke of Candelabra in the lovely, yet sinister, Kingdom of Rutabagia."' Miss Piggy had the right idea. A hat that can deliver all that is well worth the hundreds that a bespoke hat costs today.

The right hat can be a bit of magic, which we sometimes need to be reminded of. I like the story of the customer who complained to that great master, Christian Dior, that the price for a hat he'd proposed was exorbitant, given that it was merely a bit of tulle and some feathers. The master took the hat apart, gave the customer the materials and said with a grave bow, 'The materials, madame, are free, it is the genius that costs.'

Philip Treacy is a genius and a master craftsman, the modern equivalent of a Dior. He changed the way we looked at hats. 'Hats,' he said, 'were associated with old ladies and I thought that was crazy. Everyone has a head [observant fellow], so everyone has a possibility to wear a hat.' People, he also noticed, feel better for wearing a hat, which is true, too. It's hard to get a handle on the cost of a bespoke Philip Treacy hat from his atelier (69 Elizabeth Street, London SW1W 9PT; 020 7824 8787; www.philiptreacy.co.uk), though anecdotally it seems to vary from about £600 to £3000, let alone be sure of getting the personal attentions of Philip Treacy himself (he travels a great deal). However, you can buy into some of his magic by getting one of his range of occasion hats at department stores such as Selfridges and Harrods. Prices start at about £200.

Otherwise, I love the minimalist refinement of Patricia Underwood's hats. They're in the finest, most divine straw and – in winter – sometimes in felt, in simple but beguiling shapes. She's decamped to America now, where you can buy them at

Bergdorf Goodman on 5th Avenue, but in London a selection is stocked at Fenwick, New Bond Street, London W1A 3BS.

Gabriela Ligenza (5 Ellis Street, London SW1X 9AL; 020 7730 2200) also does exquisitely fine straws and deliciously pretty little cocktail hats.

Cozmo Jenks (21 New Quebec Street, London W1H 7SA) offers a bit more razzmatazz (perfect for mothers of the bride), which is no doubt why Jay Kay of Jamiroquai, Kylie Minogue and Leah Wood, amongst many others, seek her out. She'll make you a hat from scratch to suit your face or outfit for something like £600 upwards (telephone 020 7258 0111 for an appointment). She also does ready-to-wear hats (they're all blocked in Luton but every one is hand-trimmed in her Knightsbridge studio), which can be found at Selfridges, Harrods and Coco Ribbon, the cute Notting Hill boutique. Her ready-to-wear ranges in price from £285 to £575.

Marie Mercie has a cute hat shop at 8 Knightsbridge Green, London SW1X 7QL; 020 7589 7534, where they'll make you a brilliant little cocktail hat to order.

A new hatter to watch is Katharine Goodison, who used to be a lawyer and now does wonderfully innovative bespoke hats. Telephone 020 7828 6498 for an appointment.

At the cheaper end, remember that many a designer does diffusion or ready-to-wear ranges, and good department stores such as Fenwick of New Bond Street, Peter Jones, Selfridges and Harrods carry these at infinitely more user-friendly prices.

My young friends, some of whom like to wear gorgeous

little hats much of the time, tell me that they get great bargains at both Urban Outfitters and Diesel (particularly the men's department).

* www.hatsandthat.com is a very user-friendly website with some great big glamorous hats for under £50.

COZMO JENKS ON HOW TO CHOOSE A HAT

You must try on lots, even ones you think may not suit you. Remember, you can always take it off. Then there are a few rules: never have a brim that is wider than your shoulders and most especially not if you're wearing a short skirt. If you have a short neck, choose an upturned or asymetrical brim. If you have a nose you'd rather not draw attention to, choose a shallow crown. Experiment with the angle, particularly with berets, where angle is all.

Shoes

Ah, shoes. You will have gathered that I'm rather keen on them. But I've only come fully to understand the transforming power of shoes rather late in life. Of course Carrie Bradshaw (of *Sex and the City*) and her pals cottoned on much earlier. I discovered all this by chance when I was overcome with desire – the only name for it – for a pair of grass-green Marc Jacobs shoes. I bought them even though they were a mind-boggling price. But the weird thing, as I keep telling all my friends, is that in spite of the exorbitant sum they cost – the best part of £400, I seem to remember – they've turned out to be one of the best investments I've ever made. They can transform almost anything – and I mean even the greyest, dreariest sack – into something sassy and fun. I wear them with all sorts of things. They never let me down. It doesn't matter if I'm having a fat day – they still fit. Whilst other fashion trends become increasingly unsuitable (mini playsuits, anyone?), shoes are ageless.

So I'm now very keen to pass on my new-found enthusiasm for what the right shoes can do for an outfit. Apart from anything else they can transform the attitude of others towards you. They can instantly say: ah, yes, fun, sassy, outgoing. Or the wrong pair can equally forcibly spell out: dowdy, dreary, can't be bothered, not fun to know. So think about shoes. Instead of splashing out on a new dress or jacket when you think your wardrobe needs a bit of fizz, think about some really glorious shoes. They're not easy to walk in, I know, but you can always pack them into the huge tote bags that, as I mentioned earlier, are what passes for handbags these days and put them on once you've got to wherever you're going.

When it comes to heels, I'm afraid class costs and it shows. I wish it weren't true but there it is. And what's more, shoe prices seem to be reaching the ridiculous heights of bags and to have just as much cult status attached to certain brands. To buy more cheaply you need an astute eye. Office, Dune, Topshop and New York immigrant Aldo are all worth checking out as are Zara and New Look (it's not for nothing that it sells a pair every second).

Keep your eye on the magazines to see what is currently fashionable and then look for the nearest equivalent in the cheaper outlets. Often the difference between fun, funky and classy, and cheap and vulgar is a mere fraction of a centimetre or a minuscule colour shade. So be alert.

THESE ARE THE SHOES THAT HAVE WORKED FOR ME:

My wonderful Marc Jacobs: grass-green with platform soles, peep toes and a whopping great 'jewel' in the middle. Yves St Laurent has compulsively desirable shoes, as does Prada, but if these are really outside your means (though I do think cheap shoes never cut it quite like expensive ones) then look at Kurt Geiger a bit further down the price chain, or L. K. Bennett (she knows how to get the look of the moment but her shoes don't quite have the finish and attention to detail of the pricier brands). I also love Christian Louboutin shoes, which are incredibly sexy without being vulgar – you can always spot them by their bright red soles – and he does the best espadrilles in the world. At about £130 a time they seem expensive but you can wear them all summer long and they come with ribbons, beads and sequins in almost every colour you could think of. For fancy villa parties they're just the thing. In certain circles Louboutin is taking over from Blahnik and Jimmy Choo as the shoe of the moment and like both those labels Louboutins are vertiginously expensive but a pair a year is perhaps a supportable extravagance.

Every wardrobe should have a pair of red shoes. They have a power and a magic of their own. My own fabulous red pair (by L. K. Bennett, as it happens) – open-toed, with a funky high heel and a cross-over strap around the ankle – are my winter evening standbys. Any black dress is transformed by them. I will never be without a pair again.

Robert Clergerie has solved my winter daily shoe conundrum. His high wedge heels give me height (I'm only five feet two inches), they're so comfortable that I can walk and even run in them, and the high closed front made of dark elastic material gives them an elegant look. Dames Judi Dench and Maggie Smith are both addicted to his wedges and he brings out a version of them every season. Robert Clergerie has two shops in London, at 120 Draycott Avenue, SW3 3AH, and at 67 Wigmore Street, W1U 1PY.

If you want some really cutting-edge, avant-garde shoes that aren't mainstream, look out for Costume Nationale. There's not much of a selection in the UK, but check them out in Barney's of New York. Their shoes are quite simply fab and almost nobody else will have them.

Audley, at 72 Duke of York Square, London SW3 1AJ; 020 7730 2902, is a bit of a well-kept secret. It doesn't go in for high fashion but offers attractive, moderately fashionable shoes in lovely colours at reasonable prices. However, its great USP is that it'll make to order for a very reasonable sum indeed, and it's specially good for wedding shoes.

Thanks to Kate Moss, who is photographed all over town wearing their sparkly ballet pumps, French Sole, at 6 Ellis Street, London SW1X 9AL; 020 7730 3771; www.frenchsole.com, has become a bit of a cult label. Since their pumps are only about £65 a time (a mere flea-bite when compared with the prices of Christian Louboutin, who is not many streets away), customers tend to buy them by the fistful.

Taryn Rose (www.tarynrose.com) is a name worth remembering. She is a charming American from Beverly Hills who trained as an orthopaedic surgeon. In the course of her work she saw so many feet deformed by bad footwear that she decided to do something about it. Her aim was to create a range of shoes that would be fashionable, comfortable *and* give the foot proper support. Also, being a very young and attractive woman herself, she wanted glamorous shoes but didn't want to end up semi-crippled. Although her shoes may not be quite in Christian Louboutin's or Manolo Blahniks' league when it comes to glamour, they are handmade in the softest leather and do offer a high degree of chic as well as proper support. She says that for everyday wear, heels should be no more than two inches high. High-heeled stilettos should be the footwear equivalent of a chocolate pudding – delicious but only to be indulged in on special occasions. She also says that if a shoe pinches when you first try it on, don't buy it – it shouldn't have to be broken in. For the moment her shoes are stocked in the UK only at Harrods in Knightsbridge, London, but she has her own boutiques in Beverly Hills, New York, Las Vegas, San José and Seoul.

Boots: every wardrobe should have them. There are, of course, just two types of boot. There are the warm, cosy type for country weekends where practicality and warmth are what really count, even if from time to time they seem to gain a weird kind of fashionable kudos. Take Uggs, which do the job brilliantly and which Kate Moss made – briefly – a cult boot. For practical use, though, some people prefer Le Chameau, those French cotton-lined green wellies (very chic, from www.wellie-web.co.uk). Then there's the fashion boot. They can come in awfully fancy prices – Ralph Lauren or

Chloé will set you back more than £500. They're also a moveable feast. Each year tastes and fads change. It helps to keep your eyes peeled or grab *Grazia* at the hairdresser if you want to keep up to speed. Knee-high boots are particularly useful if you're wearing a short skirt, as they make it seem much more modest, which means that as you get older you can get away with short skirts for longer. They're also great – obviously – for covering up thick ankles or fat calves. High-heeled ankle-boots, when in fashion, are surprisingly sexy.

If you have trouble zipping up your boots (all that ballet when young), then www.plusinboots.co.uk should sort you out. Selve (www.selve.co.uk) will make boots to measure.

Penelope Chilvers is a bit of a cult name. Her boots are sold in good shoe departments and The Cross, 141 Portland Road, London W11 4LR; 020 7727 6760; www.penelopechilvers.com, but her USP (worn by Elle Macpherson, Kate Middleton, Jemima Khan and many a Notting Hill yummy mummy) are her 'long boots' – classic Spanish riding boots made of cowhide, with a tassel on the zip and a corrugated rubber sole.

Handbags

Whole theses have been written on handbags and their semiotics. Designer bags now regularly cost more than the monthly mortgage repayment. The current price of the famous Birkin by Hermès is something like £4,000, depending on the leather. I know fashion assistants on small salaries who spend phenomenal sums on handbags, feeling improperly dressed unless they have one of the latest numbers swinging on their arms. They can all tell their Roxys and their Novaks from their Lariats and their Mombasas. Bags, it seems, are the new jewels or rather, as one *New Yorker* writer pointed out, they're like 'dowries, signs of possession and responsibility and flaunted power'. All this is relatively new. The handbag is no longer a useful, quite attractive accessory. Rather it has become an object of acute desire, a way in which the 'having it all' generation of women reward themselves for all those hours at the coal-face. Last winter, a journalist describing London Fashion Week wrote, 'Everybody – everybody – is talking about handbags with the intensity of cardinals appointing a new Pope.'

It seems to have been Silvia Venturini (she of the Fendi dynasty) who changed the handbag landscape in the late 1990s when she brought out the Fendi Baguette, which turned out to embody in its odd oblong shape (like the baguette that Frenchmen tuck under their arms) the desires of noughties women. It changed the market irrevocably. Prada, Gucci, Louis Vuitton, Christian Dior, Chloé, Marc Jacobs – you name them – followed in Fendi's footsteps and they seem to have tapped into an ever-widening circle of desire. Bag wars arrived. Some of us, though, are more susceptible to their charms than others. I love some of the designs but the notion of spending the vast sums of money required to keep up with the latest 'it bag' seems to me so obscene that I opt right out and look for little niche numbers that seem to me more interesting, better priced and, best of all, nobody, but nobody can tell where they came from.

I seem to own somewhere between twenty-five and thirty bags, a shamingly large number in my view, but a mere pipsqueak of a collection compared to the true fashionista's pile. Not so long ago the owner of a cult handbag brand did some serious research and found that only two or three of the more than a hundred women he interrogated about their handbag habits owned fewer than twenty-five bags. Of the Voguettes, you will not be surprised to learn, none owned less than twenty-five, most owned more than forty-five and a few owned more than a hundred. But even in less rarefied fashion arenas, he found that many a secretary owned fifty or sixty bags, and one middle-aged, very proper PA to a chief executive admitted to having well over a hundred. A secretary, he discovered, would easily spend between £300 and £400 and, if she got a real itch to own something, she'd spend even more. Each season, it seems, women would start thinking quite early which would be the 'must-have' bag of the moment. Some kept their bags in the proper 'care bags' in which they're sold and, because they had so many and they couldn't remember which was where, they took Polaroid pictures of each bag and pinned them on the front so they could quickly lay hands on the one they wanted (good practical advice there, I'd say).

 A new idea imported from the States is to rent instead of buy handbags. This means you can have a new handbag each month. Tap into www.fashionhire.co.uk, where membership is just £9.95 a month, which enables you to hire a very trendy handbag at a price that varies depending upon the popularity of the bag, but seems to work out at something like about £90 a month. It is still expensive, but nothing like as expensive as buying them all.

Personally I like my bags slightly funky. To be sure, I am devoted to my wonderful python Chloé Betty, which rattles with zips and chains – it's great for bringing out when one's entering into competitive fashionista turf. But one of my all-time favourites comes from the shop at the Musée des Arts Décoratifs in Paris. It's made entirely out of recycled plastic and is embellished with strips of Hermès silks. It's made by Luisa Cevese as part of her Riedizioni collection and it cost something like £170. But I can't take it everywhere. In designery circles it goes down a bundle, but I wouldn't take it, say, to Ascot. In the UK, Designers' Guild (275–277 King's Road, London SW3 5EN; 020 7351 5775) sometimes has some Luisa Cevese pieces.

I have another seriously funky bag bought from the Contemporary Applied Arts shop at 2 Percy Street, London W1T 1DD; 020 7436 2344, which is made from a man's pinstriped suit fabric and the front is covered in buttons. It's by Edson Raupp, who seems to have a thing about buttons (or is it tailoring?) and I love it, most particularly because nobody ever knows where it's from. And it cost well under £200.

I nearly always have an Anya Hindmarch on the go. She does great totes; her bags look fashionable but don't shout, and for young mothers what could be nicer than her Photo Bag – a canvas tote with a picture of children and/or husband? Serious working women love her Bespoke Ebury.

For travelling I have a wonderful Meli-Melo, a great soft carry-all by Melissa de Bono (they're so soft that they pack flat, so you can take an extra one for bringing back the shopping), into which I can fit the requisite pashmina, book, change of shoes, toiletries and other in-flight essentials.

For evening I have three favourites: a delicious little snakeskin number from Tanner Kroll with handles made of rough aquamarines; a small, very chic, plain black satin number with the frame edged in crystal and a slinky long handle by Judith Lieber of all people (she's mostly known for her exuberantly glittery bags but she can do elegant very well when she wants to); and finally one of Susan Benjamin's beautiful little leather clutches, which is printed all over with darling flowers (available exclusively from Laura B, see p. 35).

Japanese designer Shizue (her shop, at 93 Mount Street, London WIK 2SY; 020 7491 3322, is a jewel in itself) creates little bag masterpieces. Some have a touch of the Japanese love of kitsch, others are over-the-top sumptuous and yet others are just plain elegant. Almost all are like jewels and if you add one to, say, a black evening outfit, it's as big and bold a statement as a brilliant necklace. If you haven't yet discovered Shizue, she's the designer who was the first to think of adding something as simple and practical as a light to her 'opera' bag.

Cheaper Options

Debenhams has some terrific bags at good prices and Jasper Conran's collection in particular is well worth a look. If you like the Birkin but can't afford its price tag, one of Jasper Conran's leather bags is a very good alternative. Furla and Osprey are two good names to look out for that do fashionable shapes, use good leathers and don't cost a fortune. There are lots of good middle-range names. Look at our own dear Jaeger, for instance, which has come up with some stunning bags which, whilst they're not cheap, are a whole lot better priced than the current 'it' handbags from the fancier names. My own view is that if you can't afford leather, don't go for vinyl or plastic (unless it's really kitschy plastic, not plastic that is pretending to be leather); you're better to look for a fabric bag. I'm a fan of Accessorize, whose windows are a source of neverending delight, filled as they are with brilliant colourways and intricate embroidery and beading. They always have a fantastic selection of inexpensive bags. And hang on to this fact: the divine Kate Middleton looks a dream and is usually to be seen carrying nothing more pretentious than Longchamps and Bric's.

Bag Shoppers

Natalie Massenet, who runs net-a-porter.com, that compulsive site for the fashionaholic, has learned that there are three sorts of bag shoppers.

1. The CLASSIC BAG SHOPPER – the woman who goes for bags such as the Hermès Birkin bag. 'This is the sort of bag that looks right any time, any place, night or day. It's big, it's extravagant and it says loud and clear that you're rich, you're clever – and, most of all, you're lucky.' It's the bag we buy ourselves when we've got a promotion, or have done a great deal, or it's the treat our husbands or partners buy for us if we're fortunate. The Chanel quilted 2.55 and Tomas Maier's Intrecito tote for Bottega Veneta will probably become new classics, as will most things by Marc Jacobs and Bottega Veneta.

   And – a great tip – there's also the L.L. Bean tote bag, which Natalie Massenet calls 'the Birkin of totes' ('It says you're rich and you're chic; you're just not quite so lucky'), which costs something like £20 and is an all-time classic. You can buy it online (www.llbean.com) and the price includes your name being embroidered on the bag.

2. The SEASONAL BAG SHOPPER – the very smartly dressed woman who believes in having one or several new bags every season, all the very latest 'must-haves' (probably

most seasons this would mean a Chloé, a Prada, a Louis Vuitton, a Chanel, a Marc Jacobs and a Mulberry), and then she sells them off in places like Réciproque in Paris or Sign of the Times in London when the season's over. Though how she could sell something as personal and intimate as a handbag is something of a mystery to the rest of us – as Natalie Massenet puts it, 'I couldn't – it'd be like giving away a child.'

3. The shopper who needs A BAG TO SUIT EVERY MOOD – old, new, vintage, classic and wacky, practical and girly, funky and bold.

Sharp girls around town who can't afford the latest 'it' bag often opt for utilitarian bags such as satchels and man bags, which seem to say, 'I've seen all the others but I chose something much more cool and street than anything "fashiony"'.

A very good Massenet tip: 'The young look great with something like a little Chanel handbag – the classic assurance of the Chanel bag is a good balance with funky youth. It looks as if it's her first big treat and it reads like a fashion statement. Contrarily, an older women, I think, looks better with a cooler bag – it looks less staid. If she were to carry the Chanel bag it would seem more like a status symbol than a fashion statement. It's all about balance.'

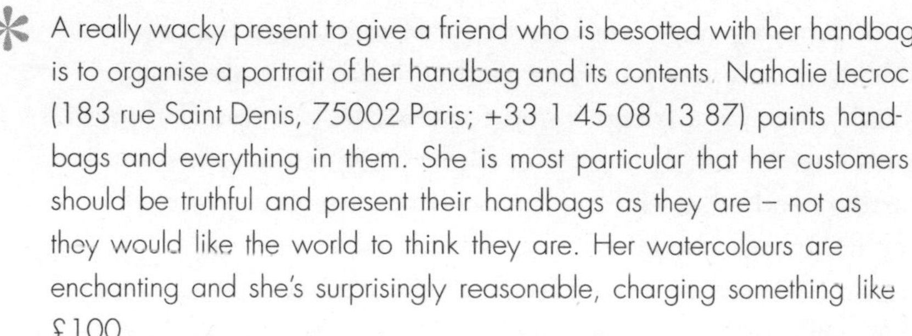

* A really wacky present to give a friend who is besotted with her handbag is to organise a portrait of her handbag and its contents. Nathalie Lecroc (183 rue Saint Denis, 75002 Paris; +33 1 45 08 13 87) paints handbags and everything in them. She is most particular that her customers should be truthful and present their handbags as they are – not as they would like the world to think they are. Her watercolours are enchanting and she's surprisingly reasonable, charging something like £100.

Jewels

I love a bit of bling – not because it's expensive (which it needn't be) but for its decorative value. I don't have expensive heirloom pieces (sob, sob), because I didn't come from that sort of a family, though my mother gave me a very nice double string of pearls and my stepmother left me a wonderful diamond cluster ring for which I thank her daily. My husband has given me some lovely pieces but mostly of a rather contemporary nature because he knows my tastes veer towards the funky and the quirky. I used to collect pretty bits of Victorian jewellery but I lost most of them in a burglary. Now I have one gorgeous string of grey-tinged South Sea pearls (bought from the divine Bob Reed of Linneys, Dampier Terrace, Broome, Australia, and you should do the same if you're passing by), plus a couple of really good earrings. Otherwise it's mostly bits and bobs that I've collected since the burglary. My own favourite pieces include some amazing huge irregular blobs of red amber that I've already mentioned, which I bought in Oman, some great rough emeralds a friend found for me in Colombia (I think), a necklace of rough turquoise, some Georgian amethyst earrings and a bracelet that is a coil of clear lime-green acrylic. In other words, I have eclectic tastes and most wardrobes need variety. Part of the point of all this is to say that while real can be wonderful (an amazing diamond or coloured-stone piece from one of the great jewellers – who would say no?), it can also sometimes be quite staid and ageing. Costume can be infinitely jollier, particularly when it comes to jewellery with attitude. A whole row of great bangles looks terrific – even cheap ones from markets in India, which cost literally pence. Accessorize also does them brilliantly.

Jewellery used to be all about status and wealth but these days it is fundamentally there to be decorative, to light up the face, to enliven a sober outfit. An austere trouser suit can be given life if worn with some diamond studs in the ears for day and some glittery chandelier earrings for evening. Big cuffs are gorgeous, and fantastic brooches look great on jackets and dresses. But none of it has to be real. This winter I wore some glorious crystal and diamanté chandelier earrings that I bought from Hennes for under £5 and several times had people compliment me on them and ask where I bought them.

Mlle Chanel, remember, used to swathe her neck in great ropes of fake pearls and her wrists in huge cuffs, and she always looked a million dollars. She understood that most of the point of jewellery lies in its ornamental value, not the price tag. These days cuffs are back in fashion. You could buy a whole wristful of them at Claire's Accessories for under £20, whilst even most department stores sell big, bold cuffs and bracelets at very reasonable prices.

When travelling, a small wardrobe of some well-chosen costume jewellery means you can ring the changes with far fewer clothes. Come the evening, bring out the glitter – the dangling earrings, the fantastic necklace or the giant brooch. The trick, though, is not to pile it all on at once. A good rule, if you exclude wedding and engagement rings, is probably to stick to not more than two pieces at a time – earrings and a bracelet, a necklace and a bracelet, or earrings and a brooch. Just don't pile on the lot.

If you're doing costume jewellery though, don't do dinky. What's the point? It looks timid and uninteresting. Wear great chunky plastic discs or rough stones. A young girl I know has a wardrobe of huge swinging earrings that never fail to flatter and to catch the eye. If you ask her where she bought them, the answer is invariably Accessorize or Claire's Accessories. To buy – and wear – costume jewellery takes a bit more courage and something of an eye. You can't take refuge in the knowledge that it is by a grand designer but therein lies the fun.

Good Places to Buy

THE GOLDSMITHS' COMPANY (www.thegoldsmiths.co.uk) has an annual fair at the Goldsmiths Hall, Foster Lane, London

EC2, which brings together jewellers and silversmiths from all over the country. The prices are often astonishingly low and the designs original and fascinating.

THE CONTEMPORARY APPLIED ARTS shop at 2 Percy Street, London always has interesting craft jewellery.

For weddings and engagements it has to be real, I think. Try the auction houses first (CHRISTIE'S, SOTHEBY'S, BONHAMS and even the provincial auction houses) for what the Americans call 'estate jewellery' – the prices seem astonishingly good. Then there are some fabulous antique jewellery shops, of which my favourites have to be PHILIPS at 139 New Bond Street, London W1S 2TL; 020 7629 6261, and NIGEL MILNE at 38 Jermyn Street, London SW1Y 6DN; 020 7434 9343. But up and down the country there are good shops selling second-hand jewellery and the prices there are often surprisingly reasonable. Cheaper, and offering the additional thrill of a possible big 'find', are places like GRAYS ANTIQUE MARKET in 58 Davies Street and 1–7 Davies Mews, London W1K 5AB; 020 7627 7034, or ANTIQUARIUS in the market at 131–141 King's Road, Chelsea, London SW3 5EB. CAMDEN PASSAGE in Islington (www.camdenpassage islington.co.uk) has lots of little antique shops worth exploring, not to mention its Saturday morning market where I've bought inexpensive silver, watches and jewellery.

ALFIE'S MARKET, 13–25 Church Street, Marylebone, London

NW8 8DT, is another great source of antique costume jewellery (as well as handbags and clothes).

BUTLER & WILSON, 189 Fulham Road, London SW3 6JN; 020 7376 5981, has fabulous costume jewellery, lots of bling and masses of funky brooches, necklaces and earrings.

ERICKSON BEAMON, 38 Elizabeth Street, London SW1W 9NZ; 020 7259 0202, is a favourite with lots of fashionistas, selling pretty, delicate things at good prices.

KIKI MCDONOUGH, 77C Walton Street, London SW3 2HT; 020 7581 1777, has mastered the knack of giving the working woman the sort of jewellery that has just enough bling to give that frisson of pleasure and desire but not so much that it can't be worn in the boardroom. Droolingly desirable pieces in brilliant stones (she puts peridots with amethysts, for instance) at good prices.

CATHERINE PREVOST, 109 Walton Street, London SW3 2HP; 020 7581 8674, is another favourite. She gives her jewellery a slight ethnic twist – lots of Navajo turquoise, semi-precious stones, jade, amber and the like. Gorgeous.

PIPPA SMALL (www.pippasmall.com) is the fashionista's current jeweller of choice and I love her stuff, too. She takes rough stones and turns out huge interesting rings or asymetrical lozenges of turquoise to form a necklace. Another necklace has a roughly cut diamond as a centrepiece. All fascinating. She has just opened her own shop at 11 Colville

Mews, London W11 2DA. Find her at The Cross, 141 Portland Road, London W11 4LR; 020 7727 6760, and also at Kabiri, 37 Marylebone High Street, London W1U 4QE; 020 7224 1808 (a great jewellery shop, incidentally).

If it's just diamonds that turn you on, go to WINT & KIDD, 237 Westbourne Grove, London W11 2SE; 020 7908 9990. Choose your stone and then get one of their designers to set it just the way you'd like it.

NEIL DUTTSON (www.duttsonrocks.com) will bring diamonds to your house.

You can also buy diamonds online, the theory being that you get more diamond for your money because online retailing doesn't have the same overheads as retail shops. Try www.cooldiamonds.com.

Jeans

I've come to the conclusion that it is really is worth investing in a good pair of designer jeans. Provided your figure is in reasonable shape (and I don't mean you have to be a beanpole), it is amazing what a well-cut pair in a good dark washed denim can do. I now see why they're such a hit with the model set. Shoes are key – low pumps for a casual look, wedges for day and high heels for night make jeans wearable all day long. To solve the problem of the changing heel height, Radcliffe Denim has come up with a brilliant (patented) solution in the shape of a cufflink that allows the wearer to change the length of the leg, lowering it for a stiletto, raising it for a pump. Older women, it goes without saying, shouldn't bare their midriffs. Wearing longer tops helps to make jeans look more grown up as well as balance the lean silhouette below. Good jackets turn jeans into classy daywear. The wash is important – a dark plain wash is the most sophisticated.

The semiotics of the premium jean are intricate and change almost daily. Tracking down that holy grail – a pair that makes one's behind look perkier, one's legs longer and one's stomach flatter – isn't easy so here are some places to get help.

The Perfect Jeans

Although it's a trend that really arose on the West Coast of America, who better to ask than Suzy Radcliffe, founder of Radcliffe Denim, the first British designer jeans brand? Here she gives her guide to finding the perfect pair.

1. Try on as many different brands and pairs as possible. Find a store that has lots of different brands, grab every pair in your size (to start with) and try everything on. Don't even look at the brand name, just focus on finding the perfect pair.

2. Try different sizes – measurement differences are very subtle and vary according to the different denims and washes used. So if you think you are a size 28 waist, also try a 27 and a 29.

WHERE TO BUY

In the US, **Saks Fifth Avenue** has 'denim doctors' to help their jeans-obsessed customers orientate their way through the denim jungle.

www.ilovejeans.com and **www.truejeans.com** (started by a man whose wife was reduced to tears because she couldn't find jeans that she really liked), two advisory websites that are a mine of useful information. Both guide you to the best jeans for your body shape.

Start, 42–44 Rivington Street, Hoxton, London EC2A 3BN; 020 7729 3334, is a boutique where the owner/buyer takes jeans very seriously and sells a pared-down, well-judged but evolving range of brands.

The Cross, 141 Portland Road, London W11 4LR; 020 7727 6760, has a special line in yummy mummy tastes so, if that's you, you know where to go. It's good on grown-up brands.

Bodymetrics at Selfridges, 020 7152 9617; www.bodymetrics.com, makes jeans to measure for £250 a time. A machine measures the body electronically, then you choose the fabric and wash, decide on where you want the waist, and whether you want bootcut or straight jeans.

Also try on two or three pairs of the same size as there will be minute differences between each pair, which may make one pair of size 28s fit better than another.

3. Always think about comfort. What you don't want is a pair of jeans that make you want to change out of them the minute you get home into something more comfortable. A great pair of jeans should not only look good but be as comfortable as your favourite pair of sweatpants. Key things to look out for are stretch denim (which will contour to your shape) and soft denim, i.e. that feels soft to the hand.
4. Spend as much as you can (or buy expensive jeans in the sales). There is a reason why some jeans cost more than others. Premium brands will use expensive European and Japanese denims. They will also contain high-quality stretch fabrics that will retain their shape.
5. Have different styles for different occasion, don't just think, 'I can only wear bootcut'. Try trouser jeans, or a narrower pair with boots – this gives you a lot more wardrobe choices. Also try black and grey denim. Again, although you are still wearing jeans, the look is very different.
6. There are styles suited to different body types. As a general rule, bootcut (with a slight flare from the knee down) is universally the most flattering style. The bootcut balances out the hips and makes your legs look longer and slimmer. With narrower jeans (or skinny jeans) you need to think about boots and a heel but you don't need to be

really skinny to wear these, especially if you team them with a long top or jumper.

T-Shirts

The White T-shirt Company (0870 043 4880 and at www.thewhitetshirt.co.uk) does a whole range of T-shirts in really good pure cotton. C & C California's T-shirts are brilliant and come in lots of colours. I'm also a fan of Marks & Spencer's versions, as when I find them in the right colour and shape I know the quality will be good. Otherwise look out for James Perse and Velvet labels, both of which have a great range of colours, with James Perse tending more towards the classic, and Velvet towards the more fashionable shapes and colours. And don't forget Gap.

And remember, under the T-shirt you'll need a well-fitting seamless bra. Keep the lacy ones for another time.

Cashmere

. . . and How to Look After it

One of my big new mantras is to adapt to the world of fashion that old Mies van der Rohe classic saying that was formulated for the domestic interior: 'Less is more'. I'd rather have fewer sweaters but most of them in cashmere than shelves full of lambswool. I work at home and my favourite working garment in the winter is a gorgeous grey cashmere sweater dress by Shirin Guild. It's my comfort blanket.

These days cashmere needn't be expensive – Marks & Spencer and Tesco sell it for ridiculously low prices, and mail-order companies such as Pure offer lots of classic cashmere lines. Brora always has charming girly lines, lots of little ballet cardigans and baby outfits, all of which make adorable presents. Which isn't to say that quality doesn't count – it does. The cheaper cashmere tends to fluff and ball far more than more expensive versions (it's usually made from the yarn from the back and the legs of the goat, which is coarser than that from the underbelly), whereas fine, expensive cashmere is not only made from the finest, white cashmere yarn but it is also properly treated and finished, which adds to the expense. Having spent all that money and loving on the garment itself, you don't want it to shrink or to be eaten away by moths. So here are my tips for looking after it.

You can wash it, if you dare. I have friends who wash it by hand; others put their cashmere in one of those laundry bags meant for delicate things and wash it on the delicates programme in their washing machines and it comes out looking terrific. I'd recommend using a special cashmere soap – either the Wool and Cashmere Shampoo from The Laundress (it is sulphate free, comes in a choice of four scents and costs £14.50 from www.globalandgorgeous.com) or the one from Belinda Robertson (£2.99, 020 7838 9170; www.belindarobertson.com).

* If you're nervous of washing cashmere yourself, check out The Laundress website (www.thelaundress.com), where the two girls who started the company give a riveting animated demonstration of how to wash cashmere. They also answer questions – very promptly – online.

Belinda Robertson does delicious cashmere that is always delivered in its own protection bag with a cedar block. But if you already own cashmere and it didn't come in a bag, what do you do? First of all you get it properly cleaned. I would only ever use a really good laundry for this – my own happens to be Jeeves (www.jeevesofbelgravia.co.uk), which brings things back beautifully cleaned and wrapped, and they haven't shrunk a cashmere or a pashmina yet. Belinda Robertson also offers a service which, for £25 per garment, will wash and revive them (send to Belinda Robertson Edinburgh, 13A Dundas Street, Edinburgh EH3 6QG). The price may seem high but it's better than losing your cashmere to moths. When you get your cashmere back from being cleaned, buy some plastic bags in which to store it (don't dream of doing this if you've already got moths – they'll have a field day inside the bag), either from Belinda Robertson (at £5 a time), or from Morplan (0800 451 122), or from www.essentialbits.co.uk, which sells the requisite bags for £6 a time. Belinda Robertson will also sell you, at £2.50 each, the aromatic cedar blocks that promise to keep the moths at bay. I'm also told that putting cashmere in the freezer for at least twenty minutes is a good way of killing off all moths and their eggs.

If you already have moths and several holes (as I do in my beloved cashmere Shirin Guild sweater dress), do as Jeanetta Rowan-Hamilton of www.nettlescashmere.com does, and revive and customise the item by covering up the holes with charming pieces of old fabric edged with ribbon, embellished with buttons, stars, beads or lace.

Julia Dee, who runs a wardrobe care service (see also p. 100), believes in storing cashmere in acid-free paper (from Morplan; 0800 451 122).

Specialist Help

Personal Shoppers and Wardrobe Advisors

I believe in them, not all the time (unless you're so rich or so busy that you pay one to do all your shopping for you) but to freshen up one's wardrobe. If you book a session with one of those on offer in most department stores (including, most excitingly, Topshop) they also cost nothing. You can just wave away anything you don't like and make them go on looking until they come up with something you do like. They look at one with a different eye and can, if they're good, wean one away from the safety of the tried and tested and give one a whole new look – or at least a few great new garments.

The big caveat is this: wardrobe advisors and personal shoppers are only as good as their advice. It sounds obvious, I know, but if you turn up for a personal shopping appointment (as I once did) and are met by a chap in the sort of suit you hoped never to see on a man you cared about, then you know you're not going to get the sort of advice you'd dream of taking. *But* when they're good, they're terrific. I've been given whole new looks and have been bought exciting garments that I'd never have thought of through good advisors but it's absolutely key to make sure your taste meshes with his/hers.

Ones who've worked for me are CELIA CLARKE AT LIBERTY – she found for me a fabulous Missoni coat that cost a bomb but has earned its keep time and time again, as well as a grass-green Armani jacket that is to die for and that I'd never have dared to pick out on my own, as well as a brilliant greyish/blackish/brownish cloque evening jacket by the Turkish designer Ischiko. MARTINA WAGENER AT SELFRIDGES found for me my favourite skirt in the world – a black Ischiko one with huge black silk roses in a cluster on one side – as well as a brilliant steel-grey satiny Marni coat with bracelet sleeves and a little stand-up collar that will look good for the rest of my life. *Very* Audrey Hepburn. All this advice came free – though the bill for the clothes was another matter. However, I console myself with the thought that I love the things I bought and I know I wouldn't have found them on my own.

There are lots of personal shoppers who will come to the house, look through your wardrobe, tell you what to keep and what to throw away. Then they will hold you by the hand and take you shopping to fill in the gaps and freshen the whole lot up. If they're any good, they will know the merchandise in a whole host of shops, have good relationships with many of them and so can arrange to have things put aside, and often they can get you to private sample sales and previews. This kind of service can be wonderful but it isn't usually cheap. And remember the big caveat: they are only as good as their taste.

The best way to find a good one is by asking friends. Here are a few I can recommend:

AMANDA PLATT (020 7229 8109) is style guru to legions of Notting Hill yummy mummies as well as to elegant middle-aged professionals, tycoons' wives and others far too famous to tell on. More to the point, she's also used to dealing with those of us who aren't as young, tall, blonde or fashion savvy as we'd like. She's also *very* nice: none of this 'My God, where did you find that skirt?' line, which would have most of us cowering in a corner in no time at all. You can safely go to her with the frumpiest of wardrobes and she'll have you organised in two shakes. She costs £550 a day, and for that she will sort out your wardrobe, tell you what is hot and great in the shops at the moment, take you shopping or just make a list of things she thinks you should buy. She has fabulous taste and really knows her shops and her brands. She also gets very booked up.

CAMILLA YONGE of Y Shop (07711 277 969 and at www.y-shop.co.uk) is young, nice, energetic and knows her stock. She'll come to the house, suss your style and then find you stuff that you'd never have found by yourself.

LEESA WHISKER (0870 043 4126 and at www.whiskeragency.co.uk) is rumoured to be the style consultant behind Kate Middleton's very ladylike look, which is – when you think about it – perfect for the role she had to play. People who've tried Leesa Whisker tell me she's terrific with a great sense of style. She isn't cheap but almost everybody who's used her says it was great value. She costs £300 for a home visit and £400 for a full shopping day.

JO POOLE (aka The Dress Doctor, 07855 032 705 and at www.thedressdoctor.co.uk) is a costumier at the National Theatre and also works for the BBC. She runs a wonderful mobile fitting and alteration service. She'll come, look at your wardrobe and tell you what's worth keeping and what's not. Furthermore, she will alter and – get this – drastically remake something that you love but that no longer quite works. She costs £240 for a day's worth of advice and my young colleague at *The Times*, Alice Olins, swears by her.

WWW.DRESSME.BIZ (07734 870 567) will do as much or as little as you'd like. Somebody will come to the house, sort your wardrobe, tell you what they think works and what doesn't, what you should wear with what, and show you how to make the most of the things you already have. They can restyle, reorganise and either go shopping for you or take you shopping. You choose.

SHONA MAC (020 7349 7225 and at www.shonamac.com) charges £55 an hour for which she'll come to the house, go through your wardrobe, tell you what to keep, what to throw out and – even better – she'll help you sell the discarded clothes (on eBay) and, obviously for a fee, revitalise and update clothes worth saving. The classic rule for wardrobe sorting always used to be 'If you haven't worn it for two years, throw it out'. I'm not much of a believer in that since I'm currently wearing things that have lain dormant for much longer than that. So an experienced second eye from somebody like Shona Mac is, in my view, well worth having.

How to Get Rid of Unwanted Clothes

Since most fashion writers would have one believe that in order to hold one's head up in what passes for society, one needs to be carrying the latest bag, wearing the hot shoe and be clad in something seen not so long ago on the catwalk, it follows that those who adopt this advice will either have to live in a mansion or else colonise whole rooms that should ideally be used for purposes other than storing their clothes. In my opinion the only answer to wardrobe chaos is regularly to edit the contents. I'm not much good at this myself and have been known to search desperately for the right skirt/jacket/shirt for an unconscionable amount of time simply because the wardrobe is too full or too chaotic.

The golden mantra when contemplating, say, a new pair of cropped trousers, has to be: ask yourself firmly (a) do I need it? (b) is it better than its close relation already in the wardrobe? and (c) when will I will wear it? Only if you have satisfactory answers to all three should you buy it. *Then* you must make up your mind to throw out its earlier, less useful/attractive counterpart.

If you have designer gear to sell, eBay is the current favourite of choice if you can manage the technology – taking the photograph, signing up and then posting it on the site. If you can't, there is a company called auction4you (www.auction4you.co.uk) that will do it all for you. The downside is that they keep 30 per cent of the sales price, whereas if you can do it yourself on eBay you keep the lot.

Shona Mac (see p. 98) will also do this for you.

Cleaning, Alterations, Repairs and Storage

JULIA DEE of Designer Alterations (220A Queenstown Road, London SW8 4LP; 020 7498 4360 and at www.designeralterations.com) – or one of her team – will come and sort out your wardrobe. They'll mend, clean, repair and – a huge boon for those who live in small spaces – they'll store your off-season clothes, thus allowing you to have a wardrobe twice the size. The perfumer Jo Malone, who lived in a small flat in her earlier days, told me that Julia Dee enabled her then to have a decent wardrobe. Jo kept each season's clothes at home and when the season was over she got Julia Dee to collect, clean, wash, repair and stow them away. At the same time Julia would bring the new season's clothes out of storage, all fresh and ready to wear.

LINDA AGRAN (0845 083 0111 and at www.lindaagran.co.uk, or email on info@lindaagran.co.uk) offers much the same service but at the Rolls-Royce end. Clothes are collected, mended, cleaned and otherwise restored to their pristine state. The ones you don't need are stored in 'a precisely controlled environment' until you need them again. Clients get little albums, with digital photographs of all their garments, so that they can remember what it is they actually own and summon it for the right occasion. When they need an item, they either ring or check in online and the garment can be returned at a couple of hours' notice if need be. However, you can't stow away just the odd sweater. There's a minimum charge of £300 worth of storage per quarter *but* that includes one free collection and delivery. Express delivery is extra – £50.

STORAGE AND STUFF

These are great companies for good hangers, acid-free paper and proper storage containers for clothes.

Morplan (www.morplan.com) for proper hangers, plastic containers and the like.

Lakeland (www.lakeland.co.uk) has everything to keep the moths at bay as well as wardrobe organisers and clear boxes to store shoes or sweaters.

www.essentialbits.co.uk sells storage containers in rather smaller quantities than Morplan.

The Holding Company (telephone 020 8445 2888 for a catalogue) has all manner of storage suggestions, including trays to help keep socks, tights and small items in order, plus an array of products to ward off moths.

The Sales

I'm not a big fan of them: the pushing, the shoving, the ugly faces and the even uglier fracas. On the whole I'd rather do without than face the sheer awfulness of it all. However, there are some things really well worth buying in sales and they're usually still there after the first hectic days are over. If you're either very small or very tall, there are fantastic bargains to be had in the clothes and shoe lines. Clothes apart, lots of fine staples are always reduced: stationery, soap, luggage, linen and electronics, not to mention things like washing machines and dishwashers with the odd immaterial scratch.

Here are my golden rules for clothes shopping in the sales:

1. Only buy something you really love or actually need.
2. Buy the bit of magic you couldn't otherwise afford.

3. If it doesn't fit in the shop, that won't change by the time you get it home.
4. Never buy anything too small. Only buy something too large if you have a crackingly good tailor.
5. Avoid the boring classics – it's better to buy them in your own good time in a solid high street shop where there is no danger of being panicked into a buy – and where you know you can always take things back.
6. Keep away from anything in a bin or with 'special purchase' attached to it.
7. If there's something you've really set your heart on and you know it's going to be reduced, then plan your venture like a military recce. Case the joint first and then plot the quickest route to your quarry.
8. Don't be tempted to buy something in a wild colour that you'd never wear simply because it's 50 per cent off.
9. If you're liable to be tempted, take a good and honest friend with you – if she says don't do it, then listen up.
10. Before you part with your hard-earned cash, check the shop's refund policy.

How to look good

Why it Matters

I'm not – and never have been – a specialist beauty writer, but I'm awfully keen on looking as good as I can. I've also written and edited what these days are called lifestyle pages in newspapers for more years than I'm going to tell you about here and beauty has always been part of my beat. So though I'm not an expert I've been inundated (oh, bliss) with goodies from efficient PRs getting me to test their wares. I've tried a lot of things, met an awful lot of 'experts', visited countless labs and interviewed more purveyors of lotions and potions than I can possibly count. I've been swathed in oils in India, stood on my head in Bali, been hosed down in Hampshire, wrapped in hot towels in Paris, had sound therapy with gongs in Africa and lots, lots more. I wish I could say with certainty that I always know what works and what doesn't, but to be truthful, I can't always tell. Some things you just *know* work for you, and even if they don't they're so enjoyable that you don't much care. Others, you may have a hunch are doing their job and others may leave you mystified.

The beauty business isn't an exact science. You can never be sure how you would have looked if you hadn't tried a specific cream/regime/treatment. When the rather cynical men on the newspaper for which I worked used to imply that the whole beauty industry was bunkum, merely a way of generating huge sums for their manufacturers, I always had the same reply: 'I can't give you rational, scientific proof but just look around you. The evidence is there. Those who take trouble look a whole lot better than those who don't.' I certainly know that I look better for taking the best care of my skin that I can, and as for wearing make-up, speaking personally, I do not step outside without it, even to go to the supermarket.

So I'm of the opinion that it's worth taking some care of oneself – both the inner and the outer being. It was George Burns who famously remarked: 'If I'd known I was going to live this long, I'd have taken better care of myself.' Well, many of us – praise be – are going to live much longer than our forebears so we might as well make it as enjoyable as possible. Being fit and healthy, and looking as good as we can, seem to me an essential component of the good life. Apart from anything else, healthy, good-looking people add to the gaiety of the nation – it's a form of politeness to others. Being unfit and overweight, short of breath or – worse – unable to walk unaided – isn't jolly. Although some ill-health is not always avoidable, if we try to eat the right things and stay away from the bad ones most of the time, if we take a modicum of exercise and keep an eye on the warning signs (high blood pressure, high cholesterol, obesity), then we are at least giving our bodies more of a chance to last the course without disaster overtaking us. As a doctor put it on the *Today* programme recently: 'We probably can't extend people's lifespan much longer than we already have, so our efforts now are concentrated on trying to enable people to be as healthy as possible for as much of that lifespan as possible.'

I don't believe in being obsessive (there's nothing so unattractive and miserable as women who won't eat a thing after 5 p.m. – or who toy with a few lettuce leaves whilst everyone else longs for a decent glass of wine) but I do believe that light, delicious food that goes easy on the fat and sugar is not only healthier than junk food but makes one feel better and more alive. I also know that moderate exercise is hugely enjoyable (at least it is for me; there's nothing I like better than being on a ski slope or a tennis court, though jogging bores me to tears) and it keeps the muscles firm, the heart in good shape and the mind alert.

But one shouldn't confuse looking good with trying to look younger than one is – they're not the same thing at all. The French seem to understand that better than we do and whilst one sees older French women who are enormously chic, as a rule they seldom look ridiculous. Women who take a modicum of trouble can look good at any age without trying to pass themselves off as anything that they are not. On the other hand I don't think trying *too* hard is attractive either. It speaks of narcissism and vanity, of a lack of proportion in one's life and of other, proper interests. We've all seen those 'Noo Yorkers', Tom Wolfe's famous X-ray skeletons, whose over-made-up elderly faces and frail figures look quite scary. The aim surely should be to try to get the balance right, to work out what suits one and what doesn't, and then to get on with the more interesting parts of life.

Nevertheless there are lots of wonderful treatments available that really do make a difference – not just to how one looks but, perhaps more importantly, to how one feels. After I was mugged some years ago, which left my mouth lopsided and out of kilter, two plastic surgeons – Howard Sobel in New York and Barry Jones in London – between them kindly put the whole thing right, and the difference it has made to my morale is huge. My smile will never be quite what it was but at least now I show the same amount of teeth on both sides when I smile. So I'm a fan of plastic surgery (about which more later). I'm also a fan of treatments that work. I've had letters from women who were almost in tears of joy at the uplift to their spirits when their broken veins, brown spots, under-eye bags and crêpey décolletages were attended to. They weren't excessively vain; rather they were understandably mourning the loss of their youthful skin and looks, and the discovery that some of the damage could be repaired restored their self-esteem no end.

Like many, I am a great fan of *Feel Fab Forever* by Josephine Fairley and Sarah Stacey; their latest news is always worth checking out on www.beautybible.com.

I'm not attempting here to give you a rundown on the complete beauty market place – whole tomes would be needed for that alone. I'm passing on only what I've learned over the years and mentioning only therapies or products that have really worked for me and my friends.

Skin

I'm starting here because it matters most. With naturally gorgeous skin you can get away with almost no make-up but my advice is, don't take it for granted. Do all you can to make sure it stays as good as it can. The key to good skin is keeping out of the sun, eating well, drinking lots of water (whilst keeping off tea, coffee and alcohol if you can; I personally can't!) and then following the three mantras of cleanse, tone, nourish. And these days we have to add exfoliating to the list. Exfoliating gets rid of the dead cells; our skins shed them at a fantastic rate each day – though more slowly as we get older – and if they accumulate they make the skin look dull. Remove them and the skin instantly (and I really mean instantly) looks more radiant. And one more thing: if you care about your skin, you shouldn't go near a cigarette – ever.

If you have a few brown spots, broken capillaries or other imperfections, remember that today there are brilliant ways of dealing with them. IPL lasers deal beautifully with both red veins and brown spots. Almost all good dermatologists and aestheticians now have access to these lasers so there's no need to suffer in silence.

Cleansers

I don't think soap and water cuts it. I've tried it but it leaves my skin feeling harsh and dry. However, if you're hard up, I don't think that it makes sense to buy an expensive cleanser. Even the simplest (e.g. from Boots, Marks & Spencer and the Body Shop) do a really good job. If your budget runs to it, here are a few of my favourites.

SHU UEMURA'S CLEANSING OIL appears at first to be very oily, but as soon as it hits the skin it turns milky, removing every scrap of make-up whilst at the same time leaving the skin feeling as if it has been nourished as well as cleansed. Clever old Mr Uemura got the idea for it way back in the 1960s when he was making up the stars in Hollywood. He observed that Marilyn Monroe, Liz Taylor and Shirley MacLaine (not to mention – though whisper it quietly – Frank Sinatra) all had to resort to oil to remove the heavy make-up needed for the cameras. He therefore set about refining oil to make it more user friendly. The current cleansing oil – and there are two versions, one for dry skin, one for oily – is made from olive oil, sunflower oil, jojoba oil and a couple of other secret ingredients.

GUERLAIN has some brilliant new cleansing products called

Secret de Pûreté. They contain lotus flower (which is claimed to be known for its purity and its restorative properties) but, more to the point, they leave the skin feeling divine. There are creams, milks, foams and gels. I recommend the eye and lip make-up remover. (You need to be particularly careful about what you use to remove eye make-up – I only ever use a cleanser specifically meant for eyes.) I like the texture of Guerlain's milky cleanser best.

LIZ EARLE'S NATURALLY ACTIVE CLEANSE AND POLISH HOT CLOTH CLEANSER (it comes as a little bottle plus two muslin cloths) is wonderful and not expensive, about £11.50 (www.lizearle.com).

EVE LOM'S CLEANSER, which lots of women I respect swear by, also comes with little muslin cloths. It's a cult product that many are addicted to. Find it at Space NK (www.spacenk.co.uk).

Exfoliators

There's a bit of controversy over these in that some women think they're a bit harsh on the skin. As I've already pointed out earlier, exfoliators remove dead cells that can clog the pores and prevent the skin looking its best. I'm a believer. Deep cleansing and exfoliating are partly the point of a facial and I notice that my skin always looks infinitely more radiant afterwards. Although I don't use them every day, once a week is just right for me. If you're prone to broken veins and have very sensitive skin, go carefully and use only the gentlest versions. My skin can't take anything harsh so I like Liz Earle's Naturally Active Gentle Face Exfoliator, but there are lots on the market at every price range. You can also buy exfoliators in pad form – particularly useful when travelling; you simply use one a day – or as lotions or creams. At the cheaper end, Origins Modern Friction is, with good reason, a cult product, and Valentine Alexander (my make-up guru, who tries almost everything that comes on the market) tells me that Olay's Definity Pore Redefining Scrub (£4 from Boots) is brilliant. At the posher end of the market, Givenchy's Black Mask is good whilst Dr Hauschka's Rejuvenating Mask makes the skin look more radiant. Take your pick. If it suits your skin, stick with it. If it leaves it red and irritated, try something else.

Toners

I'm not too fussy here and wouldn't think it worth going for a high-cost toner. Just make sure to choose one that isn't too astringent and is alcohol-free.

Moisturisers

It depends on your skin type which one is for you – dry skins and older skin need richer moisturisers than oily skin and young skin – but absolutely key is to make sure it has an SPF of at least 15 (preferably more) and that you wear it every day.

In your twenties that's probably all you need but the older you get, the more you should ask of your moisturiser. Look for hydrating properties in your thirties, anti-ageing ones in your forties and, after that, choose ultra-rich, deeply moisturising versions. They'll cost more but here spending a bit more really buys extra benefits. If you have good skin with an even skin tone, you may be able to get away with just wearing a tinted moisturiser that matches your skin colour.

Nourishing Creams

You can spend peanuts (on something like Nivea or Boots' own range) or you can spend, literally, hundreds of pounds. I think nourishing creams make a big difference, particularly as you get older. Those targeted at ageing skin have active ingredients that help cell renewal (the main reason for skin beginning to look dingy is that the rate of cell renewal decreases greatly with age). They also boost collagen production, plump up the skin and penetrate deeper into the epidermis. I don't think there are such things as miracle creams but I am absolutely convinced that regularly nourishing the skin keeps it softer, plumper and slows down the rate at which wrinkles develop. I do *not* think that the whole beauty industry is one big con – serious research goes into these creams and cutting-edge ingredients cost more than run-of-the-mill ones. I would no more dream of going to bed at night without using a night cream than I would miss cleaning my teeth.

If you want real proof of what good creams can do, a few brands (the Japanese company SK-II for one, DCL or Dermatologic Cosmetic Laboratories, and Elemis) use high-tech Visia Medical Imaging Systems to photograph the skin before and after treatment in order to track the changes in wrinkles, skin texture, brown spots *et al.*

It's almost impossible to single out one cream from amongst all the others, for what suits one person's skin doesn't suit someone else's. *But* the problem is that trying out all of them is an expensive business – who wants to spend £250 on something and then find it doesn't suit their skin? The best advice I can offer is to suggest you consult Josephine Fairley and Sarah Stacey's *Feel Fab Forever* (published by Kyle Cathie, £14.99), in particular the chapter titled 'Tried and Tested Miracle Creams', the result of a trial of some 1,600 women aged thirty-five or more.

Some inexpensive products work brilliantly well – Boots own No 7 Protect and Perfect Beauty Serum (£16.75) came out top in a recent television programme that looked seriously at the matter of skincare. But it is worth bearing in mind that the more expensive houses – Estée Lauder, Guerlain, Sisley, La Prairie – may appear from the labels to use the same ingredients as cheaper makes, but there are cheap liposomes and expensive liposomes, cheap essential oils and expensive ones, and the grander names do, usually, use better ingredients. Also you don't need to slather the stuff on. Use it sparingly. The younger you are, the less need you have of these age-defying creams.

Here are some of my own favourites:

CHANTECAILLE'S BIODYNAMIC LIFTING CREAM isn't cheap (about £245 a pot) but it has a cult following. It is stuffed full of natural ingredients but they have been carefully researched and have a proven effect. One of the key ingredients (the one that has elicited the 'liquid Botox' quip) is hexapeptide, which interferes with the messages that tell muscles to contract and therefore inhibits frowning and lines. Another, tocotrienols, which are said to be some fifty times more potent than Vitamin E, help fight free radicals and protect collagen elasticity. There are also lots of lovely, delicious essential oils – magnolia, rose and many more.

GUERLAIN'S ISSIMA RANGE is one that I love, in particular its Midnight Secret – it feels richly nourishing and yet not heavy.

NATURA BISSÉ'S DIAMOND EXTREME CREAM is a current favourite with me (as it is, apparently, with Sienna Miller, Naomi Campbell and Keira Knightley) but it is phenomenally expensive (about £200 a pot, from Harrods). I love both its texture and its delicious slightly herby smell, although it's too expensive to use all the time so I'll move to something less expensive when this pot is finished.

SISLEY GLOBAL ANTI-AGE is another expensive one (nearly £200), but brilliantly rehydrating and nourishing.

ESTÉE LAUDER'S RE-NUTRIV ULTIMATE LIFTING CRÈME is

another enormously expensive cream but it has a whole cocktail of active anti-ageing ingredients and it feels very good to use.

LANCÔME'S NUTRIX ROYAL is not too expensive (something like £30) and is a long-time favourite of many mature women so it must have something going for it.

SK-II'S FACIAL TREATMENT ESSENCE is a cult cream in Japan. It contains 90 per cent pitera, an ingredient discovered by a Japanese monk visiting a sake brewery in Kobe who happened to notice that elderly workers there had extraordinarily soft, young-looking hands. He embarked on five years experimentation, during which he eventually discovered that pitera, a nutrient-rich by-product of yeast fermentation, contained a collection of vitamins, minerals, amino and organic acids that had a remarkable effect on the skin. SK-II's Facial Treatment Essence was the result. It has remained unchanged in formula – and in price (at the time deemed astronomical) since it was launched just over twenty years ago.

CRÈME DE LA MERE is enormously expensive and, confusingly, it is referred to as a moisturiser but in fact it really does the job of a nourishing cream. Many women swear by it. Its formula has a serious basis. Years ago, aerospace physicist Dr Max Huber suffered a horrific accident – a routine experiment exploded in his face – which gave him severe chemical burns. Neither science nor medicine offered much promise of help, so Huber decided to help himself.

Twelve years and 6,000 experiments later, he perfected the cream that would help give skin a dramatically smoother appearance. At the heart of the Crème is a highly potent Miracle Broth™. There is nothing miraculous about its ingredients – sea kelp, calcium, magnesium, potassium, iron, lecithin, Vitamins C, E and B12, plus oils of citrus, eucalyptus, wheatgerm, alfalfa and sunflower. For Huber, it wasn't the ingredients but the way those ingredients were distilled that made all the difference between a good moisturiser and a small miracle. No doubt Huber understood the ancient science of bio-fermentation. He discovered that as these ingredients changed from individual components into a rich Miracle Broth™ (a process that took three or four months to complete), they did indeed transform into a whole far greater than the sum of its parts.

At the less expensive end of the spectrum, apart from BOOTS NO 7 PROTECT AND PERFECT, which is a star product, there is NEAL'S YARD REMEDIES FRANKINCENSE NOURISHING CREAM, costing something like £12.

Sarah Stacey, beauty editor and co-author (with Jo Fairley) of *The Beauty Bible* and *Feel Fab Forever*, reveals her own favourite night-time miracle workers. She recommends that you apply them all with gentle upward strokes from neck/décolletage to hairline. And, she says, around the eye bone you should merely tap the cream in.

For daily use in summer, or all year round

Balm Balm Rose Geranium Organic Face Balm (just £5.99 from www.lovelula.com, an organic apothecary that sells online).

This is a fantastic value, heavenly smelling, totally organic balm that works on skin anywhere, as well as taming flyaway hair. My desert island must-have. Brilliant at night, or for daytime *if* you're not using a matte anti-shine foundation because it takes a wee bit of time to sink in, with the result that you look shiny and your base can slip off, but it's fine under tinted moisturiser.

For extra help in winter

Aromatherapy Associates Renew Rose & Frankincense Facial Oil (£28.50 from www.spacenk.co.uk).

Again, there is a lift-your-spirits fragrance in this oil from a leading aromatherapy company. Rose and frankincense essential oils are legendary for soothing, repairing and reinvigorating skin. You need only a couple of drops, so it lasts nearly for ever.

To soup up tired 'blah' skin

Dr Bragi Age Management Marine Enzyme, (£120 for a 50ml dispenser).

This is hugely expensive but you need to use just one or two pumps per application. I keep it for when my skin really looks in need of help. This marine-based 'penzyme' (penetrating enzyme) was developed by a leading professor of biochemistry at the University of Iceland as a treatment for wound healing and arthritis. Its light gel formulation is truly anti-ageing, making skin amazingly smoother, tauter and brighter, in my experience. And stacks of testimonials attest that it is effective, too, for problem skin conditions including acne, rosacea and eczema. Dr Bragi also says it will help scarring and dark circles.

The War against Wrinkles

IN YOUR TWENTIES: wear sunblock and, when out in the sun, a sunhat as well. The skin can still repair itself but light exfoliating with an alpha-hydroxy acid product will remove dead skin and give the skin a smoother look.

IN YOUR THIRTIES: greater nourishment is needed and retinol products will help plump up fine lines. If your skin starts to look dry, use a really good moisturiser.

IN YOUR FORTIES: look for richer nourishing creams with anti-ageing properties (suitable creams and lotions will all carry this label). Some therapists recommend very light, glycolic acid-based peels once a month to reduce fine lines and facial brown spots or uneven skin tone.

IN YOUR FIFTIES AND OVER: you should be using products specifically labelled anti-ageing or one of the cult creams referred to above. Creams containing retinol have been proven to improve the look of wrinkles by boosting the production of key skin-building compounds such as glycosaminoglycan and collagen. You might like to consider the newer serums, which generally contain cocktails of antioxidants and alpha-hydroxy acids, and should be worn under your usual moisturiser. Many women swear by them. Particularly recommended is Cellex-C High Potency Serum, and I also very much like Origins Mega-Mushroom Face Serum, especially around the eye area, where they are less irritating than rich nourishing creams.

I have seen photographic evidence of amazing results from chemical peels, dermabrasion, laser resurfacing and micro-dermabrasion – with deep wrinkles almost eliminated and the skin looking completely refreshed – *but* they should be applied only by a proper dermatologist who can assess whether these procedures will work for you. Some can leave the skin very sensitive and red for weeks. Most dermatologists now recommend a series of mild peels rather than one really deep, medical peel.

Remember that some wrinkles are not only inevitable but not necessarily unattractive. Older faces where all lines have been eliminated by face-lifts, Botox and their ilk look curiously unlived in.

Treats and Facials

To cheer up the skin, head to the Organic Pharmacy, 396 King's Road, London SW10 0LN (telephone 020 7351 2232 for an appointment), or to Michaeljohn, 25 Albermarle Street, London W1S 4HU (for an appointment telephone 020 7629 6969), which has linked up with the Organic Pharmacy to offer some of the same treatments, using its beautiful, mainly natural products. Ask for the Rose Crystal Lymphatic Facial. Too many late nights and too much alcohol leaves the lymph system stressed. The combination of rose crystals and acupressure massage to move the toxins around the lymphatic system revitalises the skin. Also included in the treatment is deep cleansing, exfoliation, steaming, extraction and four luxurious masks (Rose Hip, Seaweed, Honey and Jasmine, and Collagen) as well as massage of the hands, arms, feet, face, décolletage and scalp, which incorporates a nourishing hair serum. The result is really glowing skin (and very messy hair – book a hair appointment for afterwards). It takes ninety minutes and costs £100.

BLISSLONDON, 60 Sloane Avenue, London SW3 3DD (telephone 020 75843 3888 for an appointment), offers a Triple Oxygen Facial Mask (not cheap at £130 for eighty-five minutes but then needs must), which is a brilliant reviver of dingy skin.

NATURA BISSÉ, which hails from Barcelona and makes gorgeous products, is a newish brand to the UK. Its facial (at the Urban Retreat at Harrods, 020 7893 8333) leaves the skin looking truly radiant.

EVE LOM, at 2 Spanish Place, Marylebone, London W1U 3HU; 020 7935 9988, is the gold standard for facials – her fans book up months in advance. If you can get her it's worth it, not least as a great introduction to her famous Cleansing Balm and her little muslin cloths.

ANASTASIA ACHILLEOS has a jewel of a salon in the basement of the San Domenico Hotel, 29–31 Draycott Place, London SW3 25H (telephone 07939 331 889 for an appointment). It's filled with all manner of delicious lotions and potions, with which she works many kinds of facial and massage magic, charging £150 for ninety minutes.

VAISHALY PATEL, 51 Paddington Street, London W1U 4HR (020 7224 6088), is a young, up-and-coming, much-sought-after facialist.

DO-IT-YOURSELF

If you can't get to the salons I've mentioned, here are some products that will do a similar job. **The Organic Pharmacy's Collagen Boost Masque** (£35), although not as brilliant as the Rose Crystal Facial (nothing else is, in my view), is a good do-it-yourself rescue remedy. Try, too, the delicious-smelling Rose Plus Face Cream – though expensive at £85, it really seems to lighten and plump up the skin.

From **BlissLondon** (www.blisslondon.co.uk) there's the **Steep Clean Mask** (£32), a fifteen-minute do-it-yourself facial in a tube. It'll unclog the skin, remove dead cells (the chief culprit in making skin look dull), refine the pores and brighten the surface of the skin. Its **Instant Mattification Gel** (£28) is a sort of gel powder, which gives a beautiful finished look to the skin. But for really instant brightening, try the **Laboratoire Remède Super Oxygenating Booster** (£75). It pumps out fresh oxygen as well as alpha and beta hydroxy acids, which, say the boys and the girls in the white coats, is what brightens up the skin. You should notice a difference straightaway. It can be applied morning and evening and is particularly good if your skin is oily or prone to spots. If you can be bothered, there's also a **Laboratoire Remède Skin Exacting Mask** (£72), which exfoliates (removing all those dead cells that you don't want hanging about), refines and smoothes.

I'm also a fan of **Jurlique's Recovery Gel**, which really is a tonic for those days when your skin feels duller than the grey sky.

Eyes

I am unable to endure much in the way of creams and lotions anywhere near my eyes, as they make them red and weepy. But there are a whole host of specialist creams that claim to do wonders for that sensitive area and undoubtedly some of them are effective for some women – just not for me. If your eyes are sensitive like mine, look for beauty lines that are hypoallergenic. What I do find works are the new generation of serums, which specially target the thinner, more sensitive skin around the eyes. Eye gels, too, are lighter and seem to irritate my eyes less.

However, there are lots of things that can make your eyes look great.

First, get your brows professionally done. You can always tell a high-maintenance woman because her brows are always perfect. Eyebrows and pedicures have, for my money, to be amongst the cheapest of beauty treatments that really do make an impact. Getting your brows done at somewhere like Linda Meredith (36 Beauchamp Place, London SW3 1NU; 020 7225 2755; www.lindameredith.com), eyebrow plucker to the stars, only costs just over £20 but, oh, the difference. These days you can walk into many department stores and get your brows done as soon as a technician is free. Londoners can go to Harvey Nichols' Beyond Beauty on the ground floor and get Blink's Indian threading service for £15. Fenwick of New Bond Street offers a similar service. At Selfridges, Groom will do eyebrows and lots more. (They offer high-speed treatments for those short of time where two therapists will work on a customer at once – one doing, say, eyebrows and a facial, the other doing a pedicure.)

If your eyebrows are beginning to thin out – oh, the woes of getting older – Debra Robson-Lawrence (144 Harley Street, London W1G 7LE; 0845 230 2021; www.permanent-makeup.com) does wonderfully natural-looking tattoos. Be warned: for the first two weeks they look a bit strong – more Alistair Darling than Greta Garbo, but they quickly soften and look very natural. Debra specialises in permanent make-up of all kinds and will also tattoo very gently round the lips, giving you an amazingly plump-looking mouth without the need of fillers (so no risk, then, of looking like a gasping goldfish).

Bobbi Brown always says that you should use eyeshadow to define the brows rather than a pencil.

Tips for Eyes

White eyeliner inside the inner lid, if you can stand it, is brilliant for masking the pink of the inner eyelid. Estée Lauder, in particular, has a great Artist's Eye Pencil (£14).

Eye-tec (www.eye-tec.co.uk) goes in for what it calls 'eyelash enhancement' – that is, adding false eyelashes to your own to make them look lusher. Although very effective, they only last as long as your own eyelashes.

For puffy eyes, facial lymph drainage therapy is worth a try and most good facialists offer this during the normal course of a treatment. Carmel Phelan (at 69 Harley Street, London W1G 8QW; 020 7486 7211 and Princes Risborough, Buckinghamshire; 07788 115 545 for an appointment) specialises in this area. (She also offers proper therapies for those who have had their lymph nodes removed during cancer treatment and have lymphoedema as a result.) Her therapy boosts circulation, and helps to eliminate toxins as well as make the face look firmer.

Necks and Chests

Nora Ephron, that wonderfully witty author of the screenplay for *When Harry Met Sally*, has, with her latest book, *I Feel Bad About My Neck*, given vent to one great cry of anguish about the sags, wrinkles and droops that come with the territory of being middle aged. Quite obviously, it's her neck that bothers her most. (She's photographed on the cover wearing a black turtleneck sweater, a good ploy that the rest of us might copy, at least until global warming hits us.) 'Dear Nora', I feel like telling her, 'there are things that help' (though, to be truthful, the only cure for very saggy skin on the neck is plastic surgery, about which more later).

As one gets older, the two hardest areas to fix are the tops of the arms, and the décolletage and neck. Though we can cover them up for long chunks of the year, come summer holidays, heatwaves, time on the beach or around the pool, all is revealed.

Upper arms (if you can face it – it doesn't quite seem worth it to me) can be dealt with by Smartlipo (a quick, lighter form of liposuction). But much can be done, you'll be happy to hear, to improve the décolletage. I had mine done at the Soma Centre, a charming spa and gym in the basement of the Royal Garden Hotel at 2–24 Kensington High Street, London W8 4PY (07765 850 924), but lots of clinics now offer specialist techniques. Dr Jules Nabet, a French cosmetic doctor, and Joanne Evans (an aesthetician) have joined forces to offer a double-pronged attack on this vexed area. They use a combination of Botox and laser therapy. The two treatments together cost about £400, so not cheap, but they make a serious difference. They remove brown spots, plump up the skin and deal with creases. You need to plan ahead because, to begin with, there will be some reddening and darkening of the spots, and it takes two weeks for this to clear completely.

Dr Nick Lowe, the well-known consultant dermatologist at the Cranley Clinic, Harcourt House, 19A Cavendish Square, London W1G 0PN; 020 7499 3223, offers similar treatments for rejuvenating the neck and chest. Restylane Vitale is very good for surface wrinkling, whilst he uses Botox to deal with wrinkling caused by muscle action, and photo-rejuvenation techniques to tackle sun spots and red or brown blemishes on the surface of the skin. He also recommends using a prescription-strength retinoid such as

Retin-A (a cream) or Tazarotene (a gel), and utters the usual mantra: 'Don't go out in the sun without a proper sunscreen.'

Then there are neck creams. Some women swear by them and I'm of the view that all nourishment helps the skin, but I find them too tricky to use. It's just one step too far for me and the cream seems to get onto one's clothes. However, I'm quite sure that if one was a committed beauty junkie and could find the time to deal with every niche problem, it would probably be worth it. Me, I like a simpler routine and I'm afraid my neck is rather left to look after itself as best it can.

Make-Up

The chief thing to remember is that *you can always wash it off*. Some women seem to treat make-up as if it were a dangerous innovation that might leave them permanently impaired. Most skins look better, in my view, with some make-up. As we get older our colouring tends to fade and make-up helps to lift the face. Those with sallow complexions that need a little lifting and added colouring benefit particularly. Good foundations (there are masses but my two current favourites are Giorgio Armani's Designer Shaping Cream Foundation SPF 20 and Estée Lauder's Resilience Lift Extreme) even out the skin tone, hide light blemishes and give the skin a certain luminous quality. The older one gets, though, the less good one looks with powder – it settles in the creases – so these days I'm very fond of Serge Lutens Teint Si Fin, a compressed all-in-one make-up in eight different shades that is dabbed on with a sponge and gives a smooth, flawless, natural finish. It's all part of his very edited small range of make-up called Nécessaire de Beauté designed to give that Holy Grail of the make-up world: the no make-up look (see p. 133).

Every face is different and skin tones vary enormously, so most of us need to experiment to find out what suits us. All the big make-up brands are a wonderful source of information, though only for their own products. You can get your make-up done at their counters for free, which is a wonderful service and shows you just how make-up should be applied. Turn up at a big store – Harrods, Selfridges, Harvey Nichols or one near where you live – take your turn in the queue, if there is one, and you can learn a lot. Otherwise there is nothing for it but either a bit of personal experimenting or a lesson from a make-up artist.

Possibly the most important thing to get right is foundation. If the colour is wrong, it spoils the whole look. Textures vary considerably, too, and I'm afraid that only trial and error can help you find the right foundation for you.

Primers

Primers are a relative newcomers on the beauty scene. The point of them is that they help prepare the skin, refining the pores and smoothing the skin, providing a better surface for the foundation so that it 'takes' more easily. I have friends who swear by primers from Trish McEvoy and Laura Mercier. I'm using one by Trish McEvoy, and it does make a difference.

Radiance

Radiance, you might think, has been around for a long time. Natural radiance has, yes, but when it comes to cosmetics, new technical discoveries – most particularly light-reflecting particles – have helped the beauty companies develop products that are specifically targeted at giving you a more radiant skin. I'm keen on them – and who wouldn't be?

Look for products that have magic words like 'light reflecting', 'luminisers' or 'brightening'. There are radiance-boosting moisturisers to apply under make-up, like Estée Lauder's Daywear Plus Sheer Tint Release Formula, which definitely gives the skin a more luminous look, as well as plenty of others. Just look out for those key words.

Here are three products that I believe really help: Guerlain's Midnight Star, Liz Earle's Brightening Treatment and B Kamins Diatomamus Earth Masque.

A great tip for adding radiance, which comes from an eminent Hollywood make-up artist: put a little of your foundation into the palm of your hand, add a tiny (and she means tiny) drop of glycerine, and mix well before applying. It will give a gorgeous glow to the skin without making it greasy.

For the No Make-up Look

Tinted moisturisers are all some skins need. For instance, Estée Lauder's Daywear Plus Multi-Protection Antioxidant Moisturiser Sheer Tint (with an SPF of 15) is a good one. Many other beauty companies produce very light formulations for those who don't need much cover. Origins' Nude and Improved Bare Face Make-up (with an SPF of 15) is good because it offers just a little more cover-up than most, and comes in five shades (www.origins.co.uk).

Chantecaille's Real Skin (which has an SPF of 30) and Future Skin manage to be incredibly light whilst evening out skin texture and covering up blemishes.

The chief tactic in the no make-up look is to apply foundation (or perhaps even just a good concealer) only where you have blemishes, broken veins or brown spots, and leave unblemished skin clear of make-up altogether. Blend the foundation or concealer carefully so that it's impossible to tell where the skin starts and the foundation ends. I think foundations that are a mix of cream and powder together – there are now many – look lighter than those that need powder to fix them. If you must use powder, choose a transparent one and brush it on lightly. Finish with a light lip gloss.

Need a Bit of Cover-up?

Avoid (unless you have deep port-wine birthmarks) all those medical cover-up creams – they're much too heavy. These days there are lighter, cleverer ways to conceal.

There's a whole new generation of concealers that make some of the old favourites look heavy and mask-like in comparison. Guerlain's Issima Precious Light Smoothing Illuminator has high-tech pigments and pearly particles that make it a pretty magic product. It masks blemishes and lines as well as offering a good base for those with skin problems.

Otherwise Jane Iredale (www.jiproducts.co.uk) is the magic name to remember if you need to cover up anything from acne scars to red veins. A good moisturiser to start with is her Absence, which has an SPF of 15 (£29) and in-built oil control. Its light-reflecting properties seem to diminish as well as fill in the scars. If there are any outstanding blotches or scars, stipple on Jane Iredale's Circle Delete (£20). Finish off with Iredale's Amazing Base (£33) in a shade to suit your skin tone. The Organic Pharmacy, (396 King's Road, London SW10 0LN; 020 7351 2232; www.theorganicpharmacy.com) sells her products.

Beauty on the Cheap

Great make-up brands to look for if you want to save the pennies are Bourjois (which is made by Chanel – say no more) and L'Oreal (which make-up guru Valentine Alexander says is very similar to Lancôme). Both can be found at Boots and Superdrug. Nivea, Olay and Roc are the best inexpensive, low-priced, skin-care ranges.

Make-up Specialists

Here are a few that I know to be good from personal experience:

VALENTINE ALEXANDER is, in my view, worth every penny of the £250 she charges. She sees the face as a canvas and treats it in rather the same way Renaissance portrait painters did. Because she isn't tied to a particular beauty house, she uses what she considers the best products for the purpose. Since some of these are very expensive, she can help you avoid buying the wrong one. She comes to London a few times a month and offers advice at 11 Cadogan Gardens, London SW3 1AX, and in Paris. Telephone her on 07956 846 909 to book an appointment.

STEPHEN GLASS AT FACE FACTS is very nice indeed and gentle, and he does make-up brilliantly. Like Valentine, he cruises all the beauty houses for what he considers to be the best products. Contact him on 07753 616 617 or email him on contact@stephenglass.co.uk.

MAGGIE HUNT has addressed the make-up problems of such luminaries as Shakira Caine, Helen Mirren, Baroness Thatcher, Vanessa Redgrave and Maggie Smith and if she's good enough for them I'm sure she's great for the rest of us. 'It's from forty-five and upwards,' she says, 'that my clients need most help. They're usually using too heavy an eyeliner, lots of mascara and too heavy a foundation whilst missing out on the blusher.' Her best product for lips? Lip Infinity by Max

Factor. Her studio is in Hampstead, where a two-hour make-up lesson costs £275. Telephone 020 7435 5049 for an appointment (also at www.maggiehunt.com).

NEISHA HIBBERT will devise make-up regimes for clients in her own South Kensington house (telephone 07768 078 766 for an appointment) for £75, but if you live in London she will also come to your house for £150.

DANIEL SANDLER, who's been doing faces for photographic shoots for many a long year, will also come to your house (or send one of his own personally trained make-up artists) to hold a master-class in how to apply make-up. A more glamorous kind of Tupperware party, if you like. You need a minimum of five friends and he charges £90 per person, which includes a glass of champagne. He not only goes through the make-up you already own (be prepared for some stringent comments) but passes on all those little tips that only insiders usually acquire. He guides you on how to find the right colour of concealer (most of us choose too pale a colour – it should match our foundation), how to sculpt cheekbones, and lots, lots more. Telephone 01923 845 370 or check www.danielsandler.com.

SARAH CHAPMAN is a make-up artist much favoured by *The Times* fashion desk (07050 097 796).

JOHN GUSTAFSON at Fenwick of New Bond Street (020 7629 9161) has a waiting list longer than my arm, but you could plan ahead and book way in advance.

Teeth

Good teeth do more to take the years off than almost anything else – and they can also be life-changing, affecting both career and romantic prospects. There are now clinics all over the land that will whiten your teeth, straighten them, cap them and – if you can afford the gold standard – give you light, pearly-perfect veneers. Whilst teeth whitening with a laser costs about £700 all in, crowns cost £650 per tooth and pearly veneers £545 per tooth. So this kind of dentistry is not cheap but if your teeth are bad, my goodness, the difference it makes.

I had my teeth whitened by Dr Joe Oliver at the Welbeck Clinic (0870 241 6903 and at www.thewelbeckclinic.co.uk). Dr Oliver's Power Whitening treatment takes one and a half hours from start to finish and it really works, though the result may vary from person to person.

Dr Oliver has also developed a fast system for veneers, which he calls his 'perfect smile' in a single day. Most veneers take a minimum of two weeks to make, which is usually enough for most of us, but if you have a serious emergency (a film première? a wedding? a vital job interview?), they can be done in a day. It's more expensive, costing £1,075 per tooth as opposed to the usual £595. If you have uneven, crooked or gappy teeth, you'll probably need between eight and ten veneers. The quality is identical to that of the usual veneers and they usually last about fifteen years. See him one day, pick them up the next.

Hair

Nothing – not even a pair of Manolo Blahniks or a blissful shearling coat – does more for the morale than a spanking new haircut that really works. (We will pass lightly over those occasions, an inevitable part of the female rite of passage, when one rushes scarlet-faced straight from the hair-dresser to the washbasin at home.) A great cut can transform the plain into the glamorous, the scruffy into the glossy, and the merely pretty into a beauty. Think of Princess Anne on her wedding day. Some women find their style early on and stick with it – look no further than Anna Wintour, Raine Spencer and our own dear Queen. Others reinvent themselves eternally.

The secret of the right cut, though, is elusive – not helpful, I'm afraid, but true – for it depends more upon art, a sensitive eye and intuitive scissors than just technique. Tastes need to mesh so that the crimper's idea of chic or glamour matches yours. There are a few legendary cutters around – John Barrett in New York, for whom jet-setters run up phenomenal quantities of hair-miles, and Christophe in Paris, for whom several Londoners regularly cross the Channel. Nearer home I have friends who have been transformed by Charlie Chan at Michaeljohn, Robert at John Frieda in New Cavendish Street, and Nathalie at John Frieda in Aldford Street. John Sahag of New York also has a cult following and gave my best-dressed New York friend a haircut to die for, although he didn't to do the same for me. Some years ago

Richard at the 4th Floor, 4 Northington Street, London WC1N 2JG; 020 7405 6011, gave me the cut that most transformed my look, creating a shortish helmet of hair that swirled and shone, and made something of a stir back in the office. (I try to forget the other time that a haircut caused a kerfuffle at conference time, when one of London's well-known crimpers gave me a disastrous perm.)

These days I'm devoted to Hari at Hari's, 305 Brompton Road, London SW3 2DY (020 7581 5211), where Rebecca (who does my colour) is a genius and Hari effortlessly somehow turns my not-very-promising locks into something passably chic. He now has a hair spa, which translates into a whole lot of TLC for the hair. Turn up and they'll tell you which of their many treatments will restore it if it is stressed, tired, overworked or simply freaked out by environmental damage.

The golden rule about hair has to be that if you see somebody with a haircut you admire, ask who did it. After Richard gave me that wonderful short helmet (I was *much* younger then), I was endlessly stopped and asked – most notably whilst boarding a plane in Hong Kong – and was always flattered. Then go for it. Don't hang on to straight long tresses because once, long ago, somebody admired them. Nothing is more ageing or dates one more. Sometimes the transformation is effected in one fell swoop. Sometimes it takes a few visits to the hairdresser before enough trust has built up to let the cutter have his or her wicked way. Watch carefully what he does for others – if you like it, the chances are he'll suit you, too.

As for colour, go for that too, if you need it. The fashion at the moment is for thick chunky streaks (known as 'slicing' in the trade) rather than ultra-fine ones (check out Trinny and Susannah's hair to see what they look like). A great cut, a new colour, with some of the splendid new products that help preserve the shine, can update a look more quickly than a Marc Jacobs jacket.

But don't always stick to conventional thinking about hair. Take the example of Evelyn Lauder, wife of Leonard Lauder and a formidable person in her own right. When I interviewed her a couple of years ago, she told me that she had recently decided to 'reinvent myself. I'd been wearing my hair short for years and one day when I had a brilliant cut at Coppola in Milan [the branch near the main Armani store, in case you're interested], I just decided it was so good that I didn't want to cut it short again.' So she gently grew it out and it gave her a new softer, very pretty look – overturning the convention that as you get older you should cut your hair shorter. 'The key,' says Mrs Lauder, 'is keeping your hair in good condition so that it shines. I do colour my hair but use no peroxide.' In New York, Kao at AKS on Madison Avenue, she told me, kept it looking good.

As one grows older, getting the colour attended to can take years off one's appearance. As the hair changes colour so, too, does the skin – you need a really gifted colourist to get it right. A few women look wonderful with their hair a particularly chic shade of steel-grey, but most of us turn a mere speckled grey and white and quite often the grey is yellowish, not a pretty look! So don't just drift along – get it attended to. If you spend money on nothing else, spend it on your hair. Don't hold back out of timidity. If you don't try something new, you'll never know whether it will work or not and at the end of the day you can always grow it out.

SERIOUS HELP

Almost every hairdresser offers good masks and conditioning treatments. I believe that if you can afford it, it's worth having them – they're rather like facials in that they nourish and restore. These, however, are almost the easiest treatments to do yourself at home, which is so much cheaper. Kerastase is about the best home-hairdressing range around. For real hair loss (alopecia), you need medical help.

Hands

Hands are a big give-away on the age front, although that might not worry you. After all, most of us aren't trying to con the world into believing we're younger than we are; we just want to look the best we can – but hands that aren't looked after can actually look a whole lot *older* than we are, which I think it's perfectly permissible to dislike. If you had nothing else to do, you could wear Bliss Glamour Gloves every night (they come ready infused with a nourishing grapeseed and ceramide gel to moisturise and nourish, check out www.blisslondon.co.uk), as well as exfoliate your hands, use peels and scrubs on them, and pamper them with enriching creams. Most of us have rather more interesting (or pressing) things to do so it's worth simplifying things a bit.

First, get a hand cream (we all need one, don't we?) that has a high SPF so that your hands are protected from sun damage as much as possible. It's the sun that mostly causes the ageing brown spots. Given that prevention is easier than cure, if you're young and don't yet have age spots, you should start using hand creams with in built SPFs *before* they appear. We all think it's only other people who get these things – but believe me, it's not true.

If you already have brown spots, it's probably worth investing in a few serious treatments; getting rid of them makes a big difference. Go to a good aesthetic treatment centre (they are now all over the country) and get them zapped. It's dead easy. Microdermabrasion and IPL treatments will really improve the look of your hands and will boost their collagen, too. Afterwards, just take care to nourish your hands regularly, look after your nails with a good hand and nail cream, and keep the UV rays at bay.

Hand creams that I like: Clarins' Hand and Nail Treatment Cream; Lancôme's Caresse Mains; and Liz Earle's Hand Repair, which has a good texture and smells pleasantly herbal.

Nails

I was much comforted to learn that the late Liz Tilberis, an editor at *Vogue* and *Harper's Bazaar*, never had a manicure until she reached her fifties. Brits are only just beginning to match their American cousins on the grooming front and, when they do start going in for manicures, you can always tell, because they start waving their hands about as if doing semaphore. My own aren't a very good example. I've never successfully cracked the problem of nails that split and although I find that nail polish makes them look wonderful whilst it's on, my nails are much more brittle and dry a few weeks later. I find the Barielle group of products for nails the best (020 736 0234 and at www.barielle.co.uk). I once consulted one of in:spa's nutritionists (Lorraine Perretta) and when I took the vast quantity of nutritional supplements that she prescribed, my nails were noticeably better. The downside was that they all took a lot of swallowing each day (there was zinc, calcium, potassium, plus an array of vitamins) and I rather feebly gave up.

French manicures are now considered naff but I still think it useful to run Rimmel's White Nail Pencil (£2.99) under your nails to give a good clean look at the tip. Track down a good manicurist and get your nails regularly looked after. It isn't very expensive and well worth it.

Legs

The things that make a difference are:

1. GENES, about which you can do nothing.

2. EXERCISE, about which you can do a lot; some is

essential to keep legs well toned.

3. EATING WELL, lots of fresh fruit and vegetables, and drinking lots of water. This is not always compatible with real life, but there you go, that's this beauty lark for you.

4. BODY BRUSHING, yes, really. I've never had the patience to do it but those who daily brush their legs very lightly (just enough to move the lymph along), brushing upwards from the feet towards the heart, report marked improvements. This is especially essential for those with the dimpled skin that we call cellulite.

5. CREAMS. I've never had the time, patience or will-power to apply daily creams that are specially targeted at improving skin texture or dealing with cellulite. However, more dedicated seekers after perfection than I report that if you keep at it stolidly (and I really mean stolidly: it takes something like six months), you will see some improvement.

6. MASSAGE, particularly for those with cellulite, as it helps move the toxins along.

7. MESOTHERAPY. Some people believe in it although when I tried it, it did nothing for my most troublesome area (my stomach), and it also requires lots of treatments before you see any real improvement. Worth a go, but I'm a bit dubious myself.

8. GROOMING. Most obviously of all, keep your legs well waxed and, in summer, brown, using bronzers or home-

tanning sprays or creams. (All the yummy mummies tell me Rodial's Brazilian Tan lotion is best.)

Feet

These days Brits are much more alert to the joys of a proper pedicure than ever before. Partly this is due to the rise and rise of vertiginously expensive shoes (Jimmy Choo, Manolo Blahnik, Gina and all the other usual suspects), which has meant that it seemed like sartorial sacrilege to put ugly, gnarled old toes into such delicious concoctions. There are now good nail clinics on almost every high street and pedicures aren't rocket science, so most of them probably do a good job.

If you want a really special experience, though, go to Iris Chapple at the Nail Studio, 3 Spanish Place, London W1U 3HX; 020 7486 6001. Her delicious pedicure (£45) involves peppermint soaks, rubbing off the dead skin, dealing with anything that isn't truly nasty (in which case you need a podiatrist), followed by filing and painting the nails. She also says you can give yourself a pedicure perfectly well at home (though since she only costs £45 and pedicures, in my experience, last for almost two months, why bother?)

IRIS CHAPPLE'S ADVICE:

'Brush your skin when it's dry. Never use nail hardeners. They're the worst because they dry the nails out. Keep some almond oil by the bed and put a drop on each nail (hands and feet) every night. Cut nails straight across. Never use corn plasters – always go to a podiatrist to have corns treated. Many of the inexpensive products are just as good as the expensive ones. Maybelline polish, for instance, at about £6 a bottle, is just as good as more expensive makes and it has a brilliant high shine.'

Although I'm not good at this as I'm always in too much of a hurry, I'd add to that, try to rub the hard skin off your feet regularly. On their website, Jo Fairley and Sarah Stacey rave about the Alida Foot File (£9.95 from www.victoria health.com), saying it is the best foot file they've ever come across. It's ergonomically designed and easy to use.

BLISSLONDON, 60 Sloane Avenue, London SW3 3DD; 020 7584 3888, has lots of special foot treats, including its Rosy Toes (sixty minutes for £60), which involves resting your feet on warm stones and soaking them in rose-petal-strewn water.

If you have calluses, there's the 'Hot Milk and Almond Pedicure' (sixty minutes for £55), which offers 'intensive dry-buffing with a fierce callus fighter'.

THE AVEDA URBAN SPA, 174 High Holborn, London WC1V 7AA (020 7759 7355), has a vibrating chair and two therapists who'll do your hands and feet simultaneously.

HEAVEN AT HOME (020 7937 4333, and at www.heavenathome.net). If you're the girly sort, you can throw a pampering party where you all experiment with foot soaks, exfoliators and different polishes. Heaven at Home offers a menu of different pampering treats (including pedicures) and you get two therapists for three hours for £300, which sounds like fun.

Pedicures Around the World

Bastien Gonzalez is probably the world's most famous specialist, the Bastien experience being unlike any other. He did my feet when he still had a treatment room at Claridge's and it is much, much more than a pedicure. In fact, he doesn't even paint the nails. He buffs and smoothes and shines the feet so that they don't even *need* to be painted. He's a bit peripatetic so you need to track him down to make an appointment in advance. Check into his website at www.bastiengonzalez.com and email for an appointment, or ring 020 7565 0869.

Mr So at the Mandarin Hotel, 5 Connaught Road in

Central Hong Kong (www.manderinoriental.com), is another cult name. Those who have his pedicure swear that their feet become a whole size smaller and many a client books in their feet when they book a hotel room.

At the Paris Four Seasons, 31 Avenue George V, 75008 (www.fourseasons.com), they do the most blissful French finish, whilst at the Ritz-Carlton in Key Biscayne, 455 Grand Bay Drive, Key Biscayne, FL 33149, (www.ritzcarlton.com), there are armchairs that vibrate with speed and heat settings, and two therapists give you a simultaneous manicure and pedicure.

Top Beauty Tips

1. Keep out of the sun. Use a sunblock like DDF's almost chemical-free Organic Sunblock (available at Harvey Nichols) and, when possible, wear a hat as well.

2. Use a lip balm. The best are Kiehl's (from Space NK), Smith's Rosebud Salve (from www.ukshopping.com) and Rose Petal Salve from the Rose & Co Apothecary (84 Main Street, Haworth, West Yorkshire BD22 8DP; 01535 646 830; www.roseapothecary.co.uk).

3. Best red lipsticks: Chanel's Rouge Noir and Yves St Laurent's Rouge Pur Lipstick No. 19.

4. Use a lip pencil to deal with lines around the lips that cause lipsticks to bleed (Mac's Spice is a wonderfully

accommodating shade), but never use one darker than your lipstick. A make-up artist taught me to outline my lips *outside* the lipline with a concealer (Chanel's Correcteur Éclat or Yves St Laurent's classic Touche Éclat) to make your lips look fuller.

5. Take care of your skin when travelling. Elizabeth Arden's Eight Hour Cream has been going since the 1930s and many a beauty still swears by it. I also love Prescriptives Flight Cream. Calvin Klein is apparently a great fan and buys it by the boxful.

6. Use an eyelash curler. The best is from Shu Uemura and is curved like eyelids.

7. Need to mask a spot or small flaw? Bobbi Brown's Creamy Concealer comes in lots of shades so you can match your skin colour exactly. Cheaper still is Rimmel's Hide the Blemish.

8. If you need a real pick-me-up for the skin before, say, a wedding, a seriously big date, an appearance on the catwalk or the red carpet (well, you never know), CACI Chroma-Oxy is rumoured to be the treatment that Renée Zellweger had before the Globes. It offers first a microdermabrasion followed by an oxygen facial. It takes ninety minutes, costs £75, and leaves the skin looking fresh and glowing. There's no down time at all. The flagship salon is the C2 Clinic in Hampstead, 11 Heath Street, London NW3 6TP; 020 7435 1554.

9. Chanel's Cils Magique Waterproof Mascara famously survived a birthing pool – it really does stay on through most watery occasions.
10. Sleep, sleep and more sleep.

If you ever catch sight of yourself in a mirror looking a bit slouched you'll never do it again. Stand and sit up straight – it takes years off.

Evelyn Lauder

Vitamin Injections

I first heard about vitamin cocktails from the lovely Janan Harb, ex-wife of the late King Fahd of Saudia Arabia and a famous beauty. She took one look at me and hauled me off to the Pasha Clinic for a series of seven. Janan is so keen on them that she'd have them every day if she could. She first discovered them when she had some facial burns after a fire at her home and the vitamin injections healed the burns so well that she was left without a single scar. The treatments consist of a tiny little needle injecting micro amounts of nutrients into the skin all over the face. It is only mildly uncomfortable and it doesn't take long – about fifteen minutes, at a guess. According to Dr Menevse Kargin, a wonderful Turkish doctor turned aesthetician who runs the Pasha Clinic, the cocktail she uses has a broad range of essential micronutrients (amino acids, vitamins, mineral salts and nucleotides) that are needed for the many complex cellular biochemical processes that are the basis of normal cellular activity.

I can only tell you that after my treatment I ran into somebody whom I've known for years who asked me what on earth I'd done as I looked so good. And a make-up artist who was doing my face for a professional photograph kept commenting on how well plumped up my skin was.

The Pasha Beauty Clinic is at 37 Maddox Street, London W1S 2PP (020 7409 7354), and at 97 Green Lanes, London N16 9BX (020 7226 7950). A single session costs £150, but a course of seven sessions is £500. You'll need seven for proper results.

The Non-surgical Facelift

These days there are many techniques to help in the anti-ageing war without resorting to the knife. The face ages largely because we lose plumpness from under the skin, which causes the skin to sag, rather like air going out of a balloon. It follows that if you can reflate the balloon (i.e. the skin), it will look plumper and younger, and the lines will fill out.

There are now many different fillers – Restylane, Botox and Sculptra to name but three – which are used to fill out the sagging skin. The other technique in the age war is, of course, the facelift, which works in the opposite way by cutting away the excess sagging skin and tightening it up.

When I heard that Dr Steven Victor, dubbed Dr Lookgood by his New York patients and allegedly the model for the favourite 'derm' of the 'Bergdorf Blondes' (in Plum Sykes' book), was bringing to London his techniques for what he calls his 'non-surgical facelift', I was there in a flash, volunteering to be a guinea pig.

This is how it works: first, the patient is given a series of injections rather like those at the dentist. They don't hurt – much – but they do render one's mouth area numb. Then he sets to work with his fillers.

This is what he did for me in his medi-spa at Daniel Galvin (as I write, he is deciding on new premises): Botox in the forehead, between the eyes, round the nose and eyes, as well as round the eyebrow to lift the brows and the upper eyelids. I was given injections of Sculptra in the dermis, fat and muscle layers of the cheekbones to plump up the area and so 'lift the face'. (Knowing which layers to inject into is, it seems, a vital part of the procedure's success.) This was followed by deeper injections of Sculptra into the fat layer and superficial muscle layer of the nasolabial lines (the so-called laugh lines), as well as superficial injections of Restylane into the dermis. The lips were plumped up a little with silicone to help fill in a downturning of the mouth.

You go home looking worse than when you came in, with red marks, a numb mouth, a bit of bruising. But it all subsides in a couple of days and after a week you really begin to notice the difference. My face looked a lot fresher and younger. I had higher cheekbones. The lines, particularly running from nose to mouth, were much reduced and he managed to inject the Botox so that my eyelids didn't droop (my big fear about Botox). Lines on my forehead had disappeared so I could wear my hair off my face again (my forehead had been very lined for some time). I think it truly made a difference and several friends have remarked on how well I look.

The cost: about £3,000.

How long does it last? Well, it varies. The silicone in the lips will last ten years, the Sculptra about two years, the Botox from three to six months and the Restylane from six to twelve months. So to keep looking this way isn't cheap.

Dr Olivier de Frahan is another artist when it comes to fillers (Botox, Restylane and the full facelift) and the person that many a French film star turns to for all serious beauty advice. He works in London and Paris – telephone respectively 020 7730 7928 and +33 6 09 55 77 77 for an appointment.

Warning: as one New York dermatologist put it to me, simply because techniques are there doesn't mean it is always wise to avail oneself of them. My experience tells me that before submitting yourself to any of these procedures, you should investigate very carefully the work of the aesthetician. Do not just turn up at any salon and ask for work to be done. Botox in the wrong place, too much Restylane or too much Sculptra can result in the trout mouths, bizarrely high cheeks and startled looks or drooping eyes that we're all, sadly, becoming more accustomed to seeing. The techniques are easy to master but the aesthetics of judging how much and where to put them require a fine and sensitive eye. In the right hands, they can make a huge difference for the better. In the wrong hands, they can wreak disaster.

Plastic Surgery:

Should You or Shouldn't You?

I've never understood why some people get so po-faced when the matter of plastic surgery is up for discussion. It's almost as if it were a matter of deep moral import, with the implication that there is something inherently morally superior about allowing the wrinkles to wrinkle and the frowns to furrow and the droopy bits to get droopier. Not unlike some intellectuals who think it's a sign of a superior brain to dress in drab clothes.

Plastic surgery seems to me to be fundamentally a physical issue and, providing you're not proposing to pay for it by swiping the bread from your children's mouths, I cannot see that it is a moral issue at all. What good plastic surgery does is to cut away sagging bits of skin. It removes bags from under the eyes, droopiness from the top eyelids (not a good look, bloodhound eyelids), sagginess from the chin, and generally tightens up the skin. That's it. Now where's the problem with all of that? Of course, if it's badly done, it's a hideously expensive mistake, but these days it seems to me that surgeons are getting better and better at it – heaven knows they're getting more practice. The general notion that it would be better to put up with age spots, red veins, droops and sags when there is something that can be done about them seems to me just plain daft.

Nobody who looks at the before and after pictures of such success stories as Mary Archer, Julie Christie or Sharon Osbourne could surely still take the view that in their shoes they wouldn't have done the same. All three – and there are thousands of others like them – look a million times better and happier now that the damage the years can do has been held back a little longer.

The usual charge by those who get all sniffy at the very idea it is that speaks of vanity. Well, first I see nothing wrong with vanity. Vanity makes us try harder; vanity makes us strive in many areas of our lives; vanity makes us look better, which adds considerably to the gaiety of the nation. But there is more than vanity at stake. Quite often these days it is often a matter of job survival. As we all live longer and longer (hurrah!) we want to go on living full and busy lives, and if we want to do that, it is no use denying that looks count. Whether you're behind the counter in a shop, working in a lawyer's office, trying to hold your own in the world of fashion or running a small business, how you are seen by the outside world will affect your prospects.

These days there is a bewildering array of often very technical options for us to choose from, ranging from the surgeon's knife to lasers, light pulses, fillers, acid peels – the list is endless. Many things can now be treated: from sun-damaged skin to brown spots, red veins, dubious moles, excess hair and many other afflictions. And if treatments exist that will deal with the things that indubitably make women feel less confident about themselves, I cannot for the life of me believe that it is anything other than a good idea to have them attended to.

Some of you may be frightened of the surgeon's knife – and not without reason. Mistakes are sometimes made (it must be almost impossible to estimate the damage that Mrs Wildenstein alone must have done to the world of cosmetic surgery) and the problem is that once made, they are hard to put right. But the answer to that isn't *no* cosmetic surgery – it's *better* cosmetic surgery, more finely tuned lasers, more skilled technicians. The key has to be to take the time and trouble to find surgeons with a good track record. As more and more women who have had 'work' done begin to speak out and tell their friends the good news, it will become easier and easier for those who are nervous to hear at first hand about who is good and who is not.

As to those who claim that cosmetic surgery is undignified and that they themselves would never do anything quite so drastic, when you take a good look at them they nearly always turn out to be twenty-something beauties who haven't the faintest idea of what it feels like to look in the mirror day after day and see one's reflection gradually going to pot. Just wait, I long to say to them, and see if you're quite so adamant when your own looks begin to fade. Read Nora Ephron's rail against the trials and tribulations of growing older in *I Feel Bad About My Neck* and those who are either male or gloriously young will begin to get some idea that getting older, as Gore Vidal once put it, 'isn't for cissies'. But praise be, these days there are things – highly technical, skilful, successful things – that can be done and for that I think we should all be duly grateful.

But – and here I cannot stress this enough – it is absolutely key that you get the best surgeon you can. The difference between fine work and bad work is the difference between happiness and deep regret. Ask around amongst your friends. If you hear of a good plastic surgeon, ask to see before and after pictures.

I asked Mr Barry Jones, plastic surgeon to any number of grateful women (who mostly keep deathly quiet about it) as well as, more importantly, to any number of desperately sick children and cancer patients, about the key questions that you should always ask your plastic surgeon before you embark on a facelift. This was his answer:

Questions to Ask Your Plastic Surgeon

1. Are you on the General Medical Council's specialist register as a plastic surgeon?

2. Where did you train in plastic surgery and when did you qualify?

3. Do you hold or have you held an appointment as a consultant plastic surgeon in the NHS and, if so, where?

4. Are you a member of the British Association of Aesthetic Plastic Surgeons (BAAPS), the British Association of Plastic Reconstructive and Aesthetic Plastic Surgeons (BAPRAS), the International Society of Aesthetic Plastic Surgeons (ISAPS), the European Association of Plastic Surgeons (EURAPS) or the American Society of Plastic Surgery (ASPS)?

5. Do you have a specialist interest and, if so, can I reference any of your publications in peer-reviewed journals (e.g. *Plastic and Reconstructive Surgery* or *The British Journal of Plastic Surgery*) that would reflect it?

6. Having explained to you what I would like to achieve, is there a procedure that you would recommend?

7. What scarring can I expect?

8. How much swelling and/or bruising will there be?

9. How much pain might I expect?

10. How long need I stay in hospital?

11. How long will it be before I can return to normal activities?

12. What complications may occur and what is their frequency?

13. How many of these operations do you do each year?
14. Which hospital do you operate at?
15. Does this procedure involve general anaesthesia or sedation, and if so, who is your anaesthetist and may I see a copy of their CV?
16. How much does it cost and what exactly does that cover?

Health

I'm not a medic, but I have learned a few things over the years. When I'm slimmer, I feel better and, of course, I look better. It's a bit of a struggle (no, I lie; it's a titanic struggle) for me because I'm only five feet two inches tall, and I have an underactive thyroid, and I love cooking, and I like wine, and I like eating with family and friends. And if you live in London, as I do, a lot of one's pleasures are sedentary – eating out, theatres, music – and writing, as I've always complained, is a very fattening occupation.

But losing weight isn't complicated. Although we all know what to do (eat sensibly and exercise more), sometimes we could do with a bit of help. For instance, I've never been to the Mayr Clinic (Dellach, Marie Worth on Lake Worth, Carinthia, Austria; +43 4273 2511) but intend to one day. Everybody I know who has been has said it was as tough as Hades but paid off in spades.

How to Detox and Love it

I detoxed by mistake. I'd heard that in:spa was a fun place to go and that they were running a week at Trasierra, Charlotte Scott's beautiful *finca* just outside Seville, with lots of pampering, massages, some lovely walks through the olive groves, exercise and great healthy food. It sounded divine, so the husband and I went. *But* I hadn't read the small print. It wasn't until we got there that we discovered that, for the entire week there was to be no wheat, no dairy, no tea, no coffee, no alcohol, no red meat. I blanched at the news but what I discovered was that it's *only* the compulsory removal of these things that makes the detox process – relatively – easy. We had no choice. The in:spa team made it fun and we had one of the most rewarding weeks of our lives. I don't think I lost as much weight as I would have liked (or thought I deserved) but I felt wonderfully well at the end of it and, for those who needed to get their eating and exercise on track, it was very educative (in the jolliest sense of that word). For instance, one guest was a highly intelligent, high-earning girl who was really seriously overweight. (She didn't think she had a weight 'ishoo' until she started losing it, which was when she realised how wonderful that made her feel.) However, she had no idea that avocados, whilst brilliantly nutritious, were laden with calories and should be eaten in small portions.

Everybody left at the end of the week with clearer skins, brighter eyes, and a great determination to take more exercise. I couldn't recommend it more highly.

In:spa takes its nutritionists, personal trainers, yoga teachers *et al.* to a series of divine locations, whether Ibiza, mainland Spain or Marrakesh. Ring them on 0845 458 0723 for details or visit www.inspa.co.uk.

The fundamentals behind detoxing are simple: to rid the body of the overload of toxins (alcohol, caffeine and tannin, to name but a few) with which most of us assault it daily. It can easily – if you've got the will-power – be done at home. Everybody who tries it feel energised and cleansed afterwards. It usually involves a twenty-four-hour fast – nothing but water – followed by some two weeks or so of nothing but fruit juices, herbal teas and fruit and vegetables. Clearer eyes, cleaner livers and much increased energy are the usual benefits.

So You Want to Be Fitter?

> Running is the best and, I think, the only cure for depression. Linda Ronstadt, American rock singer

Taking exercise is the key to a healthy life and – more of an incentive perhaps to the vain amongst us – it's also key to keeping in reasonable shape. You don't want to become so overweight that you put your health at risk and you can't do the things you enjoy. So join a gym, get a personal trainer, take up tennis, ballroom dancing, cycling, swiming or yoga – anything so long as it gets you moving. The trick is to find something you like as otherwise you won't stick with it. We all know by now – don't we? – that exercise releases chemicals called endorphins, which reduce feelings of anxiety and depression. It also makes one feel more alert and better able to cope with stress. You don't need to go overboard, although it can become awfully addictive: when some years ago my husband and I found ourselves running around the local pond late at night after the opera, I realised things had got out of hand. You should really aim for a minimum of thirty minutes a day doing something that makes you breathe slightly harder and feel slightly warmer than usual.

I happen to love both tennis and skiing. I play tennis with my husband and friends – not as often as I'd like but enough to keep me in reasonable nick. Skiing is trickier. My erstwhile skiing companions are all beginning to get 'knees' or other ailments, and anyway it was never possible to do it for more than a couple of weeks a year.

I haven't found a gym near enough to me that I really like so my solution – I know, I know, it's spoiling – is a personal trainer. Twice a week I have the wonderful Niki Day and, although it seems like an indulgence (when I tell my friends 'she takes me walkies, like a dog', they fall about laughing), it does get me out. She gets my heart-rate up, and makes me jog and stretch, and since I've paid for it I make a point of never missing a session.

There are personal trainers in every corner of the country and if it's the only thing that makes you exercise it's worth every penny. If you can discipline yourself to exercise on your own, well done – keep it up, and think of all the money you save.

So You Want to Be Thinner?

If you can't lose weight on your own (as I say, it is – relatively – simple: eat fewer fats, carbs and sugar, and take more exercise), let me recommend Professor Clark, an Edinburgh man who came to be interested in nutrition via his speciality in diabetes. He discovered that by controlling patients' diets, he could lower their insulin levels as a result of which their weight usually fell too. He's not primarily in business to help people lose weight – he's there to help them be healthy, and the process of eating healthily usually results in their losing weight. His regime normally reduces the so-called 'bad' fats in the blood as well.

Professor Clark starts off by ordering a blood test to see just where everything is at – thyroid, cholesterol, insulin and all the other vital factors. 'Everybody's biochemical profile is different. I've had very slim women come to me who have terrible biochemical profiles because they're in effect starving themselves of nourishment.'

The principal weapon in the healthy diet is lowering insulin levels. Counting calories, he says, isn't what matters. It is much, much more important to reduce the intake of refined carbohydrates. They stimulate the production of insulin and it's insulin that converts those carbohydrates into fat. Those who are overweight often become locked in a vicious circle in which the refined carbohydrates that they eat mean that they manufacture more insulin, which in turn increases the desire for more carbohydrates.

I was given a diet sheet that was simple to say the least. I had to cut out all refined carbohydrates (cakes, biscuits, bread, pasta, rice); eat plenty of lean protein and lots of vegetables ('This is not a low carbohydrate diet,' he points out, 'it's high in carbohydrates but the unrefined ones that are mostly found in vegetables'); cut out saturated fats; go easy on the alcohol (a glass or two a day of red wine); and that's it. It is, of course, our old friend the low GI diet, fine-tuned to meet my individual needs after Dr Clark has studied the blood test results.

I can tell you that it works and it isn't onerous. When I followed it conscientiously, I went down from ten stone three pounds to nine stone. My insulin levels fell by 49 per cent, my triglycerides by 18 per cent and my LDL (low-density lipoproteins) by 10 per cent, whilst the HDL (high-density lipoproteins – the so-called good fats) were up by 10 per cent. I found it enormously helpful knowing that somebody would be checking my weight every fortnight. As the hand reached for the odd chocolate, it would be stayed by the knowledge that the evidence would be all too easily spotted by Professor Clark.

If you find it difficult to control your weight, Professor Clark could well be the answer. He's in London for a few days every week. His practice is at 14 Devonshire Place, London W1G 6HX. Telephone 020 7935 0640 for an appointment. He charges £190 for the initial consultation and £140 for each return visit.

> If you have formed the habit of checking on every new diet that comes along, you will find that, mercifully, they all blur together, leaving you with only one definite piece of information: french-fried potatoes are out. Jean Kerr, American writer

Massage

If you thought massage was a delicious optional extra, think again. Massage is seriously good for your health – and the older you get, the more you need it. According to Oz Garcia, who runs the brilliant Longevity Lounge in New York (a practice entirely given over to important things like nutrition and exercise to help people keep healthy and so go on feeling well and looking good for as long as possible), once you hit your fifties you should, if possible, have two massages a month. He says it keeps the muscles flexible, the toxins at bay, helps along a sluggish lymphatic system and prevents the build-up of knots of tension in necks and backs. In London, Dr Ali, who treats many of our most famous citizens, thinks that massaging the neck and shoulder area helps the functions of the pituitary gland (the headquarters of hormone control) by improving blood flow to the brain and he, too, thinks that twice a month is about right.

There are good masseurs in many places and it may take time to find one near where you live. I like Pure Massage (3–5 Vanston Place, London SW6 1AY; 020 7381 8100; www.puremassage.uk.com), which is in an unfashionable part of Fulham but it is sweet and clean, and has lovely spacious and calming treatment rooms. Although it has no grand pretensions, it has a serious purpose. Its founders, Beata Aleksandrowicz and Jean-Marc Delacourt, decided to concentrate solely on massage. To simplify the matter, they offer a small range of clear-cut options, all of which aim to be beneficial to health and well-being; they are not merely pampering, though they are that too. Beata offers seven different sorts of massage, most of which are a flexible combination of Thai massage, Swedish massage and Indian head massage, using all the acupressure points, and which she has adapted to suit almost all clients. She uses massage to help with back problems; with migraines (often, says Beata, caused by strain and tension in the back); to relieve stress and tension, particularly in the neck and back; to help with lymphatic drainage, which keeps the immune system in good order; and to keep the joints and muscles flexible.

Like my New York friend, Oz Garcia, she believes that a one-off massage is fine, and better than nothing, but for optimum results you should go regularly and then see the difference it makes. 'Each time you come back, the practitioner can go deeper into the muscle tissue and you can release more toxins.'

If you can't get to Pure Massage there are organisations everywhere, as well as independent masseuses (we use the wonderful Sibyl Darrington, 07801 018 967 and at www.holisticbodywork.co.uk) who will come to your house. Perfectly at Home (020 7610 8000 and at www.perfectly athome.com) mans the telephones until 10 p.m. and will send its trained masseurs to anywhere in London. Dstress Direct (020 7727 0490 and at www.dstressdirect.com) will also will send masseurs to addresses in the London area.

Scent

Looking good is also about another very important intangible: scent. It is so fundamental to how I feel about myself that I can't imagine life without it.

I'm not ashamed to say that I'm a scent snob. I love the classic, complex, subtle scents of the great French houses – Caron, Guerlain, Nina Ricci, Dior, Creed, Chanel. I hate the cheap chemical smells, the harsh and strident concoctions that abound today. And, since I might as well make my prejudices clear, I personally can't be doing with most florals (though I make an exception for Guerlain's L'Heure Bleue) but I recognise that some of them are finely made and are some people's lifelong passion. The *raison d'être* of a fine scent is to reawaken a transitory, half-remembered world where memory and nostalgia, misty hopes and dreams all intermingle. The world it nudges into being should be rich and complex, haunting and insubstantial, but redolent with possibility, sensuality and desire. I like scents to remind me of satins and furs and boxes at the opera, and dancing the night away, and falling in love, and all the things I cherish in life. In my experience, it's only the great classic scents that can do this.

Roja Dove, Professeur des Parfums and *éminence grise* of the perfume industry in the UK, thinks scent 'should be all about hedonism, indulgence, utter luxuriousness', which is why his Haute Parfumerie on the fifth floor at Harrods is one of the world's best places to learn about scent. There you will find not only the world's finest scents but some that are stocked by nobody else. 'I've allowed my whimsies full rein in my Haute Parfumerie,' says Roja, 'and haven't allowed commercial considerations to influence me one jot.'

If you have one great signature scent that you love, the best way to wear it is to buy both the eau de toilette (80 per cent of what you apply at 8 a.m. will have dissipated by noon) and the parfum (50 per cent will stay on the skin for twenty-four hours). Combine four or five pumps of the eau de toilette with a touch of perfume on the wrist, inside the dip of the collarbone, behind the knee and behind the neck.

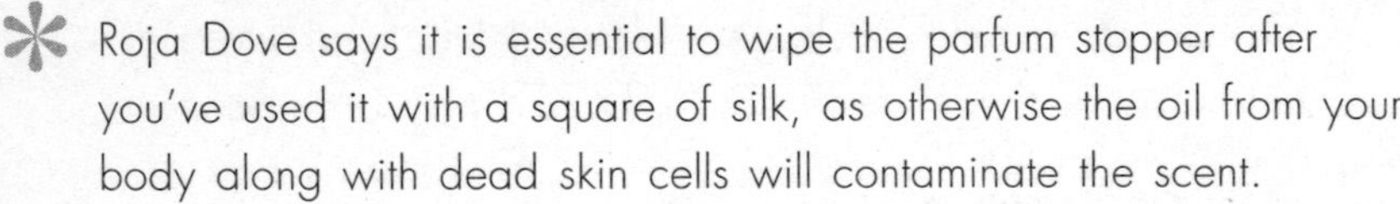

Roja Dove says it is essential to wipe the parfum stopper after you've used it with a square of silk, as otherwise the oil from your body along with dead skin cells will contaminate the scent.

Finally, there's the matter of the bespoke scent – one made specially for you, which I have never tried. This can be inordinately expensive (usually from £3,000, whilst if you want the master himself, Roja Dove, it'll cost you about £20,000) and my hunch is that it isn't worth it. There really are gorgeous scents around, some of them not worn by all and sundry, and to pay all that money and risk finding you don't like the result – it scarcely bears thinking about. I think the risk is too high.

Finally there is the matter of price. Really great scents aren't cheap. If you can't afford good ones it is better to wear nothing and do as that master hotelier, Gordon Campbell Gray does, simply smell divinely of nothing but fresh soap.

Not many women seem to know that the sun and scent combine to cause nasty pigmentation. Keep scent for when you're indoors.

Roja Dove's Guide to Choosing Scent

Perfumes can be divided into three main categories:

FLORALS: this is the largest and most varied category, ranging from simple florals (Diorissimo by Dior or Fracas by Robert Piguet) to big mixed bouquets (L'Heure Bleue by Guerlain or L'Air du Temps by Nina Ricci). The aldehydic florals (Lanvin's Arpège or Chanel's No. 5) shimmer and sparkle whilst others (Vent Vert by Balmain or Truly by Stephen Burlingham) are crisp and fresh. All will have a sweetness that people either love or can't stand.

Florals are most liked by those of a happy, uncomplicated disposition, for whom every day is a sunny day.

CHYPRES: these are based around oak moss aided by cedar wood, vetiver and patchouli, counterpointed by hesperidic (citrus) notes. Chypres have a dryness about them and are the most understated, pared-down formulas, which gives them their elegance and sophistication. These are the perfumery equivalent of a plain black evening gown from Valentino or a plain navy dress by Jean Muir. In other words, they take confidence to wear and are not for the faint-hearted. Amongst the great chypres are Mitsouko by Guerlain, Tabac Blond by Caron, Farouche by Nina Ricci, Cabochard by Grès, La Perla by La Perla, Miss Dior by Dior and Femme by Rochas.
Chypres are mostly chosen by strong-minded women who tend to see life in black or white terms, who know their own minds. If you're a minimalist at heart, then chypres are for you.

ORIENTALS: these are based around vanilla (a psychogenic aphrodisiac that not only enhances pleasure for the wearer but has a very specific effect on others), sandalwood, gum resins from trees and tonquin musk (from the tonka bean). They're rather hedonistic and self-indulgent – when they're good, they're wonderful, but when they're bad, they can be cloying and pervasive, verging on the vulgar. The great orientals are Shalimar by Guerlain, Opium by Yves St Laurent,

MY FAVOURITE SCENTS

Guerlain's Shalimar used to be my all-time favourite, but now they seem to have changed the composition (partly, as I understand it, because of EU rules and partly because of the difficulty and expense of getting some of the rare ingredients) and now I find it too heavy and unsubtle. I still love Guerlain's Jicky, Vol de Nuit, L'Heure Bleue and Mitsouko.

- Quadrille by Balenciaga (a great classic now revived).
- Narcisse Noir (a favourite of the Ballets Russes), and Tabac Blond, a wonderfully sensuous chypre, both by Caron.
- Ormonde by Ormonde Jayne.
- Ambre Soie (rich, dark and warm, with hints of cinnamon, cloves and Chinese ginger), and Bois d'Encens, both by Armani Privé, and only to be found in the best Giorgio Armani boutiques and at Harrods.
- Bel Ami by Hermès.
- Ambre Sultan by Serge Lutens.
- Feminité du Bois by Shiseido.
- Shocking by Schiaparelli, because it's the first scent my father ever gave me. It brings back happy days in Aldeburgh and walking along the estuary in the long summer evenings.
- Yerbamate and Spezie by Lorenzo Villoresi.

In summer or on holiday I often wear something lighter. Diptyque's Philosykos smells divinely, subtly of fig. I also love Jo Malone's Ginger and Nutmeg.

Must de Cartier, French Can Can by Caron, Bal à Versailles by Jean Desprez, Vol de Nuit by Guerlain and Nuit de Noël by Caron.

They are worn by women who are larger than life and generally like to be noticed. These are women who know how to use their femininity to their own advantage and know exactly which shade of lipstick, height of heel and length of hem suits them best.

So now you're ready to start the search.

1. Allow yourself time. It could be the start of a lifelong love affair.

2. Choose your store carefully. Those that have separate counters for every perfume house are not the best environments for this particular exercise. Go to a specialist shop (see p. 173) where there is somebody who cares passionately about scent.

3. Go wearing no scent but armed with a pen and pad to note names.

4. Smell some florals, chypres and orientals, and by a process of elimination, decide which group pleases you most. Most testers are marked on the back with the words 'fleuri' or 'florale' (indicating florals), 'chypres' and either 'orientale' or 'amber'.

5. Think of the scent strips as hangers for clothes. Only when you put on the clothes (scent) will you really know

whether it suits you but in the meantime you can judge quite a lot whilst it is still on the hanger (scent strip). Take about five or six strips to test the different scents. Don't smell them right away. Walk away and then smell them two at a time, one and then the other. Ask yourself which of the two you prefer and put aside the one you like least. Then compare your preferred strip with another and again discard the one you like least. You will soon come to the one or two you like best. Keeping these, go and sit somewhere quiet to compare and contrast. When you decide which one you like best, spray it on your wrists (do *not* rub it in), a little bit on the collarbone and a mist around your hair. Then leave the store and go home. 'Just like a lover, you'll only know whether the love affair will last if you spend the night together, so take some home. Otherwise you could end up with a *mésalliance*.' If you still love the scent the next day, go and buy some. Lastly, you shouldn't 'quite like it' either – you should fall madly, passionately in love.

Some Special Shops for Scent

London

ROJA DOVE'S HAUTE PARFUMERIE on the fifth floor at Harrods, 87–135 Brompton Road, London SW1X 7XL (020 7897 8797), or one of the three Roja Dove perfumeries in House of Fraser stores.

FORTNUM & MASON, Piccadilly, London W1A 1ER (020 7734 8040). A really good perfume department with some scents that you won't find anywhere else.

L'ARTISAN PARFUMEUR, 17 Cale Street, London SW3 3QR (020 7352 4196), is a delightful shop with lots of small niche perfumes.

LES SENTEURS, 71 Elizabeth Street, London SW1W 9PJ (020 7730 2322). James Craven has a passion for scent and is seriously knowledgable. The shop also has a brilliant catalogue with great descriptions of the perfumes it carries and will send out up to six little sample phials at £2.50 a phial.

ORMONDE JAYNE, The Royal Arcade, 28 Old Bond Street, London W15 45L (0207 499 1100). Linda Pilkington is a relatively new perfumer on the block but her products are lovely. Fans are mad for her grapefruit candles and I love her Ormonde fragrance. Her bath oils are gorgeous, too.

JO MALONE used to have just one shop in Walton Street in London. Now I've lost count of them all but I still love her grapefruit candle and her Ginger and Nutmeg fragrance. Check her out on www.jomalone.co.uk.

OUTSIDE LONDON, there's Ogle, 1 High Street, Pershore, Worcestershire WR10 1AB (01386 552 890). Also, Scent of Boston, 12 Dolphin Lane, Boston, Lincolnshire PE21 6EU (01205 351 155).

Paris

There are some gorgeous places to visit in Paris.

CHANEL is best known for Chanel No. 5 (with Marilyn Monroe declaring it was all she wore to bed, how could it fail?) but not everybody knows that if you go to its boutiques (and there isn't a better one than Boutique Chanel, 31 rue Cambon, Paris 75001, where Coco herself held court), you can buy some very special scents that aren't sold anywhere else. Cuir de Russie is my favourite but I also like Bois de Iles and No. 22, whilst Gardenia is for those who are into florals. Six more special, boutique-only scents have just been launched, known as Les Exclusifs, and all by Jacques Polge, Chanel's 'nose'. Worth investigating.

SERGE LUTENS was for years the creative director of Shiseido and he helped develop many of its scents, in particular the gorgeous Feminite du Bois. Now he has his own line, all of which are divine, though as perfume is such a personal thing, you'll love some more than others. Me, I love most of them but particularly Borneo 1834 and Ambre Sultan. Go to his jewel of a shop, Les Salons du Palais Royal Shiseido, Jardins du Palais Royal, 142 Galérie de Valois, Paris 75001, and leave yourself time to try them all.

FRÉDÉRIC MALLE (Editions de Parfums Frédéric Malle, 37 rue de Grenelle, Paris 75007; +33 1 4927 0909), whose grandfather founded Parfums Christian Dior, has some wonderful perfumes, including Le Parfum de Thérèse. It was made by the great 'nose' Edmond Roudnitska for his wife during the 1960s and he gave Frédéric Malle the right to make it after his death. It's lush and languid, and has a cult following.

LA MAISON DE GUERLAIN, 68 avenue des Champs Elysées, Paris 75008, is a gorgeous boutique that has all the glamour one expects of the grandest of all parfumiers. Here you can not only try all the greats but there's a series of boutique-only experiences and scents that 'vaut le détour'.

ANNICK GOUTAL, 14 rue de Castiglione, Paris 75001.

Florence

LORENZO VILLORESI, Via de' Bardi 14, Florence 50125, is for my money one of the greatest living perfumers, but you must make an appointment to visit – telephone +39 5 5234 1187 or email info@lorenzovilloresi.it. Villoresi is from an old Florentine family and in his laboratory at the top of a medieval palazzetto overlooking the Arno he mixes up wonderfully complex and exotic perfumes. These capture the smell of cut grass, the Mediterranean (sage, rosemary, myrtle, thyme), tobacco, and wild poppy, amongst many others. There are divine room candles and pot-pourris too. Some are available in the UK (at Fortnum & Mason), but if you're in Florence you'd be foolish not to visit his little atelier. He will also make you a bespoke scent in about two hours for £1,000, which is infinitely cheaper than anybody else.

FARMACIA DI SANTA MARIA NOVELLA, 16 via della Scala, is one of the world's oldest pharmacies or herbalists, dating from 1612, with divine soaps – the pomegranate especially – lotions, colognes and powders. It's an experience just to see the shop even if you buy nothing.

love, marriage and happiness

Love

Speak to me of love; I thirst for it.

Alexander Pushkin to Anna Petrovna Kern, 22 September 1825

Most of us need love in our lives in order to feel alive, let alone happy. We need to love as well as to be loved, and if we can achieve both we are immeasurably blessed. For most of us it is the one true essential, the basis of our lives. But there are so many different kinds of love and different ways of loving. There's nothing like the adrenalin rush of 'being in love', which is, of course, a kind of madness, an intoxication that can turn out to be a fatal attraction that causes days, months, even years of grief . . . or it can be the stepping stone to a more grounded, enduring sort of love that leads to a lifelong marriage. But love was ever a mystery. It works in deep, unknown ways and there are no certain answers to any of the big questions: 'Why does he not love me any more?' 'Why has he/she left me?' Love changes – indeed, it must change if it is to endure – and it can take many forms.

How can we tell real, enduring love from its more intoxicating cousin, infatuation? That's the big question. If we knew *that*, the world wouldn't be littered with broken hearts and failed relationships, and half the world's literature would never have been written. But just as there are no pat answers, there are no formulaic rules. And there is comfort to be found in the fact that pain and heartbreak are the other side of caring, and the more you care, the more it hurts. This applies to any form of love. Every mother will tell you that from the moment her child is born, whole new acres of possible suffering – as well as joy, of course – are opened up.

But for those for whom long-lasting love has never happened, who have been widowed or divorced, who for one reason or another find themselves alone, there are all sorts of other ways of loving. There are children and godchildren to love, there are mothers and fathers, brothers and sisters, friends and the big wide world to channel all that love into.

All I know is that love comes out of the blue, sometimes when you least expect it, and that the key is not necessarily to go looking for it but to keep your mind and heart wide open to the larger horizon. Those who keep looking outwards, who can find it in themselves to reach out to what life brings them, who feel that sense of possibility in the air, are those to whom things happen.

✻ READING

Let me recommed *Everything I've Ever Learned about Love* by my old friend and colleague Lesley Garner, published by Hay House, and Erich Fromm's *The Art of Loving.*

Marriage

God grant me the serenity to accept the things I cannot change, the courage to change the things that I can, and the wisdom to know the difference. Reinhold Niebuhr, 'The Serenity Prayer'

We have only to look around us to see that there is no blueprint for marriage. Every marriage is different. We see (a few) so-called traditional wives who prefer to defer to their husbands, who are happy for them to do most of the earning and most of the decision-making, and for the two people in that particular marriage it seems to work. And then we know of other people who would find it so stifling and claustrophobic that one or other would have run away screaming into the night after just a few months.

Other couples evolve completely different sort of partnerships. Sometimes the woman is an equal partner financially and plays a pro-active role in all the major decisions involving the family. In others, she may sometimes be the sole earner and the couple have mutually decided that it suits their circumstances best for the husband to play what used conventionally to be the female role – the child-carer, the domestic rock and the financially dependent partner. There are as many psychological and practical arrangements as there are couples.

All we know is that if there is a formula, nobody's found it yet.

Good marriages are all about 'fit', about the degree to which each partner's hopes, expectations, talents and dreams can be allowed to grow and flourish – and, of course, they are also about love. At first sight the institution doesn't seem to be in the most robust health. Most of us have only to think about our close and immediate circles of family and friends to see divorce on a scale that would have been thought socially unacceptable for our parents' generation. I myself grew up with divorced parents in the South Africa of the 1940s and 1950s, and it always made me feel a child apart, for I was for many years the only child I knew whose living parents were no longer married. Today, however, divorce is commonplace.

The statistics bear this out. Two out of five marriages at the moment are doomed to end in divorce – though to look on the bright side that means that three out of five survive. Three out of the four children of our own dear Queen have been divorced. Add to this the number of people who aren't bothering to get married at all, and the numbers of children born to single women or women who are in relationships with 'partners', and it appears that the institution of marriage is in deep trouble.

In my close circle, one of my dearest friends tells me that her children – attractive, clever, in their thirties with great careers – aren't even considering marriage for, as they remind her, 'You and Daddy have seven marriages between you [which she has to admit is true] and we don't know many people who have stayed married, so we can't quite see the point.'

One of the things that has changed is that in the practical

sense women don't need a man in the way they used to. The old joke that 'Marriage was the price men paid for sex whilst sex was the price women paid for marriage' seems so archaic now as to belong to another world. Women can earn their own livings, have a perfectly jolly social life, enjoy the pleasures of sex and even have children without tying the knot. IVF, sperm banks, financial independence and multiple fluid relationships – all things unthinkable merely forty years ago – have played their part in changing the way we relate to our friends, our families and our children.

I recently read of a young woman who, feeling that her biological clock was beginning to tick, decided that whilst she was perfectly resigned to not having a man in her life, she could not reconcile herself to life without a child. In years gone by this would have been an insoluble dilemma. No more. She found no fewer than three different men who were only too delighted to meet her need for an arm's-length, sanitised form of parenthood: a young gay man, a much older married childless man and a single straight man of her own age. Problem – at one level – solved.

It seems so flexible, so modern, but I have my doubts as to how deeply these new arrangements meet the psychological and practical needs of either men or women, let alone the children. For this loosening of old attitudes has had a dramatic effect on the plight of children. In the UK some 42.9 per cent of children are currently born out of wedlock and whilst the phrase itself may seem harsh and out of date, the reality is that most children flourish best in what we have learned to call the family. It is obvious that loving care – and this clearly *can* be provided by loving parents who are not married – is what children need to grow into healthy, well-adjusted human beings who have self-respect and respect for others. When you read the stories behind the Asbo set that we have created today, nearly every one is a poignant human tragedy, of children who have not been loved and nurtured, who live with mothers who may have several children by various vanished fathers, who seem not to know how to be proper wives or mothers. The jails are full of people who come from dysfunctional families who were not mostly, or even usually, born bad but who were not given that essential start in life, that age-old security that only love and care, which seems best provided by a mother and a father who are married to each other, can provide. This loosening of ties and lack of social boundaries has led to too many men and women having children for which they don't provide proper, stable homes.

It would be wrong to ignore the upsides – women no longer need allow themselves to be bullied and marginalised; their talents need no longer be neglected; they have paths to professional fulfilment and economic freedom; there is a chance for greater honesty in relationships – but we also see that more and more women at least are beginning to sense that professional success and economic freedom often come at a great price. We see women who are made lonely by their freedom, their lack of ties, their financial independence. I remember well being at a professional meeting where there were some highly successful women round the table. Somebody mentioned that one of our previous colleagues had got married and had retired to be a mother of three in the country. One of the most successful of all the women said with a voice full of envy, 'Oh, wow . . .' And it rapidly became clear that for the farmhouse, the kids, the dogs in the back of the car, the husband, the busy round of a family life, she'd give it all up tomorrow. Underneath she felt a deep longing that was something she couldn't help, an old biological recognition of the need to bond, of one man to commit to one woman, and to create a safe haven for each other and their children. A longing, too, to be, as my friend Sandy Boler, the ex-editor of *Brides* magazine, put it, 'to be safely gathered in' – something that marriage in its best and most reassuring form can do.

Which is possibly why I detect in the air, in the *Zeitgeist*, something of a seismic backlash. Women – and marriage has always been more in a woman's interest than a man's – have come to see that too much insistence on egalitarianism hasn't brought them the dreamed-of utopia. Insisting that a man who works long hours also does his share of the cooking and the nappy-changing whilst his wife whirls around with her own career may succeed in bringing about help with the chores but it doesn't often lead to that woman being deeply loved. An insistence on strict division of labour seems to me to smack of minding more about 'one's rights' than any notion of real love. It would, surely, often be better to do rather more than one's share of the housework and have a happy home and a husband who loves one.

One now sees high-earning alpha women who seem to be indulging in what one commentator called 'competitive breeding' – in other words, creating and building very large families (think of those two city titans, Nicola Horlick and Helena Morrissey, and they are not alone) – as if to compensate for the masculine world in which they spend their days. One senses a kind of yearning for the sort of domestic dreams and certainties that were the norm some forty or fifty years ago but which these days have got lost in dreams of breaking through glass ceilings and forging free and independent lives.

The *New York Times* columnist Maureen Dowd put it beautifully when she wrote: 'Five years ago, you would often hear high-powered women fantasise that they would love a Wife, somebody to do the shopping, cooking, carpooling, so they could focus on work. Now the fantasy is more retro: They just want to be that Wife.'

Those of us who are married know that marriage isn't always easy – though, heaven knows, it's always seemed to me so much nicer than the alternative. Since many of us are lucky enough to live much longer than primitive man was privileged to do, we know that long-lasting marriages – some of forty, fifty and even sixty years – have strains and stresses of their own, but it is hard to think of a better institution for meeting our deepest human needs. Almost no marriage is perfect (and, interestingly, if it is, the children often suffer quite badly – remember the writer Alice

Thomas Ellis's quip that 'Men love women, women love children and children love their hamsters'), but nobody has yet come up with a better way to meet our most profound longings. De facto, marriage – a serious commitment between a man and a woman, whether blessed by a priest or not – reaches far back into antiquity. It evolved because it was what men, women and their children required if society was to be whole and sane. A really good marriage should, most psychologists think, meet three crucial needs: the longing for real emotional intimacy; the need for a sense of self-worth; and a greater possibility of both partners fulfilling their goals in life.

But marriage is an ever-evolving institution. Modern ones have had to adapt and change. Many women now earn more than their spouses. The lucky, well-adjusted spouses are happy and grateful for it, but the less secure seem to require even more nurturing, so that the working wife is locked into a syndrome where the harder she works, and the more money she brings in, the more she has to show on the home front that she isn't neglecting her domestic skills and that he isn't a 'house husband'. Where both spouses are highly successful and there are children, something has to give if the marriage *and* the children are to be nurtured – and if it isn't the woman who is prepared to give up some of her high-flying years, then I see trouble ahead. It may not be fair, but what is the alternative?

Many marriages these days are second and third marriages, requiring a greater generosity of spirit, a greater willingness to forgive, to put away past bitternesses and an extra effort to make these multiple, complex relationships work. Sometimes I'm astounded at the warmth and nobility with which some new relationships can be made to work if those involved bring a real desire to create something good out of what could be destructive chaos. I see step-children who love their step-parents and their step-siblings; I see rejected wives moving on from their natural feelings of hurt and pain in order to ease the path for children and step-children. Of course one sees the reverse as well – those who can never escape their feelings of injury and rejection, whose bitterness lives on, creating yet more difficulties for those around them. But they are the ones for whom there is usually no moving on, no different other life, which those who can put away their past suffering can sometimes find.

'Food and plenty of sex,' says one high-flying wife, are the key to keeping a husband happy. If you keep both of those flowing, you can get away with a bit of neglect on other fronts. Whatever it takes, it seems to me that the rewards of having a husband or partner who loves one, who cares for his home and children, are worth cherishing. If swinging from the chandelier is what it takes, then do it – that's my view.

A Few Things I've Learned Along the Way

- Don't nag. It's not worth it. It's simpler and more conducive to a happy household to do whatever it is oneself.

- Concentrate on the things you love about him, not the things that drive you mad.
- Manners matter: politeness, kindness, tolerance, generosity of spirit.
- Try to think of things that please your other half: meals, books, adventures, small treats. All these are ways of showing love.
- Remember he has needs too.
- Don't harbour regrets or dwell on past hurts.
- Do your best to love his family – although some of them may be more lovable than others – and always welcome them to the house.
- You don't own the person you married. They are still entitled to some freedoms, to their own views and their own space. The best marriages provide a secure framework in which individuals can grow and flourish, not wither and diminish.
- It's worth making time to be together, so plan time together and little pleasures. It's particularly hard when there are small children, but grandparents or babysitters can be roped in. One couple who found that they were always so busy that they never had time to talk in a connected way made a date once a week to have lunch out – not a grand lunch, just a simple pub lunch – and they found that they began to rediscover each other.

- Find things that you like to do together. Try to take an interest in his hobbies, friends and sports and in return he should try to take an interest in yours.
- Never run him down in public.

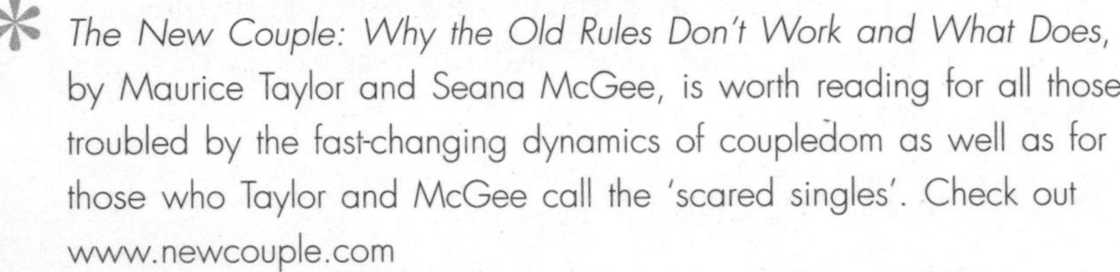

The New Couple: Why the Old Rules Don't Work and What Does, by Maurice Taylor and Seana McGee, is worth reading for all those troubled by the fast-changing dynamics of coupledom as well as for those who Taylor and McGee call the 'scared singles'. Check out www.newcouple.com

Money

We all know that money doesn't buy happiness – there are plenty of miserable millionaires and billionaires around to prove the point (though, as some wag pointed out, it's a whole lot nicer to be miserable in comfort than in penury). But some money is, in my view, essential for self-respect. I've earned my own money since I was twenty and, though I have the most generous of husbands, I would never, ever like to have to ask for every penny I needed. Virginia Woolf, in a famous essay titled *A Room of One's Own*, came to the conclusion that if a woman was to write fiction (for which read 'do anything interesting or important at all'), a woman needed her own income and a room of her own. I would say that for all women, no matter what their status, it's important to contrive to have some – not necessarily a great deal – but some money of their own and to find something of their own space to be their own person. Who wants to be the other half of a 'passenger', of somebody without a proper life or interests of their own?

A friend of mine who doesn't earn her own money (her husband earns plenty) jokes that she has compiled a 'running away' fund out of the housekeeping. She has no intention of running away – she loves her husband dearly – but she does like to know that she can. I understand completely. The idea here is that true relationships, the best relationships, are founded on a certain degree of independence, between two people who are properly whole in their own right. A friend who married a very rich – and very nice and wise – man was given £1 million on her wedding day by her new husband. He wanted to know, for his own happiness and satisfaction, that she was staying with him because she wanted to – not because she had to.

To be totally dependent on a man for money limits one's freedom, no matter how kindly and generous the man. The same is true for men – a certain degree of economic security is essential to be really free. It's why men, instead of having 'running away' funds, have what they like to call 'fuck you' money. It enables them to be courageous in difficult situations, to walk away when they need to. So I feel that women, for their own sense of self-worth, should always find a way of having or earning money of their own. Even if it's a small part-time job, it at least means that if you're set on buying something that he doesn't like, you can spend your own money on it and, more importantly, when you buy him a present you're paying for it. That apart, my view on work is that work (which doesn't necessarily have to be financially hugely rewarding) sustains one through many difficult times in life – it gives shape and meaning to one's life, expands one's knowledge and interests and sees one through periods of loneliness, bereavement and heartache.

Getting Help

Many marriages – and relationships – run into difficulties. Some of them can be repaired and here professional counselling can be an enormous help, not just to the man and wife but to any children involved as well. The organisation Relate offers face-to-face sessions with a counsellor or even, if you can't travel, counselling by telephone. There's also a couples workshop. You are asked to pay a small charge. Check into their website at www.relate.org.co.uk and you'll find a list of the standard problems that crop up in many marriages: 'I've had an affair, how do I tell my partner?' or 'My partner and I just don't seem to talk any more and it feels as if we've drifted apart', or 'I can't seem to stop arguing with my partner, what can we do?' It helps to know that, whatever it is that is troubling you, the Relate counsellors will almost certainly have seen something like it before. You are not alone.

Others find help in psychotherapy, but here it is vital to make sure of the calibre of the therapist – the good ones are marvellous, the bad ones dangerous. Try to get recommendations from friends who might know of good ones through personal experience. Otherwise contact the British Association for Counselling and Psychotherapy (0870 443 5252 or visit www.bacp.co.uk).

Divorce

Divorce is right up there as one of the most stressful events life can bring, being only less painful than the death of a child or somebody very close to you. Even the most amicable of divorces spreads ripples of pain well beyond the couple themselves – most of all to the children, if any, of the marriage. However, mothers, fathers, siblings and friends will also feel the fallout.

On the other hand, some abusive or destructive relationships, or ones that are plain worn out, where neither side can muster any affection, tenderness or respect for the other, are clearly better ended. Calling time is sometimes the only way to a better future. These days, there are two pluses: at least it can be done now without having to cast blame or exchange insults, and too, as people live longer and more healthily, many divorcees go on to make new and happy second, third and fourth relationships.

Besides dealing with the emotional pain, there are legal

and financial implications, as well as domestic arrangements, that have to be taken into account. Here the blessings of friendship really count. Talking to friends, feeling encircled by people who care, can ease the pain but nonetheless professional help is almost always needed.

Organisations such as Relate (www.relate.org.uk) and Divorceaid (www.divorceaid.co.uk) are great sources of help. Divorceaid offers counselling, as well as advice on everything from where to go for legal help (it believes in promoting what it calls collaborative law as a new and more dignified approach to divorce) to how to find support groups. And remember, the words on the Divorceaid website: 'Time is a healer. Spend some time with us. From distress to recovery you are not alone and it will get better.'

Widowhood

This is usually another deeply painful life event, particularly for couples so closely bound that they can't ever envisage another partner. But, to be truthful, I have known some widows and widowers find a completely new lease of life as the patterns of an old way of life are thrown off and a fresh life beckons.

How successfully people adapt and heal is often very dependent upon whether they still have work that is rewarding, whether they have nurtured friendships and have a warm close circle to call on, and how financially comfortable they are.

Since usually men die rather younger than women, it follows that there are rather more widows than widowers, which means that not all widows can hope to remarry. But full and rich lives can still be lived. Friendships, hobbies, travel, a warm and open heart that takes pleasure in small things, and an interest in other people, can all help to build a different sort of life.

Cruse is a non-religious organisation designed to help anybody who has been bereaved. This includes young people and parents of children who have died, but Cruse was originally set up with the aim of helping those who had recently lost their spouse. It offers support in lots of ways, including one-to-one counselling. Contact Cruse via the website (www.crusebereavementcare.org.uk) or telephone the helpline (0844 477 9400).

www.nawidows.org.uk is another organisation designed to provide support for those who are widowed or who have lost partners.

Friendship

Always anticipate your friends' needs, never wait until they have to ask. Maria Huxley (wife of Aldous Huxley)

Nurture your friendships – they matter more than you can possibly imagine. Of all the things I most regret, it is perhaps working too much and not giving enough time to my friends. When one sees the banana skins that lie await in life – the love affairs and marriages that go wrong, the illnesses that hit most of us at some time or another, and all the other more minor tragedies that make up life's great tapestry – it is friends and lovers who see one through. If you have them, you can cope with almost anything. And one also needs friends to share good fortune with – it's pretty pointless enjoying the good times alone. We all hope not to be a friend of the Gore Vidal sort, he who once proclaimed: 'For true happiness it is not enough to be successful oneself . . . one's friends must fail.'

Friendship, though, needs maintenance. It means giving time and thought to our friends and, for many of us, absorbed as we are by our jobs and our families, it is hard to find time to do as much as we would like. It is perhaps one of the consolations of the empty-nesting syndrome that as the children leave home, parents once again become more outgoing, able to renew old friendships and make new ones.

Once again they find they have the sort of time that they haven't usually had since their twenties.

How do you keep friendships alive when you're having trouble juggling work and family and there's scarcely a free minute in the day? It's difficult, but there are ways. If friends are much the same age and at the same stage in life – whether singles, what Bridget Jones called the 'smug marrieds', bogged down by their children, coping with teenagers, empty nesters – it makes it that much easier, for your interests are already aligned. Singles can go out clubbing (if that's their fancy), see plays or form book clubs together. Later, as marriage and families come along, you can do things as married couples and then get together as families for Sunday lunches and walks, football games, tennis, whatever.

But the real way to show your friendship is to be there when times get tough and to help celebrate when there's a success. We all remember the friend who lifted the phone and offered to help when one of you lost a job, who visited in hospital when you were ill, who sent flowers or a letter when some disaster hit or there was something to celebrate.

One friend who lost her husband horribly early to cancer has never forgotten the woman friend who rang every day to begin with, and later on every week, to find out how she was, to invite her round to supper or to the cinema.

Friends most particularly should be there when people they care about are ill. I learned when my brother was ill and dying of cancer that some friends found the whole thing embarrassing. They didn't know what to say, so they said nothing. It wasn't that they didn't care but they didn't care enough to get over their embarrassment. Real friendship, in my view, should have meant minding more about my brother, whose predicament and suffering was real, than their own discomfort.

Another friend was bitterly hurt when one of her closest friends seemed to abandon her when she got breast cancer. When she saw her at a reception, the friend waved an airy hand and said, 'Do ring me if you need anything.' That is *not* how you do it. You ring, you visit, you write, you try to anticipate what might help. You take a meal round to the house, offer music to listen to or books to read. You might also think of the partner of the person who is ill, who often is having a tough time, too, but real friendship involves anticipating the need and trying to fill it – not waiting to be asked.

Friendship, in the end, is simple, if time-consuming. It means doing for your friends what you hope they'd do for you.

On Being a Daughter

There are so many phases to being a daughter, ranging from those early years when one's mother is a golden goddess who can do no wrong (as my daughter once put it, 'Mother, until I was about twelve, I thought you were perfect!') to the final later years when the person who once cared for us as children and young adults now needs to be cared for themselves. It's one of the most painful of all adjustments to make but the great thing is that there is now a great deal of help at hand.

- You could start with your local GP, who will be able to point you in the direction of district nurses, social workers, home care organisers and a raft of other therapists, if they are deemed necessary.
- Your local library has a long list of agencies that can provide help, as well as useful pamphlets and leaflets.
- The Citizens' Advice Bureau is a good source of advice on benefits and bureaucracy, and can nearly always guide you to other sorts of help.
- Age Concern (their helpline is 0800 009 966 and at www.ageconcern.org.uk) and Help the Aged (020 7278 1114 and at www.helptheaged.org.uk) can both offer lots of advice.
- Remember, too, to get legal advice over tricky areas like incapacity benefit, income support and power of attorney. The latter must be sorted out whilst the elderly person is of sound mind – it is too late once they are no longer capable of making that decision.
- Universal Aunts (020 7738 8937 and at www.universalaunts.co.uk) can offer companions to read, guide, drive and escort elderly people.

- But remember, carers themselves may need help too. Don't be afraid to ask for it and don't wear yourself out – that doesn't help anybody. If you are a carer, you might like to know that there is a support group near you: contact The Princess Royal Trust for Carers (020 7480 7788 and at www.carers.org) and you will find a great deal of useful information on support services.

THINGS TO DO WITH THE ELDERLY

Take them to the cinema once a week or recreate the experience at home – play a DVD, buy popcorn, make it fun.

Get them books on tape to listen to or books in big type from the library. Contact Listening Books (020 7407 9417 and at www.listening-books.org.uk).

Find an adult education class they'd like.

Organise painting or photographic classes – or anything else that interests them.

Take them to a gallery or museum once a month.

Start a book club with like-minded friends.

On Being a Grandmother

Where have all the grannies gone? I mean the genuine, original, 22-carat articles who wore black shawls and cameo brooches, sat in rocking chairs and smelled of camphor? Keith Waterhouse

Being a grandmother is wonderful – particularly when it comes, as it usually does these days, slightly later in life than it did in times gone by, so that by the time it happens, one is good and ready (I'm not sure I'd have much liked being a 'granny' in my forties). It is a great joy to find a succession of babies, toddlers and slightly older children back in one's life after the years in between that were bereft of the sweet sounds and smells of tiny children. I'm not as good a grandmother as I'd always dreamed of being. I always thought I'd be the doting kind and though I do dote – all five of them, as far as I'm concerned, can do no wrong – I'm too busy to be doing much of the apple-pie baking or the babysitting. And I'm not alone – grannies all around us are trekking in the Himalayas, writing books or running companies, and so our children's generation is having to get used to the fact that the apple-cheeked, ever available, domestic granny is a long-gone stereotype. But that can have its upsides. All my grandsons have been promised that they will be taken to Africa when they turn ten and since I'm just back from the first such expedition (to Botswana: such fun for me and, I hope, for him), I'm glowing at the moment with the memory of it all.

As I didn't have any proper grannies myself (my father's mother had fifteen children and I don't even know how many grandchildren, so I was simply one amongst a vast, undifferentiated horde; whilst my mother's mother was too hostile to my father to take much to his daughter), I aim to be the kind of granny that I wish I'd had.

I consider myself unbelievably lucky in both my son-in-law and daughter-in-law, who seem to welcome us whenever we are around and who never keep their children from us but want us to love and cherish them, as we do. Other grandparents, I know, are not so lucky and seeing their grandchildren sometimes seems fraught with difficulties. The straight facts of the matter are that once one's children are married and have left the nest, there is a power shift: usually grandparents need their children and grandchildren rather more than the children need the grandparents. Which is why it seems not only wise but essential to try to make sure that there are no rifts or rows and also that one has a proper role to play and never becomes a mere encumbrance or a duty.

HOW TO BE A GOOD GRANDMOTHER

Never forget that they're not your children. You've had your turn – now it's theirs.

Never criticise anybody – son, daughter, the in-laws, children. As far as you're concerned they're all perfect.

Offer advice only if it's asked for.

Don't pop round all the time without being asked.

Try to make visits fun, and think of interesting things to do with the grandchildren.

Remember all birthdays and exam times, and always offer congratulations when they're due.

Always respect the rules of your grandchildren's parents.

If you see that they are in difficulties of any kind, don't criticise – offer help.

Never show favouritism. You may have favourites (grandparents are only human), but keep them to yourself and let nobody guess.

Never undermine the parents.

Never be competitive with the other grandparents – it's not grown-up and it's pointless.

Try to be useful – and fun.

Think of a role you can play that nobody else can.

I can't be a grandmother. I'm too young.
Grandmothers are old. They bake and they sew.
I was at Woodstock! I pissed in the fields.

Karen Buckman, *Parenthood*

Ten Things to Do with Grandchildren

1. Take a musical grandchild to a first concert, a ballet dancer to their first ballet, a football-mad one to his first Premier Division football match.

2. From time to time, take each one to something on their own where you can have a special time alone. Choose something that matches their interest.

3. Take one to see a couple (no more) of special pictures at a museum and talk to them about why they're special. Follow it up with knickerbocker glories at Fortnum & Mason, or your local equivalent.

4. When they reach a certain age (as I've already said, mine get taken to Africa for their tenth birthday), take them on a suitable unusual holiday – to see the pyramids, to Paris, to Rome, the Victoria Falls, to a musical festival . . . whatever.

5. Just before Christmas take them to see Father Christmas at the North Pole (www.santatripsonline.co.uk).

6. Teach them some games – whist, bridge, rummy, chess, poker, charades.
7. Teach them how to do something you're good at – such as cooking, gardening, tennis, riding, sailing, skiing.
8. Introduce them to books you've loved that you think they might like . . .
9. Take a teenage girl shopping for clothes (e.g. her first grown-up party dress), make-up, or for whatever interests her.
10. Plan a special overnight treat – such as a camping, riding or sailing weekend, or teach them to fish in Scotland, the Yorkshire dales or Devon.

* Two invaluable guides: *The Grandparents' Book* by Miriam Stoppard, published by Dorling Kindersley, and *The Good Granny Guide* by Jane Fearnley-Whittingstall, published by Short Books.

How to work and have a life

Having it All

We all hear of supermums, those celestial beings who rise effortlessly up the career ladder, whose children are immaculately turned out and whose marriages appear to be perfect. I just never get to meet them. For most of us, the most stressful time of our lives (but also – *never forget* – one of the most wonderful and rewarding too) is the arrival of a first child. Even for the few who are well off enough to give up work and attend to their child full-time, it involves huge changes from their previous carefree, childless life. I shall never forget the utter loneliness that I felt after my first child was born and my husband used to kiss me goodbye as he set off for work, saying, 'Bye – see you later.' As the front door shut I knew I was going to be mostly alone with a small, demanding, crying, hungry baby for the next nine hours. I loved her more than I'd ever thought possible, but I hadn't anticipated the sense of isolation that being left alone with a small baby brings. After the companionship of a busy office, the lunches with girlfriends, the interesting work, the freedom to hot-foot it to theatres, the exhilarating evening meetings (my husband was then much involved in politics), it was a huge shock. I was lucky in one sense in that I needed to work (at the time I didn't have the option of staying at home), so we got a nanny. I went back to my busy job and reclaimed much of my previous life, though I still feel guilty about not having been at home during the day for my children during those early years.

Since then life for most women has got more difficult, not less. Few households can buy houses, or enjoy the sort of holidays and lifestyle that modern families aspire to, on just one average salary, so far more women are having to work. Also there are far more single parents having to bring up children alone. The statistics tell us that in 2005 there were some 1.9 million single-parent families looking after 3.1 million children. For most of them going out to work is usually not a luxury or a nice little cherry on the family cake, it's a necessity. Added to which, work is usually much, much more demanding than it used to be. All during my children's growing-up years I worked on Sunday newspapers or the weekend section of the *Financial Times*, which meant that I could almost always be home for bed, bath and stories and, later on, for family suppers and talk of school, homework, practising and so forth. These days most people I know work intolerably long hours – which is a huge problem whether they have children or not. British workers work the longest hours in Europe and a recent Amicus survey found that the effects on family life of long working hours, coupled with appalling commuting times, meant that most of those surveyed were too tired to enjoy their home, their families, their friends or their hobbies.

Before this begins to sound depressing, I should also like to point out that one of the reasons that this situation has become such a problem is that the opportunities out there for women are so much greater. Life is richer and more complex, but the corollary is that it's often more stressful.

So what to do? The first thing is to accept there are no magic bullets. You can't have it all. I truly don't think it is possible to have a glittering career (if it involves very long hours and lots of travelling), well-adjusted, happy children *and* a loving marriage or relationship, I think its possible to have a medium career (that is, something that you can do in predictable hours without too much travelling) as well as happy, well-adjusted children and a good marriage. Since something's got to give, it seems to me that it's usually best for the family as a whole if the woman can bring herself to put her own career, even for a short time, on the back burner. Tough, I know, but I think that's the reality. Some women with fabulous careers ask their husbands to give up their own career to look after the children. This sometimes works, but does an alpha woman (or any woman, come to that) really want a meek, docile house-husband? I don't think so. It upsets the balance of power in the relationship in ways that don't psychologically suit either man or woman, in my view. And usually – but by no means always – it's in the family's interests for the man's career to be given most attention, for even in today's more emancipated environment men *usually* still have a greater earning capacity and wider horizons.

The choices facing women are hardest for the group that knows that slowing down or taking time out, even for just a few years, may mean giving up for ever the chance of making it – if not to the top, then probably to where they want to be. Now that women are having children later (but this, as I don't need to tell you, also comes with the downside that they risk missing out on having children at all), it's possible in some careers to get high enough up the ladder to be able to take a smallish career break without losing out on the promotion stakes. Really high-flyers can even risk taking complete career breaks – a wonderful thing to do for those whose confidence and abilities are exceptional. I know of one very successful young woman with four youngish children who went off with them and her husband for a whole year to wander round the world but she knew that she was so employable that she'd have a choice in terms of work when she got home. He ran his own businesses so he was going to be fine, too.

Most of us aren't so gifted or so sought after and so the choices are tough, though at least today (unlike in my own child-rearing days) there is statutory maternity leave and the right to get your job back if you want it.

As you can see, there are no magic solutions – I can only offer thoughts. I know that I regret enormously that I wasn't more involved in the day-to-day ordinariness of my children's lives – collecting them each day from school, taking them to the gym class or swimming class, etc. – but at first I couldn't afford to give up work. By the time I could, I'd got to like my job a lot and got paid enough to mean that I could afford good childcare.

But even full-time mothers need some down time, some

time to themselves. Nobody, I think, finds full-time child-care and domestic work a totally satisfactory way to spend their days and it's perfectly normal to want some time for your own hobbies, interests and friendships. Try to arrange for a grandparent to help, say, twice a week to give you some free time or, if that's not possible, organise swaps with other mothers – so that you have their child one afternoon a week in exchange for their having yours on another afternoon. As the child gets older, nursery school beckons, whole mornings begin to become free and the world opens up again.

What is happiness except the simple harmony between man and the life he lives. **Albert Camus**

Time to Take Stock

Maybe it's worth taking time to think more carefully about what you really want in life. Do you most want a high-powered job? Who was it who said 'Be careful what you ask for, as you may get it'? If that's what you want, then take good note of what you may very probably lose out on: a very close relationship with your children and possibly even with your husband/lover/partner as well. And are you intent on working because you have a great gift or skill (as a lawyer, surgeon, writer, stained-glass window maker, potter, gardener) or because you really need the money? If it's money, or you think it's money, think more deeply about that, too. It may well be that your income really is absolutely essential – it is for many women – but it may also be that you're suffering from what these days is called affluenza ('a painful, contagious, socially transmitted condition of overload, debt, anxiety and waste resulting from the dogged pursuit of more'). It's worth asking yourself how much money you *really* do need? After all, childhood is gone in a flash. As Ruby Wax once put it: 'How much money do you have to make before it doesn't matter that your child sues you when he's twenty-eight for being missing in action.'

Amongst my younger friends I know of several couples that consist of two high-flying bankers or two hugely successful lawyers (you get the picture), each of them earning more than enough to keep them comfortably in houses, skiing holidays and private school fees, yet they see scarcely anything of their children. One or other of them is often on a plane; both often work late; and the households are kept afloat by relays of nannies, cooks, chauffeurs, gardeners and the like. Fee-paying schools see this all the time – children who are materially spoiled beyond imagining, for whom half-terms are spent flying first class to the world's glamour spots, but who are emotionally more deprived than many children from the third world.

Take a moment to think about the correlation between money and happiness. There comes a time when working harder and therefore earning more results in less rather than greater happiness. In a fascinating survey carried out recently by London University, the researchers tried to establish what connection – if any – there was between money and happiness. Some of the findings weren't too surprising. Yes, for the very poor, enough money could measurably buy happiness, in that the difference between being able to afford your rent, food and other basics and not being able to afford them is such a crucial leap that it is literally the difference between continuous, serious angst and a sense of ease and peace. *But* once most of those basics were taken care of, all sorts of other things made more difference to the sense of well-being of the people questioned. Most important of all was good health (which, the researchers found, was the equivalent to a pay rise of some £304,000 a year), followed by marriage (the equivalent to earning an extra £54,000 a year), whilst living with somebody was even better (worth an extra £82,500 a year), and just chatting to a neighbour on a regular basis gave a sense of satisfaction equal to a pay rise of £40,000 a year. Happiness, as we all know, comes from a complex combination of things, but at the heart lies love, friendship, good relationships with family and friends, a degree of security, and meaningful work – preferably doing something that you're good at. One friend once said to me that his dream for his children was that they would find a means of earning a living that they so enjoyed doing that it didn't seem like work; it was what they wanted to do anyway. That is the dream . . . Few of us achieve it but it is possible.

It may be that you might be happier working less hard and living more simply, having more energy and time to spend with children, husband, lover or partner, with friends and family. Think about it carefully – assess what gives you satisfaction, what makes you feel good. You might be surprised at some of the answers.

It's also worth adding up what it costs you to work – because working isn't cheap. You need to pay for transport, for different sorts of clothes; you tend to spend more on fast food, cleaning, cleaners and all the rest. Again, the cost of working may amaze you.

Spend twice as much time and half as much money. A headmaster in an address to parents. It applies, he pointed out, as much to the plumber as to the banker.

It's Not All Bad News

On the plus side for working mothers, I would put the fact that both my husband and I spent every non-working minute (and we were lucky in that both our jobs involved pretty ordinary working hours) with our children and we always saw it as a treat and a pleasure, never a burden – evenings, weekends and holidays were sacrosanct. We were never looking for ways of 'dumping them'. We were also able to live rather more amply than we would have been able to do without my income.

Our children got to be self-reliant and independent when quite young. I remember one of my son's tennis coaches being stunned that a nine-year-old boy could cross London on his own, turn up on time with the right clothes and racquets, and cheerfully set off home again on his own. It makes me quail a bit to think about it now – but then it seemed quite normal.

I *think* our children like the fact that not just their father but also their mother has a life, an independence, an income of her own. I never had a day when I didn't worry about my own mother and I really don't think mine worry about me at all – which I think is a nice gift to give them. When the children have left home, work is a big consolation. The money's nice but so is the sense of purpose, the companionship and the continually expanding horizons. So whilst I miss those years when the children were at home – the happiest of my life – I'm not totally bereft now that they've flown the nest. I have another life, *and* (something I much enjoy) another income, which buys them – and their children – some pretty nice treats.

Getting Help

Sleep Problems

For working women probably the most stressful time of their lives is when the moment comes after the birth of a baby to go back to work. Sleep – or lack of it – is an all-consuming obsession. Even new mothers not going back to work find that getting enough sleep dominates their lives.

Try to establish a routine. Getting a baby used to learning to go to sleep by himself or herself is an essential survival tactic – for you and him. Babies, unless they're ill, are tougher than one thinks. After about six months, if there are no digestive problems, a baby should be able to last the night without a feed or drink.

Never let a baby become accustomed to sleeping in your bed – you'll never have a good night's sleep and it will be a nightmare trying to persuade him back to his own bed.

Some children are better sleepers than others and some mothers are naturally better disciplinarians than others. If you have problems, try to get them sorted early on – for your own sanity and the baby's. My own daughter, and several other people I know, have been driven to distraction by babies who didn't sleep, but there are children's sleep consultants who can help. In London, Mandy Gurney, at Millpond (020 8444 0040 and at www.mill-pond.co.uk), offers personal advice, either in your own home or over the phone. Those who have used Millpond say it's money well spent every time.

Andrea Grace (020 8348 6959 and at www.andregrace.co.uk or email to enquiries@andreagrace.co.uk) will come to your home, give personal advice and write up a future plan of action.

* When you're truly desperate, it's worth knowing that Night Nannies, too, will come to your rescue – for a fee. They're a godsend if you can afford them. They know just how to calm a fractious baby and soothe him or her into good sleeping habits. Check out www.nightnannies.co.uk for a list of regional contact details.

Childcare

The biggest problem facing the working mother is childcare. All those years ago, I could afford a live-in nanny on a good income but it was certainly not that of a lawyer or a banker. That has got more difficult today – nannies cost a king's ransom, with massive bribes (flats of their own, smart cars, first-class flights, etc.) from the new breed of hugely affluent City workers making it harder for those on average salaries to compete. All the evidence is that small babies need one-on-one care. Those who are looked after by their own mothers, or a dedicated nanny, granny or childminder, at least until the age of one, thrive much better than those who have to compete for attention with other babies and toddlers in not-so-good nurseries. This, I am afraid, is an inconvenient fact. Numerous other studies have shown that lack of proper parental love and care in the early years can affect children's performance and sense of psychological well-being all their life. So I worry about a whole generation of babies being brought up in crèches, however well run. It may be that in the early years you need to think of part-time work, if you can organise it or afford it, or do some work from home. Employers are becoming more family friendly and some now offer flexi-time, whilst certain quite high-powered jobs can sometimes be organised as a job share between two women, giving each of them precious time at home with their children as well as the stimulus of work and the benefit of income.

There is no pat answer to this problem. The options are few and come down to a full-time nanny (expensive but, if you find the right one, the most reassuring and flexible solution); grannies or other family members; childminders or day nurseries; and crèches. All present some risks and obviously the quality of the person you choose is key (are they reliable, kind, energetic, honourable; do they like children, etc.), so taking up references is absolutely crucial. Partly you have to go by gut instinct, partly by their credentials (childminders, for instance, must be registered; nurseries and crèches are carefully regulated) and partly by personal references. I don't think a day nursery is suitable for a child under one who still needs close one-to-one care, but I know that some mothers have no option. As the child gets older and more sociable, day nurseries have lots going for them. However, the best ones fill up fast so the time to check them out is the minute you know you're pregnant.

Nevertheless, you will still have to resign yourself to the fact that you will always feel guilty. When you are at work, you'll be worrying about the children, and when you're at home, you'll be worrying about work. It comes with the territory and I know of no way round it.

The other problem, which looms up later and which new mothers often don't take into account, is that teenagers are more, not less, needy than small children. Just because they don't have to be watched every minute of the day doesn't meant they don't still very much need close relationships with their parents. After all, nobody else can be expected to be as sensitive or as caring about their well-being or as alert to any looming problems as you, their parents. They need time with their parents; they should have frequent chances to talk to them and bring up things that may be worrying them. An au pair or a nanny who, if good, can provide for the wants of a small child is much less able to be emotionally satisfying as a carer for a teenager. So try to organise ways of keeping in as close touch with your teenage children's interests and needs as you can.

It would be terribly sad, wouldn't it, to look back on your life in films and not know your children? For me there's nothing more . . . lovely or rewarding than seeing my children grow up . . . and they only grow up once, remember.

Audrey Hepburn

Throwing Money at the Problem

Here, of course, that old bugbear – money – is important. You can't throw money at the problem if you don't have enough of it. But *even* if you do have enough of it, I think there are only certain problems for which it is decent to use money to buy your way out of trouble. It is *not*, in my view, decent to pay other people to deal with a difficult child who is probably just longing for more attention from his/her parents. It is *not*, in my view, decent to pay other people to go to his sports days, read her stories at night, take him to the all-important school interview or generally do the things that are crucial to a child's sense of being loved and valued by her parents.

But if you have the sort of job that takes all the hours that God gives and you earn enough, then for heaven's sake buy the services of the cleaner, the gardener, or the cook, so that those chores are taken care of, leaving you with as much time as you can muster for the people who should, after all, be what matter most in life – your nearest and dearest, whether wife, husband, children, siblings, or mother and father.

If you need to and can run to it, it may be worth spending a one-off sum to get the house properly sorted – unless you're one of those naturally organised people whose cupboards are immaculate and whose files are in tip-top order (see Chapter 5). A declutter expert or even a life coach could show you not only where you've gone wrong but how to get your priorities right.

If you can afford it, some of the concierge services that now abound (www.quintessentially.com to name but one) will organise things like sending presents, booking air fares and holidays, sort the house move, and anything else that can be delegated. Urban PA (020 8487 9400 and at www.urbanpa.com) will provide support services at home. They'll take over household chores, organise garden maintenance, or get house sitters in when you're away, as well as provide secretarial services at home.

Consider it Done (www.consider-it-done.co.uk), will – for a fee – take care of every domestic chore, no matter how piffling.

www.why-bother.co.uk will give the house a good clean, taking in everything from light bulbs to dusty corners.

Remember the maximum of Mr Micawber, in Charles Dickens' *David Copperfield*:

'Annual income twenty pounds, annual expenditure nineteen nineteen six, result happiness. Annual income twenty pounds, annual expenditure twenty pounds ought and six, result misery.'

Keeping control of one's spending is one of the most obvious ways of reducing stress.

Get Organised

Most of can't afford to pay other people to do these things and so we have to do them ourselves. Making lists helps enormously. The busier your life, the more you need lists. There's something so satisfying about ticking items off. One very successful man I know says he tackles his list by starting off, when he's fresh and the day is young, with the things that he least wants to do. The day, then, can only get better and better.

Planning ahead also helps. Get the shopping sorted by organising a weekly list with Ocado (www.ocado.com) or Tesco (www.tesco.com). It's a bore the first time round but once it's all set up it saves you hours and, best of all, you don't have to worry about parking or humping all the heavy stuff home.

When I ran what I call an 'establishment' (two children, a nanny, the cleaner, my husband and me), I used to plan food quite carefully at the weekends. As I cooked, say, Sunday lunch, I'd be cooking something else for the week ahead – a soup, a casserole, a cottage pie and a pudding – so that at least the first two or three days didn't need much thinking about. If I had the occasional easy weekend, I'd stock up the freezer by making, say, two lots of a casserole, one for the meal that day, the other for the freezer. A freezer – a big new excitement then – was a fantastic asset. If properly stocked, it meant that one never ran out of bread, butter or most of the basics. These days fast food has got so much better that one scarcely needs to cook if one doesn't feel like it – *but* it is infinitely more expensive than cooking from scratch.

Having a tidy house saves many crucial minutes a day (as Dawna Walters, the closet guru, once put it, 'If you can find what you need exactly when you need it you'll save hours a week'). By tidy, I don't mean the sort of anal house where nothing is ever out of place, but a basic tidiness, with cupboards reasonably sorted, so that you can find sheets or washing-up cloths when you need them, where files are in order and clothes hung up.

Tidiness can be made easier by developing a habit of tidying as you go along so that you don't let the mess develop from a minor nuisance into a major one, which means clearing a mini minefield every week, as one woman I know used to do (she let everything build up until Saturdays, which were an absolute nightmare of dirty dishes, piles of laundry, stuff all over the floor and so forth). That sort of major clearing-up effort involves big chunks of time and is seriously dispiriting. I, for instance, try to do little bits of tidying when I have a few spare minutes. Whilst I wait for a kettle to boil I might, say, tidy a kitchen drawer or do the washing-up that's waiting in the bowl. Putting things away after you've used them is one of the simplest ways of keeping disorder at bay. Above all, you don't want to have the sort of house that gets so untidy that you dread the unexpected visitor or that is so cluttered that you can't find the kettle because it's covered in junk.

Learn to Compromise

We've already seen that having it all isn't an option. There aren't enough hours in the day, so it's essential to learn to compromise. This means working out what really matters – whether time with your child, your work, a perfect home, seeing your friends, couple time, or hobbies. The balance between all these things will need to be rethought once you have children. If your work isn't all that rewarding, why not take the chance (*if* you can afford to) to take a year or so off to look after your child or children whilst you regroup your energies and rethink your career plans. You may have to see slightly less of your friends, go less often to the theatre, give up time in the gym and stop worrying about your house looking so perfect. Remember, childhood goes in a flash.

If you're a working mother, on an average income, you can't run your house as if there were a battalion of servants or as if you were at home all day. So don't try. Children would much rather you had fun with them, read to them, taught them to ride a bike, took them hiking, than that the house was a shrine to cleanliness. Nobody ever lay on their deathbed wishing they'd spent more time cleaning, whereas plenty die regretting that they didn't spend more time with the people they loved. If you're short of time, work out ways of making the provision of meals less bothersome. Children don't need elaborate food. They need fresh healthy food that doesn't have to be labour intensive – simple roasts, pastas, grilled fish and fresh vegetables can all be turned out without too much effort if you plan ahead. Children don't have to have two hot meals a day – cold food is just as nourishing as hot. Nobody dies if the clothes aren't ironed – buy as many non-iron clothes for the children as possible so that they can just be tossed in the machine, dried and put back on. If you can afford it, use dry-cleaning and laundry services that deliver (www.harpersdry cleaners.co.uk and www.letmeironforyou.co.uk).

You may have to settle on giving up for a few years some things that you mind about. I seem to remember that for a long period we were never able to go on a proper walk (small children walk too slowly) or play tennis (because it would have meant leaving them at the weekend when we wanted to be with them) and I almost never had time to read a book, but the years flashed by and soon we were into doing most things with the children (tennis, skiing, hiking, playing chess and card games and the like). The time really does go quickly, so give up some of your treats for a few critical years for the greater pleasure of spending time with your children. Remind yourself every so often how fast childhood goes and how much time (if you're lucky) you will have to yourselves after the children have left.

It's not having what you want, it's wanting what you've got. Sheryl Crow

Stress Relievers

EXERCISE: It's the best reliever of stress there is and besides, it makes one feel much more able to cope with stress than slobbing around on a sofa ever does. The secret is to find something you like (swimming, yoga, tennis, golf, hiking) and, if all else fails, book yourself a personal trainer. It's expensive and possibly self-indulgent but if it's the only thing that gets you moving, it's essential.

HOBBIES: It helps to have a passion, something you love to do that isn't connected to work. I know it's hard to justify the time if you're already trying to juggle work and family life, but perhaps it's worth each partner thinking about giving the other a present of something like two hours a week when they can do whatever they like: joining a book club, going to the theatre, having a piano lesson, having a painting or photography lesson.

MASSAGE: It's not cheap but if you can afford it there are few better ways (other than exercise!) to soothe the nerves. Quite apart from its more serious benefits (helping with stiffness, knotted areas in the neck or back, 'bad' knees and the like), it gives you an hour or an hour and a half when you have nothing to do but relax. It's been known for thousands of years that the power of touch can be a powerful healer. For the elderly in particular, who live alone and have lost those closest to them, and so no longer have any physical relationships in their life, the touch of the masseur's hand can help to reduce depression, enhance the immune system and ease pain.

SPA TREATMENTS: Apart from massage, as far as I'm concerned, most other spa treatments are entirely frivolous, which isn't to say that some people don't enjoy them hugely. If they're what make you feel better and you can afford them, why not indulge from time to time but remember that you can get much the same benefit at home for a fraction of the price. Book in some 'me' time, lock the bathroom door, light some candles, turn on the radio or the iPod or whatever gives you pleasure, and soak in a sea of Ren's Moroccan Rose Otto bath oil (available from Space NK) for as long as you feel like it.

Home Sweet home

What is a Home?

To me, having grown up in a fractured family as more or less a nomad in South Africa, without a secure family home as a refuge, my own home is now everything. It's so much more, though, than four square walls and so much more than mere possessions. It's a sanctuary for me and the people I care about. It's where I feel safe, where I'd rather spend my time than in any six star glossy hotel. It's where I like to think my family and friends can find tranquillity, warmth and laughter, where I love to share food and wine and stories. As the outside world becomes more complex, most of us increasingly need the enveloping comfort of home. The current spate of what one commentator called 'decorexia' (an obsession with the house and its contents) is, I think, symptomatic of more than just another field for competitive consumer spending; it is also an indication of our need for our own safe world. We're looking for ways to order our living spaces in ways that suit our particular lives, our families, our needs, our desires.

But a home is not a static place. It is the canvas on which we paint our personalities. As we all travel more, this influences the way we live and adds another layer to the things we surround ourselves with. In this way we change and grow, and our home evolves. For a home is also the storehouse of our family histories, a living archive that holds the treasures of our personal lives. Every picture, every book, every object tells a story. It speaks of where we've been and who we are, of what we mean to each other and of how we relate to the world around us.

I love best the sort of houses that are particular and truthful – and by that I mean that they're honest expressions of who the owners are. They've filled it with things they love and that have meaning. They haven't chosen things solely to impress or created an environment that isn't an entirely truthful representation of who they are. The houses I like lack pretension and they have no status symbols for the sake of them. That doesn't mean to say that some of them don't have some stunning and expensive pieces, but they're there because the owners truly love them, have perhaps discovered the designer/maker themselves, have brought them home in high excitement after some long journey and not merely plonked them down because they're a trendy thing to own.

I have no recipe for how to combine things. But you must be sincere. And if you are, strangely, it will succeed. Andrée Putman, the exceedingly elegant French designer

Practical observation tells me that Andrée Putman (see above) is absolutely right. Choose things you really, honestly love and somehow they'll work together. Our own house is filled with a very eclectic collection of things: a 500-year-old stone gentleman from Bali, a very recent Edmund de Waal ceramic installation given to me by my children, African masks and tribal stools, a Victorian wrought-iron child's cot upholstered and turned into a small sofa, an antique French bedstead, pictures that range from the first (frankly rather strange) print I ever bought for just £12 to one or two rather lovely drawings and paintings inherited from my father. Strangely they seem to work together.

As you can tell, I care about our home. The present one isn't where our children were born or were mostly brought up, but when we bought it they were still – just – at home and they set out from here, at an interval of three years apart, to Cambridge and the bigger, wider world, coming back often enough to make us feel that their lives and presences are part of the history of the house.

When it comes to style my tastes are relatively simple, veering towards the boho and the romantic. I admire austere simplicity when it's beautifully done, but can't quite bring it off myself. Nor do I like anything too 'Belgravia' or establishment. I do mind terribly – too much, my husband would say – how things look. I absolutely empathise (again) with Andrée Putman when she says, 'Of course, I love seven pillows behind me, but physical comfort is never the first thing. I prefer spiritual comfort, by which I mean space, light (natural, as well as artificial), contrast of textures, and pure lines. I never look for literal comfort, but for something that allows my mind to rest.' I know just how she feels. I'm irked to an irrational degree by things that don't look right and not nearly enough by things that don't work quite so well.

I think I'm pretty good at getting things to look interesting but I am, I confess, not so good at organising the practicalities. In an ideal world I'd have them both. I'd love to have loads of storage, enough working space in the kitchen, a small table and a light wherever one is needed, really comfy chairs and sofas, and all the other practical and technical things that these days make such a difference. On the other hand, perfection is often a little dull. (Remember what Truman Capote said about Babe Paley: 'Babe Paley had only one fault: she was perfect: otherwise she was perfect.') There's something about a house being an ongoing project that is rather beguiling. If it were all done in one fell swoop a certain something, I can't help feeling, would be removed from daily life. I can't imagine buying one of those 'turnkey' apartments where you just hand over a cheque and everything is done for you. Where's the fun in that?

In any event, getting it right is complicated, requiring an immense amount of planning, not to mention an address book more than a metre thick. But all the best and most interesting houses evolve over time. We married very young with no money and such cash as there was went on the children and childcare, so for years we had very little furniture and could afford few luxuries. But over the decades we have accumulated things – presents that we've given each other and that our children and others have given us; pictures we've inherited; bits I've brought back from my journalistic wanderings – and all these objects, I like to think, make our house particular and personal. So don't be impatient. The best houses take time. If they're to be true expressions of who you are, then it can't be done overnight. Build it up, layer upon layer, as your life evolves.

Here I try to pass on just some of the lessons I've learned as I've grappled with trying to keep our much-loved house looking good and working well.

Fundamentals

The thing I always remember about my mother, who never had much money but who always looked a dream (she never weighed more than seven stone from the day I was born), was that she made the small and not very prepossessing flats she lived in seem warm and welcoming because she always filled them with books and music, flowers, fruit and chocolates. (Nowadays I'd add wine, but in those innocent days I hadn't discovered its pleasures and neither had she). None of those are really expensive (particularly in South Africa) and I've always thought that in some ways you don't need a lot more than that. They are all things that we require for mental nourishment, for sensuous comfort and for aesthetic pleasure. If you've got those, you're in clover. But there are other things that make a difference: warmth (how I remember, in the days before ubiquitous central heating, the frozen rooms that greeted me when I first landed in the UK); candles; plump cushions; comfy beds; fine sheets; good soap; great coffee; a great big kitchen table. In addition to those, a certain level of order and tidiness really helps (squalor isn't restful), whilst a few touches of glamour add the magic.

Generosity, whether of the mind or the purse (and in my experience they tend to go together), is hugely appealing and so it is with houses. It shows. There is nothing more attractive than a warm and welcoming home – it's more important than worrying about whether the house is scruffy or down-at-heel. There's nothing more off-putting than the skimpy bowl of fruit, the mean-sized towels, the cheap soap, the inadequate central heating. The converse is also obviously true: great piles of fluffy white towels in a bathroom, wonderful soap and ample hot water are hugely comforting, whilst a house filled with those essentials – music, books, fruit and flowers – is so inviting that you could (almost) forget the furnishings.

And remember: it's a home, not a museum. It's for living in, not for looking at. Have the things you love.

Touches of Magic

It is my common observation that nothing spells death to an interior more than the small, the mean and the dinky. A touch of grandeur does wonders for even the smallest of homes. Just as the classic technique for any fashion brand trying to reinvent itself is to dip into its archive, to take some classic designs and play about with scale, upsizing and downsizing, the same is true for the house. Playing about with scale (what one might call an *Alice in Wonderland* ploy) can add a touch of magic to almost any room.

For that marvellously sumptuous designer Alidad, getting the scale right is where good design starts. 'If scale is not right, it can kill a room. When in doubt, overscale – it always works. I usually go to extremes. If a client has a small room and wants it to look special, I choose the biggest patterns I can find, and the large table or commode that will only just squeeze through the door. You can visually expand a room by cheating the eye; overscaling seems to push back the walls and ceilings.' This also applies to big-patterned wallpaper and to accessories. A couple of Washington-based designers, Robert Cole and Sophie Prevost, used 'the grandest, tallest, definitely over-scaled lounge chair in the tiniest drawing-room . . . and it looked wonderful. It actually made the room feel bigger.'

Tables can be given a bit of added theatre by using oversized hurricane lamps as candle-holders – small and medium just look conventional, but once you go large the change in atmosphere is dramatic. Chunky glasses, big mirrors, oversized platters and even huge fat poles for curtains with great big rings are all different ways of imbuing a house with a sense of generosity and making sure a room never looks bland.

Chandeliers – not grand, pompous ones that look as if

they were devised for formal reception rooms in so-called grand hotels but enchanting little antique ones from France or Italy – lend an enchantment to almost any room. Dining rooms and drawing rooms are obvious contenders for their charms, but some of the most sensuously welcoming bathrooms I know sport a chandelier in the middle. I have one over my own dining table and it gives me joy daily. The light is delicious (on the wall opposite we have a Venetian mirror and the light reflected back and forth is wonderful) and it is on a dimmer switch so we can have slightly mysterious half-light when we need it. Oversized chandeliers can sometimes work. Philippe Starck put a black glass chandelier in a sugar-pink room at the Baccarat headquarters in Paris and it looked fabulous. And if chandeliers aren't right think about some scintillating Art Deco lights – the glittering chrome and glass reminds one irresistibly of movies, the glamour of Hollywood, of Fred and Ginger in their heyday.

Huge mirrors leant nonchalantly against a wall are currently a fashionable interiors prop and very good they look too. A giant buddha or a statue add grace and grandeur to a room. They don't need to be expensive. The Golborne Road in North Kensington in London is a very good source of inexpensive mirrors but up and down the country there are antique shops, or what the French call *brocantes*, offering them for not a lot of money. And talking of France, the provincial antique fairs (except Ile-sur-la-Sorge, which is now almost as expensive as Bond Street) that are held at intervals all through the summer are a great source of old mirrors.

If you can't find things large enough on their own to be eye-catching, grouping them in multiples, even if they're fairly common or garden objects, gives them a visual importance that often works. One African mask can look a bit silly but five look dramatic. The interior designer Kelly Hoppen once told me that sometimes she would buy huge glass vases from Habitat in threes or fives (somehow odd numbers work better than even), group them asymmetrically and they would look divine. I copied her, bought three huge glass vases for very little and filled them with giant fake deep red amaryllis (£8 a stem from Debenhams), and put them on a landing table. They look, I think, terrific. At The Conran Shop, Polly Dickens will cover a dining table with a vast array of differently sized glass candlesticks, none of them expensive, and the mass is what makes the magic. I was once in a room that was fairly austere – lots of white paint and bare floorboards – but the mantelpiece was lined with a row of buddhas that looked interesting and exotic, and added a bit of panache. 'Where,' I enquired of the owner, 'had they come from?' Marks & Spencer she said, without a blush.

In yet another all white and cream room with painted wooden floors, the whole room was saved from austerity and a certain bleakness by the addition of a single – but very beautiful – old, carved armoire. In a conventional room with conventional antiques the old armoire would have contributed no drama but in its austere white setting it seemed theatrical and wonderful. In another equally clean-lined room one brilliant quirky piece, in this case a silvered curving chest of drawers, added the buzz that the room so badly needed.

Quite often a room can be enlivened by changing the eye-level. If all the furniture is of a similar height the effect is dull and monotonous, so lead the eye upwards (particularly in a high-ceilinged room or one where there is a particularly beautiful cornice or ceiling) by choosing a tall piece of furniture or erecting something like a high screen. And never forget candles, about which more later. Even the dullest interior can be turned, at night, into a wonderland if there are enough candles to shed their wonderfully soft, flickering light. You can buy lots of small cheap glasses (more contemporary than silver candelabra) or, slightly more expensively, lots of glass candlesticks and the light from the candles will be reflected off the glass in a magical way. Instead of small Georgian candlesticks, go for less conventional, quirkier ethnic ones – oversized, of course. If you have space – on a landing, in a corner – think about doing something that I once saw in Biki Oberoi's Udaivilas Hotel in Udaipur, which is to have a table given over entirely, come the evening, to a massed array of lighted candles of various shapes and sizes.

The important thing is for a room to have visual variety so it doesn't do to use only large pieces, the point being that you want contrast rather than uniformity. Symmetry and asymmetry also need to be balanced, because too much of either is simply dull. In very large rooms try splendid architectural pieces – carved wooden doors, pillars, huge urns, big fireplaces, even complete staircases. They can often be found at the suppliers of architectural salvage (try the London Architectural Salvage & Supply Company, St Michael's Church, Mark Street, London EC24 4ER; 020 7749 9944). Everything it sells has the immense advantage of being a one-off and so is to be doubly treasured.

Soane (50 Pimlico Road, London SW1W 8LP; 020 7730 6400) was founded by Lulu Lytle and Christopher Hodsoll entirely to provide people with architecturally inspired pieces. They have, for instance, some column tables, as well as a huge four-foot-high Doric column on which a vast urn, or even their monumental glass vase (twenty inches high), could be placed.

* If you can't afford serious art, blow up and hang on one hall a favourite black and white photograph or picture, mega-size – it'll look dramatic and twice as important. There are now plenty of companies that will do it for you (see Chapter 7, Perfect Presents).

Ilse Crawford, the designer behind Babington House and Soho House in the meat-packing district in New York, seems effortlessly to conjure up magic. She combines a sense of cool with an updated version of old-world glamour. In her very white rooms in Soho House there are zebra skins on the floors (there is something very sensual about animal skins; I suppose it was Elinor Glyn and her tiger skin rug that did it), lots of mirrored surfaces, the odd piece of baroque or quirky furniture. (If you don't fancy a zebra skin on the floor, even though the skins should come only from zebras that have died a natural death, consider a cow hide.)

Texture is another way of providing a sense of luxe, which is partly what glamour is about. Cushions are possibly the least expensive way to inject some instant allure. Many of the chain stores – Debenhams, House of Fraser and now BhS with Kelly Hoppen's new range – often have wonderfully rich cushions, silk quilts and bedspreads at fantastic prices. Have a look at www.comforthouse.com.

And finally, flowers, flowers, flowers.

Economy Glamour

Suzanne Imre, editor of *Livingetc* magazine, offers ten ways to add a touch of magic without breaking the bank.

1. Stain floorboards in the darkest wood stain you can possibly find (I use Dulux Trade Ebony stain) and paint walls and skirting boards in a fresh, pure white (Farrow & Ball's All White).

2. Fit elegant, smoked-glass doorknobs on all internal doors. Buy the most expensive ones you can afford as they will still be cheaper than changing all the doors!

3. Hang a large, mirrored disco ball in the hall (Jade

Jagger has one in her house in Ibiza; John Hiscox has one in the area that houses his swimming pool) to create a little sparkle and tongue-in-cheek amusement each time you walk into your home. (Get them from www.light-engineering.com.)

4. Glam up your kitchen with nothing more than elbow grease: polish all your stainless steel to a high shine, from plug sockets to cooking utensils. They will reflect the light and help make the room look instantly smarter.

5. Have fun with scale and never go for the middle road. Opt for the size that will create dramatic impact in a particular space: mini mosaics or huge slabs of stone in a bathroom; a narrow delicate armchair or an oversized, squashy sofa for a sitting room, or try the juxtaposition of a grand, wide chandelier in a long, slim hallway.

6. Plain white sheers at windows always look effortlessly elegant. Hang them high above the window frame and let them cascade down to tumble on the floor, creating a long slim shape that makes the ceilings appear higher too.

7. A beautifully scented home is the ultimate flirtation with the senses. After dark, dim the lights (never use anything brighter than 60 watts) and light scented candles in hallways, sitting rooms and bathrooms.

8. Give a tired, but interestingly shaped, piece of wooden

furniture a touch of Italian gloss by lacquering or car-paint spraying it in brilliant white, sexy black or deep ruby red. Find a local car mechanic who can help.

9. White kitchens are simply the best when it comes to modern interiors, but they can run the risk of looking sterile at times. Break up a plain space and add a shot of style in the form of a mirrored mosaic splashback. It guarantees instant edge.

10. Buy a number of inexpensive black picture frames in differing sizes and mount your favourite black and white photos in them. Group the frames artfully on the wall or, for a more casual look, lean them on shelves, overlapping if you like.

Mix and Match

There's something very staid and old-fashioned about having everything that matches. Think of the traditional dining table, sideboard and chairs all perfectly matched – very, very boring, very last century. Mix a traditional table with funky chairs – Philippe Starck's Ghost chair, or even his Mademoiselle chair (both done for Kartell), or the Tulip chairs that Eero Saarinen designed all those years ago for Knoll. You can even mix the chairs themselves, providing they're all in roughly the same mood. If you have a table the right size but it looks staid and down-at-heel (in an unattractive way, not a divine shabby-chic kind of way), you can get it sprayed in a brightly coloured lacquer – even deep shiny black. At the Milan Furniture Fair a few years ago, all the trendiest tables had red lacquered legs; they looked great (still do) so you could update a dull table by just spraying the legs. I saw a wonderful table the other day that had clearly once had a shabby pine top but it had been overlaid with a beaten metal top and a whole gaggle of design journalists were looking at it agog. We all loved it. It had so much more personality than something too new and shiny from a snazzy showroom. And, of course, with dining tables size and proportion are more important than looks because you can always cover the top with a gorgeous cloth.

The three-piece suite has long ago died a death, but it reminds us that a varied collection of sofas and chairs is infinitely more interesting than matching sets. It needs a good eye, though, because whilst one, say, Louis XV chair in a very modern room looks brilliant, there are some styles that just don't mix. Usually if a piece is attractive enough in itself, it will blend with other things of equal quality. It's good, too, to put the odd antique in with the resolutely modern – or vice versa. It livens the interior up no end.

China and tableware, too, are much more fun if they're mixed up together instead of that 'wedding-present', matching-set look. I first saw the charm of this more boho approach to dining tables some years ago in one of those quintessentially shabby-chic English country houses where the table was laid with a disparate collection of antique

QUICK WAYS TO UPDATE YOUR HOME

1. Change your china. This doesn't cost a fortune and can immediately change the look. Throw out (or better still store) the plain white (just a little boring now). Bring in colour and modern shapes, and mix with antiques.

2. You can't afford to throw everything out but a few brilliantly chosen quirky accessories can update the look – a floppy resin vase-cum-sculpture by Gaetano Pesce, some extraordinary glass by somebody like by Massimo Micheluzzi, or a huge elliptical vase from Lino Sabattini. Think of it as adding Jimmy Choo shoes to a Topshop dress.

3. Change the cushions. Get them beaded, embroidered, covered in buttons or pleats in colours that give the room a new look.

4. Change the look at the window. If you have blinds, consider adding some floaty sheers as well. If you have thick lined curtains, swap them for something lighter and fresher.

5. Art is what the City bonus set seem to spend their money on. So can you. You don't have to buy the big names in the posh galleries. Scour the annual student shows at art colleges and buy before Charles Saatchi gets there, or go to Frieze Art and the other user-friendly art markets that are

burgeoning everywhere. Blow up a large photograph or get The Bigger Picture (020 7636 9000 and at www.mybiggerpicture.com) or 55 Max (020 7625 3774 and at www.55max.com) to give you a blown-up version of an image of your choice to fill a whole wall. If you're a techno-whizz, you can play about the computer to create, say, Andy Warhol-like images of your own and enlarge them.

6. Change the floor. Pull up a fitted carpet and sand and paint the floorboards, or swap a dowdy rug for something more modern.

7. Changing the walls isn't expensive – you can slap wallpaper (currently really back in vogue) over existing paint or repaint over paint. A vibrant paper on one wall is very 'now'.

8. Refresh the lighting. Throw out anything dowdy. It's amazing what one wonderful light can do – a charming chandelier, say, or Ferrucio Laviani's Bourgie lamp, or an old photographer's or dentist's light from Alfie's Antique Market.

9. You can refresh the look of a chair or sofa with a throw or blanket – using, say, an all-white bedcover on a sofa if you're tired of its existing colour.

plates, silver and glass. I presumed that over the years some pieces had been broken and others had gone missing, but as it was the sort of house where there would have been plenty of different sets, I now think the owners simply put together whatever seemed to look good on the day. It looked wonderful. Shortly after that I began to collect vintage blue and white plates from the grand old pottery companies whenever I came across them. Each and every one is different. I went on collecting over the years from various antique fairs and stalls, and I bring them out when I'm not in resolutely modern mode and want a table that looks not so much chic as pretty and inviting. Wedgwood has a very modern, avant-garde take on the harlequin notion with its selection of plates, each sporting a different portion of a traditional Wedgwood pattern, yet all working together because they come in the same colour range. While it's fun to mix your own sets, try to keep the mood fairly similar. If you want to collect old china, it's worth looking at www.chinasearch.co.uk.

And then there are glasses. In our house we're big fans of Riedel's austerely elegant wine glasses (each shape is beautifully tailored to enhance the grape type, so there is one glass for, say, Bordeaux, another for white burgundies and so on) and we always restock during the Harrods sale when they are about half price. I also have a collection of wonderfully ornate seconds made in Florence that didn't cost very much. They're all in varying shades of green with rich baroque twirls of gold and come in different shapes and sizes. I don't bring them out when we're serving very fine wines (in which case, in my view, only Riedel will do), but I love them just the same. Guinevere Antiques at 574–580 King's Road, London SW6 2DY; 020 7736 2917, is a good (though expensive) source of antique glasses, as is The Dining Room Shop at 62–64 White Hart Lane Barnes, London SW13 0PZ; 020 8878 1020. Nason & Moretti (www.smallislandtrader.com) does very similar glass and if you ever go to Venice or Florence don't miss a chance to get some wonderful glass there.

Water glasses of different colours but the same style often look very pretty on a table (Graham & Green, 0845 130 6622; www.grahamandgreen.co.uk, has a particularly charming selection) and I've seen tables laid with a varied collection of antique silver all collected from antique fairs at different times. Shops such as The Pier (0845 6091234 for a catalogue and at www.pier.co.uk) have ready-made collections of glasses that come in packs of four, all in different colours (£19.95 for a green, pink, red and gold lustre glass, either simple for water or fluted). It sells shot glasses, too, also in packs of four, each a different colour.

The same principle applies to cutlery. Whilst we were lucky enough to inherit a collection of some properly matching pieces, I still can't resist buying up small bits of silver, particularly Georgian, whenever I come across them at fairs or pass a likely-looking antique shop. Buying cutlery in small doses means you don't have to fork out a vast sum all at once and gradually it mounts up. I've found pieces in Portobello, in Camden Passage antique market in Islington and at small fairs. For posh Georgian silver, Bruford & Hemming, 136 New Bond Street, London W1S 2TH; 020 7499 7644, is a great source. John Pawson, who famously owns very little 'stuff', does his buying there.

If you want inspiration on how to mix a lot of styles together, you could scarcely do better than pay a visit to Talisman at 79–91 New King's Road, London SW6 4SQ; 020 7731 4686 and at www.talismanlondon.com, where Ken Bolan blithely puts a Gustavian chair next to an Art Deco chest of drawers, or some Art Deco chairs round a chic but shabby table. There's a splendour and a grandeur to the way he mixes and matches, and it's a brilliant lesson in how to do eclectic with élan. There are also alarmingly tempting pieces to buy.

Tara Bernerd's Guide to Renovation

Tara Bernerd is a sassy and clever designer, and her company, Target Living, 020 7351 7588 and at www.targetliving.com, has carried out a large number of architectural and design projects – some for private homes, some for large corporations such as the Blackstone Company.

1. THE BRIEF

Stop, look and think about the space. The most common mistake is to launch into choosing colours and new fabrics before you've worked out how to make best use of the space. Think about how you will use the room, all the functions it will need to fulfil (eating, sitting, watching television, entertaining, whatever). It seems obvious, but if you do this it will clarify your mind and the steps you need to take. Collect images of inspirational rooms from magazines to try to identify what pleases you.

2. THE LAYOUT

Draw a scaled plan of the room. This is essential if you are considering building works but it also enables you to try out, with scale models of the furniture, how best to furnish the room. For instance, if you were redesigning your living room, you might start off thinking of a sofa and armchairs, yet through drawing up different options you might find that an L-shape sofa and larger character chair would work better. It should also help you plan a lighting and electrical layout.

3. THE SPECIFICATION

With the plan in hand and an idea of your furniture layout, you need to consider flooring, wall treatment, ironmongery (door handles, etc). You should do this before you choose the final colours and fabrics.

Think of it as building up an artist's palette. If going for a wooden floor, for instance, consider the type and colour impact that this will have on your choice of wall covering and so on.

4. FEATURE TREATMENT

You might identify an area that you'd like to emphasise or make stand out in some way – perhaps a wall with a fireplace or a large back wall on which you might put a different colour (paint or lacquer), wallpaper or even leather to make a feature of it. This is usually easiest on one wall, on columns, or an obvious stand-alone area.

5. THE FABRICS

With a layout and specification in mind you can start hunting for fabrics or leathers, the materials for the room, again building up your palette. Choose approximately three fabrics, making sure they are not all too busy. Usually one should be more detailed and the other two less patterned, and occasionally one of these may be a strong bold colour for a little edge. These fabrics will become the blinds, sofa and armchair material, and will usually be the main colour in the room. Try to get large samples, as tiny swatches can be deceiving.

6. FURNITURE

With a plan of your furniture layout, this will help focus you as well as ensuring that what you buy fits. Be wary of the spontaneous purchase that often turns out to be a real problem, either by not fitting or simply being the wrong colour. So look around, buy magazines and perhaps have a style in mind. Draw up a clear list of what you need as well as measurements.

It is helpful to have a small zipped bag with all your samples together so that you can check that things fit in with your scheme.

7. GENERAL PLANNING

Design is a logical process so consider all the various timing implications, i.e. lead-in times and installation time. Some companies have maddeningly long lead-in times.

8. BUILDERS/PROFESSIONALS

Do consider professional help – it can save you expensive mistakes. Always ask to see the previous work of companies that you're considering.

9. HAVE FUN

Once you're organised, with a layout, a spreadsheet of all your items and their corresponding prices and timings, you should try to enjoy the process and not be scared of change.

10. ACCESSORIES

Finally look at cushions, throws, plants, etc. These final details can lift a whole room: a terrific pile of funky trunks, a fantastic throw or edgy cushions. But remember that just as the wrong hat can kill a wonderful outfit, so these details can be deadly if not chosen with care. Be honest, buy sincerely here and stay with the scheme.

Paint

Until I started updating our West London terraced house about six years ago, I hadn't realised quite how sophisticated the matter of choosing paint had become. It's joined the long list of totemic products that are said to speak volumes about their owners. Even so, with the mass of choice around, it isn't always easy to find what you want if you have something very specific in mind. For instance, I knew I wanted a dark, almost black, green for our front door and chose the darkest green I could find on the usual colour charts. It wasn't dark enough. It irked me daily until a friend, with wonderful taste, to whom I bleated about my disappointment at not finding the right colour, said, 'Oh, the colour you want is Shop Front Green – you can get it from Papers & Paint in Park Walk.' She was right. It's perfect. It made me realise how hugely important it is to get colours right but because, most of us choose paint colours so seldom, we don't get enough experience to know how the colour on the chart will look in a big mass up on a wall or in combination with other colours. I can't begin to mention every range around but I list below the pros and cons of some of the companies I've used.

DESIGNERS' GUILD (head office), 3 Lasimer Place, London W10 6QT; 020 7893 7400. Whilst she can do a sophisticated neutral as well as anybody else, it's probably for her heart-lifting collection of brilliant blues, stinging greens and absolutely luscious pinks and reds that Tricia Guild is best known.

FARROW & BALL, Uddens Estates, Wimborne, Dorset BH21 7N7; 01202 876 141; www.farrow-ball.com. The first company to lift paint into the realm of a status symbol, it is most famous for producing the first historic range of paints for the National Trust and for the much-admired depth and flatness of the finishes (achieved by making paints the old, traditional way with no vinyl or plastics). Farrow & Ball recommend buying sample pots to experiment with before you decide, for colours appear to change, according to the area of the surface and any other colours near by. If you have grand, or even just pretty, cornicing, it's worth thinking of painting it just with distemper. This gives it a wonderfully powdery finish, highlights the carving and, because it can be easily washed off, you don't get that build-up of paint that flattens the detailing. There's a complete range of floor paints, too, not to mention exterior paints.

FIRED EARTH, Twyford Mill, Oxford Road, Adderbury, Oxfordshire; 01295 812 088; www.firedearth.com, has a range historic colours, as well as Kevin McCloud's delicious English Palette – some especially subtle greyish-greens.

FRANCESCA'S LIME WASH, Unit 34 Battersea Business Centre, 99/109 Lavender Hill, London SW11 5QL; 020 7228 7694; www.francescaspaint.com. Her lime washes and milk-based paints are just the thing if you fancy the look of a faded Italianate villa. They are the most traditional paints of all, made the way paint was made before the introduction of plastics, so when they dry they have that soft, velvety look that you see on the walls of grand palazzos. You can use paint grandly, as in Houghton Hall in Norfolk, or reverently, as in a host of renovated churches, or in a very modern way, as in Francesca's own flat or those of many of her friends and fans. Her range includes ninety-eight colours but she'll also custom-mix a colour to any specification. Her lime washes cost £29 (plus VAT) for 2.5 litres, but as they need to be mixed with water you actually get some five litres for your money. Her chalky emulsions are £15.92 (plus VAT) for 2.5 litres. She also has a collection of super-chalky paint shades that are fabulously subtle.

MARSTON & LANGINGER, 192 Mozart Terrace, Ebury Street, London SW1W 8UP; 020 7881 5783; www.marston-and-langinger.com. Brilliant outdoor paints – masses of shades of greens, for instance, to choose from, from palest lettuce to darkest forest – for conservatories, sheds or fences.

PAPERS & PAINTS, 4 Park Walk, London SW10 0AD;

020 7352 8626; www.papers-paints.co.uk. Just delicious colours, including the Beauvais Grey used in my kitchen.

THE PAINT & PAPER LIBRARY, 5 Elystan Street, London SW3 3NT; 020 7823 7755; www.paintlibrary.co.uk. Its Architectural Range is fantastic and now I nearly always use paints from its range. It has done much of the hard work by grouping paints in co-ordinated ranges. It has also taken some of the classic neutrals and off-whites, with names such as Wattle, Ivory, Slate, Stone, Lead, Sand and Clay, and produced each of them in four different shades. Interior designer Ann Boyd, for instance, who was once the taste behind Ralph Lauren interiors and is as sophisticated a designer as you could hope to find, almost always chooses paints for her clients from The Paint & Paper Library. 'If you're trying to do different tones in the same room he makes it dead easy. I just use, say, Wattle 1, 2, 3 and 4 in different places.' Most people use Shade 1 on the ceiling, 2 on the cornices, 3 on the walls and 4 on the woodwork but some will put 3 on the cornice and 2 on the woodwork. Whatever you do, you'll know that they're all in the same family of tones.

For £4 you can buy a beautifully produced set of cards showing all eight colours and they come with charming little architectural drawings and advice. Better still, if you find all the neutrals confusing, there is a private consultation service. For £100 per hour (and most visits don't take much more) plus travelling expenses, an advisor will come to your house and advise on colours and paint finishes. If that sounds like a lot, just compare the cost of getting it wrong with the pleasure of getting it right.

Mass-market Versus Niche Paints

When a 2.5 litre pot of Dulux paint can be bought for under £20, you might wonder how it is that some people are prepared to pay more than twice the price for something that doesn't seem to have a lot more to recommend it than a fancier, more obscure name.

The key is to know when and where to use these paints. Many interior decorators – particularly those who work on large developments where price becomes a key issue – are skilled at picking the sophisticated colours from ranges by companies such as Dulux and Sanderson. Joanna Wood and Ann Boyd, for instance, starry designers both, happen to agree that Sanderson's Soft Ivory, 5–7b, is one of the best pale bone colours there is. Karen Howes of interior design consultants Taylor Howes, says that 'Sanderson Cameo White is the best colour in the world for ceilings'.

The big brands have realised that it wasn't enough to swamp the market with choice – what the public wanted was more advice, more closely edited ranges. Which is why Dulux, for instance, has a selection of designers and consultants who can give advice on everything from colours to fashion trends. Ilse Crawford, who was design consultant to Babington House and wrote *Sensual Home*, is one of Dulux's consultants. She helps put together not only advice on trends but more importantly colour stories (such as Jungle Engineering, which homes in on a very fashionable group of greyish/greenish colours) that make it easy for the customer to choose shades that work together. One of the problems of the huge ranges offered by both Dulux and Sanderson is that the choices are almost too great. 'If you have plenty of time,' says Ilse Crawford, 'you could probably nearly always find the colours you want, but it does take time and these days for many people time is money.'

Joanna Wood, an interior designer whose clients have tastes ranging across a vast spectrum, says that she can often find neutral colours in the mass-market ranges: 'Sanderson's Spectrum range has some very sophisticated neutrals.' She often uses Quill Grey (47 – 10m), which is a very good greyish white, and Birch White (47 – 10m), another excellent slightly greyish white. When it comes to deep colours, such as reds ('It's so hard to find a red that isn't too coral or too purple in the more commercial ranges'), she opts for Farrow & Ball: 'There is a greater intensity of colour – the paint itself is thinner, so you need more layers, but there's more pigment in it.' She also often uses The Paint & Paper Library's Tarleton ('a fantastic greige') both inside – in contemporary interiors – and out. On the other hand, Tara Bernerd, who runs Target Living and has done interiors for private as well as commercial clients, has found a wonderful shade called Burgundy in the Dulux range, though she turns to Farrow & Ball for a really deep, intense black, Black Railings.

When it comes to exterior paints, Joanna Wood thinks that it's hard to find in commercial ranges the colours made by the conservatory-building company Marston & Langinger. 'Their colours are just perfect for the country – they do a fantastic deep yellow that looks lovely in Sussex, whilst they do a green that is perfect for woodwork in the Cotswolds and a bluey-green that looks wonderful against Gloucestershire stonework.'

Since Kelly Hoppen (www.kellyhoppen.com) has now designed a big collection of furniture for BhS (great value), some of the Perfect Neutrals she originally devised for Fired Earth are on sale at BhS stores at very reasonable prices. Her complete range is on sale at her shop at 175–177 Fulham Road, London, or can be bought directly from the manufacturers at www.craigandrose.com.

Commercial ranges, which in reality have to please the mass-market, have to take into account considerations such as durability, which has an impact on the formulations. The upside is that marks are more easily washed off and the paints last longer. The downside is that for many people the colours aren't chalky or subtle enough. The price you pay for the subtler colours from the niche companies, for the chalky effects, for the deeper pigments, is that they will be less easy to clean and that you'll have to repaint more often.

OBJECTIVE SOURCES OF ADVICE:

One of the best is www.paintquality.co.uk, which has useful advice on the different sorts of paints and how to use them. The Dulux website (www.dulux.co.uk) offers lots of advice as well as a service to help you plan the colour scheme for your room. Dulux will also mix up any colour you like (if you take along a example of the colour, they will match it exactly) so you can get as swanky a 'historical' colour as you like for a mass market price.

Wallpaper

If you haven't been asleep you'll know it's back big-time. There are all sorts of niche manufacturers (of which the most famous is at Timorous Beasties at www.timorous beasties.com, which takes the classic toile de jouy formula and suberts it by using gritty urban images instead of the charming rustic scenes traditionally used) but the big three – Cole & Son (www.cole-and-son.com, which had a lot of fun updating and recolouring its traditional flocked papers), Osborne & Little (www.osborneandlittle.com) and Designers' Guild – have all smartened up their acts no end with an immensely rich array for us all to choose from.

However, there two niche players I think it worth drawing to your attention. For real glamour it's hard to beat De Gournay 112 Old Church Street, London SW3 6EP; 020 7352 9988; www.degournay.com, which takes traditional Chinese scenes and hand-paints them almost any colour you'd like. The private dining room in London's Mirabelle restaurant, in Curzon Street, has a wonderful version in silver, black and grey – it's quite stunning. Their wallpaper is very expensive but very special.

Florence Broadhurst was a brilliant Australian designer of wallpapers who was murdered in mysterious, unresolved circumstances back in the late 1970s. Fortunately a couple of passionate admirers, Helen and David Lennie, have bought the archive and are now reissuing the wallpapers. They're brilliantly coloured, flamboyantly decorative and so of the moment that it's amazing to learn they were all designed way back before the 1970s. Find them at Borderline, Unit 12, Third Floor, Chelsea Harbour Design Centre, London SW10 0XE; 020 7823 3567.

Bedrooms and Bedding

I believe the reason that most of us get carried away by hotel bedrooms is twofold. First, unless we're very unlucky in the hotel we choose, the bedrooms are usually rather bigger than our own back home, and second, when we arrive we are greeted with a pristinely ordered space. There are no knickers over the chair, no piles of old newspapers (which, I'm ashamed to say, are usually by the side of my bed); there is nothing gathering dust under the bed; the surfaces are clear, the linen clean and the whole atmosphere, *even* when the decor is dire (it happens), is usually, at the very least, tranquil. That's the element that I think we should aim to reintroduce to our bedrooms back home. Clear the space. If possible (ah me, a dream that, alas, the arrangements of my own dear *schloss* make impossible), make a dressing room where the clothes, the jewellery, the essential bits we all need, can be stored.

A designer friend has a bedroom with a clever device to introduce orderliness: behind the bed itself, which is not against the wall but juts a little way into the room, is a very large screen and behind the screen is the area where clothes are kept, books stored and where all the paraphernalia that contributes to an unrestful atmosphere is hidden from the eye. It works a treat.

Hotels have shown us, too, just how much difference a really large bed can make, something like six feet wide being the minimum for a high-end hotel these days. It may be expensive to start with (and certainly the linen doesn't come cheap either), but a large bed is an investment in marital happiness and good sleep that one realises should – over a lifetime – pay for itself hands down. The Four Seasons hotel group, for instance, had so many requests from guests to buy the beds in which they'd enjoyed such happy nights that it now runs a small sideline making and selling beds. If you're interested, you should ring the London purchasing manager at the Four Seasons Hotel, Jan Hollunder (020 7907 5392), and she'll organise it all (prices are quoted in dollars – from $1,800, excluding VAT).

Biki Oberoi's sumptuous hotels in Rajasthan (Rajvilas, Udaivilas and Vanyavilas) have wonderfully seductive bedrooms. (Some of the decorative objects, most particularly the ornate 'silver' candlesticks used at Rajvilas, are on sale by popular demand and these days many other hotels have followed suit.) Those hotels illustrate the emotional appeal of the ample four-poster, the fluffed-up pillows, the television placed just so, the ethnic touches so that each hotel is anchored in a specific geographical place. But above and beyond all the decorative flourishes, it is the generous space allotted for clothes and bathing that makes the rooms such a joy to inhabit and if we can replicate that at home (not often a possibility, I know), what a difference it makes.

And absolutely key – the thing that even the very best hotels often fall down on – is good lighting. The number of times that one arrives in a so-called five-star luxury hotel and is unable to read in bed far, far outweighs the number of times that one can actually read with pleasure. Think about that when you're planning the bedroom. These days, too, there are miniature lights that allow one partner to read whilst the other dozes off – important for those whose sleep patterns don't coincide.

Guest Rooms

I happen to feel very strongly about these, having had both wonderfully comfortable experiences in friends' houses and also some of the roughest nights ever where my dear hosts clearly haven't the faintest idea of what it is like to sleep in their own spare room. I'm a bit neurotic about this since in my own family there circulates the tales of the aunt whose guest bed was so uncomfortable that it became a family legend – nobody ever went to stay with her twice.

So, first, sleep in the spare room yourself at least once. See what needs doing. Is there good lighting – good enough to read by? Are the curtains (or blind) thick enough to let guests sleep properly? It is warm enough? Airy enough? And, most importantly of all, is the bed comfortable? If it isn't, change it (this is not easy, I know, but John Lewis will take away your old one as they deliver the new one). An extra bit of luxe is a television set – nothing is so spoiling, in my view, as being able to watch the late-night news from one's very own bed. Put an extra blanket across the bed in case the guest needs it if the temperature drops. Have lots of delicious pillows – nothing looks so welcoming as huge square continental pillows encased in crisp white antique pillowcases. See below for more on bedlinen. Don't palm guests off with easy-wash, no-iron polyster – give them really delicious pure cotton. You can buy it inexpensively from Marks & Spencer, Zara or John Lewis. And make sure there is a waste-paper basket.

Little luxuries aren't expensive either – a tin of biscuits, a bowl of fruit, a fluffy white robe, slippers, a hot-water bottle, some really good books, a bottle of water, even (*quel luxe*) a little decanter of whisky.

* If you can't run to enough spare rooms to cater for everybody who wants to come and stay (we now, for instance, have five small grandsons, which means that if they all come together we run out of beds), let me recommend Argos, which does some fantastic foldaway beds at quite astonishingly low prices. Other good solutions are those single beds with a drawer below that pulls out to become a second bed when it's needed.

Linen

And still she slept an azure-lidded sleep
In blanched linen, smooth and lavender'd.

John Keats, 'The Eve of St Agnes'

I am of the opinion that one of life's little luxuries – one that a lot of us can afford – is freshly laundered pure cotton sheets (personally I prefer them to linen). I always remember asking a group of internationally recognised design gurus for their definition of real luxury and Sir Terence Conran came up with 'river-washed linen sheets'. He's not alone. Much of the Western world is getting awfully pernickety about the sheets it sleeps in. Sophisticated shoppers want to know about fibre and threadcounts, not to mention finish and esoteric little niche names.

Some years ago now The White Company (www.thewhitecompany.com) revolutionised the world of bedlinen by offering us a huge variety of pure white cotton bedlinen, some plain, some embroidered. Now a whole host of other companies have climbed on the bandwagon.

Marks & Spencer, for instance, has joined the fray and now gives us pure white cotton bedlinen made from long-staple pina cotton and a threadcount of 400 (see p. 275). I like my bedlinen pure white but with a slightly vintage look (I love some white-on-white embroidery or lace), and I've found some delicious versions at Zara Home (www.zarahome.com). This is a great source of gorgeous inexpensive things for the home but there are, as I write, only three branches: one at 127–131, Regent Street, London W1B 4HT, given over entirely to the home; a home department in the branches at 65 Duke Square, King's Road, London SW3 4L4, and at 79 Brompton Road, London SW3 1DB; and at Bloomingdale's in New York (linen fetishists should make a point of visiting its linen department when in the Big Apple). The French Company (01372 274 771 and at www.thefrenchcompany.co.uk) sells pure white cotton sheets, duvets and pillowcases, some plain, some decorative. So does the French House (0870 901 4547 and at www.thefrenchhouse.net), which deals exclusively in things, er, French and works with small artisans and family firms, bringing back white embroidered sheets that grandmère would have loved.

If nostalgia for Imperial Russia is more your scene, The Volga Linen Company is the place to look. The embroidery is done by women living in a village in the Volga River valley, where they have been working in an unbroken tradition since the eighteenth century. It is made from 100 per cent flax (linen), and prices start at £295 for a single sheet. There's lots to choose from that's plain but the linen with the red hand-embroidered cockerel is much sought after. Check it out online at www.volgalinen.co.uk or telephone 01728 635 020 for a mail order brochure.

The Linen Press goes in for rigorously plain linen sheets made from pure Irish linen – very austere, very beautiful, in white, natural or black (from £110 for a single flat sheet) – and also has lots of other linen temptations (wonderful pyjamas, for instance). Check them out at www.thelinen press.co.uk or telephone 01768 372 777.

For something prettier, Cabbages & Roses (020 7352 7333) takes vintage sheets and hand-prints them with roses – very soft, very charming.

Cologne & Cotton (www.cologneandcotton.com) has a lovely range, mostly white, some plain, some embroidered, some with lace, but also some pale stripes, some checks and a few other colours.

Otherwise never forget the John Lewis group. It doesn't usually have enough variety on the white front for my tastes but it offers wonderful quality and good prices. And still on the high street front, the Linea range at House of Fraser stores is under-recognised. Some of it is lushly beautiful and it comes at very user-friendly prices.

Two insider addresses for linen fetishists

EDITH MEZARD lives in the Château de l'Ange, in Lumières, not far from Avignon (+33 4 9072 3641). It's a favourite shop of both Viscount Linley and Mrs Rupert Hambro and one can see why. Edith Mezard helps her husband run his haulage business in the morning and every afternoon, seven days a week, she opens up her shop. She sells beautiful old linens but also combines old and new textiles to create magic cushion covers, bedspreads, curtains. Almost every piece is different. There is hand-embroidered linen, plus a range of scented soaps, candles and perfume for linen that rejoices in the name of Blanc, which, you may be sure, won't be in everybody else's linen cupboard back home.

CHÂTEAU DE BAGNOLS. If you're in the Beaujolais area, the shop attached to the hotel that Lady Hamlyn lovingly restored but which is now owned by the Von Essen group, sells many of the pieces that Lady Hamlyn commissioned exclusively for the chateau from a vast range of craftsmen, including finely embroidered linen sheets, damask tablecloths and lusciously beautiful towels with a discreet same-colour (white) monogram.

Antique Linen

I've long had a fetish for antique linen, haring off down muddy roads in France at the smallest hint of a sign with the magic word, *brocantes*. What I think I'm going to do with it all, I can't imagine. Be that as it may, I now have several old monogrammed and embroidered sheets that make wonderful tablecloths, hand towels and those heavy linen napkins that nobody seems to produce today. In old French market towns when they have their days selling *antiquités* or *brocantes*, you can still find antique pieces like this for very, very little. In posh antique shops in the UK they cost a fortune. In the Sablon area of Brussels where there are some wonderful second-hand and antique shops, vintage linen for bed and table can often be found at excellent prices.

Jane Sacchi, whose appointment-only business at her house in Chelsea was for years a well-guarded secret amongst fellow linen fetishists, is now reachable by phone or email (020 7351 3160 or at www.janesacchi.com). She always has a supply of the finest monogrammed linen sheets (they also make terrific curtains), bold red-striped ticking, and hand-embroidered towels as well as bedspreads, tablecloths, tea towels and pillowcases, often with the beautiful old monograms still intact. She also has a collection that is dyed a beautiful dusty old blue with the traditional woad or *bleus de pastel*, the dye that in the Middle Ages brought wealth to the towns of Albi and Toulouse. Prices aren't cheap – but then remember linen is almost for ever – with single linen sheets starting at about £115.

I happen also to love The Cloth Store, 290 Portobello Road, London W10 5TE (020 8968 6001), which has an amazing selection of old linen washing-up cloths, old sheets and fabrics of all kinds.

Guinevere, 574–580 King's Road, London SW6 2DY (020 7736 2917 for a brochure or check into www.guinevere.co.uk), always has a mouthwatering selection of antique linen, including those deliciously traditional red and white tea towels and tablecloths. If the prices frighten you off, you can always settle for a little lavender bag, monogrammed (in red).

THE LOW-DOWN ON THREADCOUNTS

Threadcounts: a matter of great importance to the linen fetishist and increasingly cited by hotels to lure in picky customers (Schrager hotels, for instance, specify sheets with threadcounts no lower than 350 and the ones at the Sanderson boast 450).

But there's no need to get too hung up on them. Threadcounts refer to the number of strands in a square inch of sheeting. Generally speaking, the higher the threadcount, the better and finer the sheets. However, most experts seem to agree that whilst the difference between a threadcount of 120 and 250 matters greatly, once you go above 250 you're just showing off.

Besides threadcounts, it's also finish that helps give a

soft and silky feel. Frette, many experts agree, are amongst the finest of the fine (Gordon Campell Gray uses them in his impeccably chic hotels, No. 1 Aldwych and Carlisle Bay in Antigua), and much of the mystique is to do with the finish.

More on the Bedding Front

Silk duvets are a bit of an unknown luxury. Harry Kershaw, a latter-day merchant adventurer, imports from China some amazingly plain and beautiful pure silk duvets – that is, both the covers and the innards are all made entirely of silk, the covers of woven silk, the innards of silk floss. He's rather evangelical about them. To lie in bed under silk, he declares, is to sleep in the utmost luxury. The Eastern nobles (who cannily kept these indulgeness for themselves) valued silk for its softness, warmth and its light weight. Sleeping under silk, they agreed, was rather 'like being wrapped in a soft and delicate cloud'. Its breathability, says Harry, enables it to absorb as much as 30 per cent of its weight in moisture without feeling damp, and this keeps it feeling cool in summer yet warm in winter. It is also a boon to those who are allergic to some forms of bedding, for house mites, the cause of many allergies, do not, it seems, take to silk.

The duvets themselves come in two weights: 9 togs (a

measure of its warmth) and 4½ togs. The idea is that most people would buy two – the 4½ tog for use in the summer, the 9 tog for use in autumn and spring, whilst in winter the two can be tied together (they come with silk ties). Prices range from £90 for a single 4½ tog silk duvet (£110 for a 9 tog version) and go on up to £135 for a Super King 4½ tog (£190 for a 9 tog version). For those who still believe in sheets and blankets, Harry also has some pure silk cream blankets at prices starting at £90 for a single and going up to £160 for a Super King. Check them out at www.silkwoodsilk.com or buy them from branches of Graham & Green (www.grahamandgreen.co.uk).

Ginger Lily (www.gingerlily.co.uk) also sells silk bedlinen as well as silk-filled duvets and pillows.

Bathrooms

I'm not going to talk here about the nitty-gritty of bathrooms: which bath to choose, which basin or which tap. Suffice it to say they can, and should, be glamorous, even in small spaces. One uses them all the time – certainly morning and evening – and they make a huge difference to one's morale. Even small ones can be made seductive if you keep them tidy and add candles, good mirrors (in fact, mirrors are a good way of creating glamour; a fantastic antique one, most particularly in a very modern bathroom, can soup up the look no end), divine soaps and oils. If you're sharing the bathroom, try to have two basins. For busy people, it makes such a difference and cuts out all that business of two of you both trying to clean your teeth at the same time that goes on in the single-basin bathroom.

Babington House (I think) led the way in showing us that baths don't always have to be tucked away in closed-off bathrooms. There's something deeply seductive about a bath set in a wide window as an integral part of the bedroom. By taking away the need for a shut-off bathroom, a lot of space can be released to make the new bedroom-cum-bathroom infinitely airier.

I was never convinced about power showers until we got one. Now I am. It means I can be showered, hair washed, and ready in about seven minutes flat – and I feel the dirt is being rinsed away as I shower instead of my sitting in the middle of it.

Lovely fluffy towels – at least two sizes (one a big bath size and a smaller face size) – are essential and though they're more expensive than mean-sized, cheaper versions, they're not that much more expensive. It's not an economy worth making.

Neither is cheap soap. Fine, creamy, triple-milled soap isn't very much more expensive than tawdry versions and yet it gives such a feeling of luxe in the bathroom. Buy a good make and enjoy it. Let me recommend as an occasional treat (rather than for every day) the wonderful pomegranate soap from the Farmacia di Santa Maria Novella in Walton Street in London and in Florence (for details see p. 177), but closer to home Jo Malone's soaps are beautiful too, as are those from Floris and Crabtree & Evelyn. I'm not a personal fan of those olive oil versions from Marseilles (they're a bit too rough and *artisanale* for my taste), but plain unscented soaps – in particular Simple Soaps, which smell fabulous and are wonderfully moisturising – from Boots are pretty good. Ditto bath oils. We all have different notions of what smells great. I'm currently rather in love with Jo Woods' organic range, which is small, beautifully focussed, smells divine (particularly her Usiku) and is entirely free of chemical nasties. I also love Ren's Moroccan Rose Otto with a passion. The point about bath oils, it seems to me, is that they're fabulous when they're really lovely but not worth having if they're not. Better to stick to water and a good soap if you can't afford something good.

The bathroom is also a great place to burn some delicious scented candles.

Kitchens

You can spend almost £100,000 on a kitchen without even trying (just check out the smart names such as Boffi, Bulthaup and Alternative Plans, with their fantastically seductive modern designs), but why would you? You get all sorts of fancy extras, it is true, like drawers that glide, a million different choices of internal arrangements and posh technical pyrotechnics (doors that fold swishly, extra-wide drawers for storing saucepans, that sort of thing), but let me tell you that my own kitchen comes largely from Ikea. Our builder bought the cabinets (since Ikea make them in their thousands, they can deliver terrific quality at rock-bottom prices) and then customised them to fit our space. We live in an early Victorian house and the ground floor is a big open room – a dining area at the front and kitchen at the back – so the kitchen had to look good (as it can be seen from the dining table) and in keeping with the character of the house. I wanted it to be calm, rather like a cool Victorian larder or pantry, and unflashy. We've got built-in units on either wall that emulate the sort of huge dressers that you might have found in an old pantry and a large window at the back that overlooks lots of gardens. The only slightly luxurious touch is the cooker, which is large (four hobs and a central long hob for a fish kettle plus two ovens). Otherwise we have a standard fridge (I would have loved a vast American-style one in stainless steel or sugar pink but there wasn't room), a dishwasher and lots of storage, as well as some open shelves on which we can display dishes and china. The cornice, edgings and woodwork are painted a very pale grey (Sanderson's Dusky White) whilst the main cupboard doors are painted Beauvais Grey, a shade I love (it is, in fact, a subtle greenish-grey and comes from Papers & Paints at 4 Park Walk, London SW10 0AD; 020 7352 8626; www.papers-paints.co.uk). Our builder added greyish marble working surfaces, a little early Victorian moulding to the cabinet doors and plain white china knobs. I love it and feel happy in it, and yet it cost relatively little.

The kitchen is now ten years old and if I were doing it now I'd probably go more for stainless steel and lots of open shelving but there's something about having a restful kitchen, that isn't too trendy or edgy, that is very soothing as one softens an onion or stirs a sauce with some fabulous music playing all the while. If I had young children still around, I'd arrange things differently again and there would be a big kitchen table and old sofas to sink into, but as it is it does us beautifully.

I love old things such as antique creamy linen kitchen towels with that old-fashioned red stripe running through them. I collect them when I see them at fairs and in antique shops but Guinevere, 574–580 King's Road, London SW6 2DY; 020 7736 2917, always has some (at a price). Another favourite shop for kitcheny things of a nostalgic sort is Summerill & Bishop, 100 Portland Road, Holland Park, London W11 4LQ (020 7221 4566), which sells vintage cutlery, antique linen cloths, old glass cloches, cheese stands, glass and porcelain ware.

Labour and Wait, 18 Cheshire Street, London EC2 6EH and at 020 7729 6253; www.labourandwait.co.uk, has such old-fashioned delights as wooden pencil cases, feather dusters, enamel jugs, ladles, bowls and spoons, natural linen dishtowels, a rope doorstop, a wonderful pocket knife set and many other things that make their shop a splendid trip down memory lane.

Baileys (Baileys by Mail, 01989 561 931; www.baileyshomeandgarden.com) has a very similar ethos – lots of enamelware, proper string, wire food covers, corn brooms, galvanised iron dustbins, vetro china mixing bowls, pumice stone and old-fashioned beech bathmats.

Laundry

There was a time when it looked as if Marigolds were about to become the new Blahniks – i.e. a chic accessory for the yummy mummy set. We haven't quite got there but the realisation has now dawned that there are delicious cleaning materials around and that the nasty chemical varieties (though admittedly very efficient) that smell horribly of artificial compounds are no longer strictly necessary.

BAILEYS (01989 561 931 and at www.baileyshomeandgarden.com) has some delicious-smelling, eco-friendly cleaning materials at very low prices: washing-up liquid, glass cleaner and household polish as well as lavender water for dousing linen.

ECOVER (www.ecover.com) is a new discovery in our household. The range is sold in most supermarkets (including Waitrose) and has a whole raft of ecologically sound cleaning materials. More eco-friendly cleaning things like tea towels and useful gadgets can be found at www.ethicalsuperstore.com.

LONG BARN (01962 777 873 and at www.long-barn.co.uk) is a farm near Winchester that sells delicious little lavender pillows and sachets as well as a lavender pillow spray.

THE LAUNDRESS For serious luxury I'm addicted to products from the USA's www.thelaundress.com. They're expensive but they smell more divine than any others I have come across. All their products have four basic scents: Classic (citrus, ylang-ylang and sandalwood); Baby (vanilla, musk, bergamot and lavender); Cedar (perfect for woollens – cedarwood oil, frankincense, spices and citrus zest); and Lady (amber, citrus and green herbs). Then there are products for whites, darks, baby clothes, linens and cashmeres, as well as conditioners, ironing waters, stain solutions, and two amazing products called Crease Release (spray it on your linens and the creases fall out) and Stiffen Up (as effective as starch but smelling much nicer). Fabric Fresh is a spray for the upholstery that dogs, children, cigarette smoke and the chaos of life have left smelling less than fresh. The Wool and Cashmere Shampoo (sulphate free and smelling of cedar) is what they call the 'hero' product: the one that, once tried, has a permanent place in the laundry cupboard. Prices don't seem to me high for the extra zing that they add to the not very glamorous matter of doing the laundry. They're mostly somewhere between £4.95 and £5.95, but the Wool and Cashmere shampoo is £11.95 and the Signature Detergent (for general laundering) is £14.95.

In the UK you can buy all the Laundress products through www.globalandgorgeous.com and Fortnum & Mason, but do check the website of The Laundress (www.thelaundress.com), on which you can pose your own laundry-related dilemmas to the girls. I posted mine, asking for help in getting red wine stains out of the white tablecloths I love and which our local laundry never seems to deal with (though it is highly skilled at folding the cloths so that you don't notice the stain is still there until you get it home). I sent my email at about 4 p.m. and had a reply by 9 p.m. In case you have the same problem, this is it:

Hello, Lucia,
Ah, the downfall of the fabulous red wine. We wouldn't launch our products until we were able to conquer red wine and yellow armpit stains.

This is my method for red wine.

In a sink or bin pour The Laundress Stain Solution directly onto the wine stain and rinse with HOT water. Repeat, repeat, repeat. The wine first turns gray, then yellowish.

When I get to the yellowish state I launder (with hot water) with our Whites Detergent and pour extra detergent on the remaining spot. Do not put in the dryer if the spot is still visible. Re-wash as the dryer will set in the stain. Successful on my white linen slipcovers, too many times than I'd like.

Happy Laundering!

 To liven up the laundry room, CATH KIDSTON (cathkidston.co.uk) does the cheeriest of covers for the ironing-board and, to save on all that table linen (this is for those who have children or grandchildren), she does wonderfully pretty plastic cloths that you just wipe clean.

Flowers

As I've already remarked, I've often thought that the things that really matter in a house (apart from it being filled with people one loves – the one true necessity) are books, flowers, music, food and wine, none of which need be expensive. Londoners who can muster the energy to get up early can buy huge boxes full of flowers at Nine Elms (the old Covent Garden market) for very, very little – and you don't have to be there *that* early (anything up to 8.30 a.m. is fine). Stores such as John Lewis and Marks & Spencer are getting much better on the taste front, and what I call their 'arrangements' are getting less pretentious and more attractive by the day.

The rules set down by of the old Constance Spry (and, indeed, Kenneth Turner) school of floristry ('Always form a triangle', and 'Never have even numbers of anything' were two unchanging mantras) are mostly outmoded, though the looser, more ephemeral sort of unwritten rules are more difficult to follow.

Remember, you can put flowers into a whole variety of containers that aren't officially labelled vases. Huge glass jugs, or old milk jugs in country houses look wonderful, as do ice-cream bowls, little ceramic holders, coffee cups, tumblers or even old tins – use your imagination.

For those who like rules – and they do, after all, simplify the matter – hang on to this one: if in doubt, never mix your flowers. Just have masses and masses of one thing, the more you can afford the better. Were you to be so misguided as to put some hyacinths with roses, or tulips together with daffodils or – worse – combine tulips with orchids, ooh, goodness, I can feel the shudders now. You can – just to complicate the matter – combine certain flowers (this is where personal eye and taste are everything) but experts such as Nikki Tibbles of Notting Hill's Wild at Heart (222 Westbourne Grove, London W11 2RJ; 020 7727 3095; www.wildatheart.com) say you should then stick with a one or two colour palette, for example whites and lime greens and creams, or pinks and reds, or lilacs and blues.

For somebody who isn't into the artless and romantic, and wants something on the chic side, Nikki Tibbles provides what she calls 'gorgeous wax vases' and for, say, a dinner party, she might suggest planting them down the middle of a table filled with 'a hedge of lilac roses'. The roses should be cut quite short so that the heads are just over the top of the vase and here she gives a useful tip: 'The taller the stem, the fatter the rose head, so you'll need fewer of them.' (As they cost some £2.50 a stem, this is a bit of knowledge well worth having.) Another Nikki Tibbles tip: change the water daily.

At Marston & Langinger's brilliant newly expanded showroom at 192 Ebury Street, London SW1W 8UP (www.marston-and-langinger.com), Simon Lycett looks after all the flowers. If you like a little bit of provenance with your florist, then you'll want to know that he did the flowers for *Four Weddings and a Funeral*, which we all got to have a dekko at, as well as for the wedding of Posh and Becks, which we did not, as well as for Elton John's fiftieth birthday party. Peter and Susan Marston (of the Marston part of the name) are great proponents of simplicity. 'Contorted willow is a big no-no. No weeping willow, either. And no cruelty to plants and certainly no floral bondage. Little wire spikes to hold them together or string that is too tight are another big no-no. Gerberas – no. Carnations – no.' And those once oh-so-chic zinc containers that all the Milanese florists use are very much no, too. No mixtures: 'They come from the petrol station school of floristry.' So what rates a yes? Purple hyacinths – so beautiful that you just stick them in an empty paint tin. A huge moss cushion of massed white crocuses looks great. ('How do you water it?' I asked rather mundanely; 'You sprinkle it,' came the reply – but then practicality, as Peter Marston put it, isn't what flowers are about.) Great big blowsy pale pink peonies are very much yes: 'When the petals drop just let them lie there – they're perfection.' The 'straight from the greenhouse look' is very in – just take things like fritillaries in terracotta pots straight to the table. Little tiny pots of grass, specially wheatgrass, look wonderful, all bright green and neatly clipped.

Ercoli of McQueens, who does the *Vanity Fair* party at the Oscars (126 St John Street, London EC1V 9AN; 020 7251 5505), is also of the simple school of floristry. 'I hate formulas,' he says, 'and I hate mixtures. I just love lots and lots of bulbs and the sense of smell is important – have a great rosemary plant in the kitchen, for instance, or in the bedroom and bathroom have big groups of snowdrops or daffodils. Simple things like leaves and stones look good, too.'

If you have the sort of home that sports cutting-edge B & B Italia furniture, clean minimalist lines, lots of cream, grey and black – you get the picture – then probably Inwater are the people for you. Robert Hornsby, the creative spirit behind the company, doesn't call himself a florist, dearie me, no – he's a flower designer. *Very* different. Nor does he have a shop – he has a 'design space', which readers may visit to buy his advice, containers, plants and flowers, at 70–76 Bell Street, London NW1 6SP (020 7724 9985), while the website at www.inwater.uk.com will give you a good idea of what he does. It was Robert Hornsby who first submerged flowers under water (hence the name). Nowadays this is thought a bit passé, though to be truthful I still sometimes find this ravishing (one of Robert Hornsby's tricks was – and sometimes is – to colour both flower and water with fabric dyes). He likes great big torpedo-style shapes and will sink flowers underwater on stones, or lots of just one flower crammed inside a very clean-cut container. He's also fond of big 'bombs' (perhaps in these nervy days a happier term might be 'domes') of massed roses or arum lilies. He likes to use fluorescent lime-green Perspex underneath a flower arrangement to give it a subliminal glow.

If you'd like somebody to come to your house and give you the interior design perspective on what sort of flower arrangements would work, then Anne Kahn of Anne Khan Flowers, 55 Hatton Garden, London EC1 8HP (020 7404 4048), is your woman. She works a lot with interior decorators, being called in to give a bit of Zen treatment here, something baroque and fanciful over there, and something sweetly boho somewhere else. She can offer a sort of blueprint of which shapes and colours, and which containers, would work best for you.

I think nothing is nicer than country roses, from the garden rather than forced hot-house ones, and you can get them in season, of course, from Country Roses (01206 273 565 and at www.countryroses.co.uk), a flower farm near Colchester.

There you have it: it's not rocket science, just a question of keeping it simple.

How to Make Flowers Last

1. Cut the stems off shop-bought flowers at an angle as you soon as you get them home.

2. Always use a very clean vase.
3. Keep the water clean. A drop of bleach will help keep the water sterilised and so stop the stems from rotting.
4. An ice-cube in the vase helps revive flowers that are wilting.
5. Use the the plant food the florist provides, but if you're cutting your own, add some sugar.

Scented Candles

You may be of the school of thought that hates them. I love them when they're wonderful but when they're bad, they're horrid. I'm unashamedly picky about them and like only the best and most expensive, because I'd rather the house smelled of fresh coffee, fresh flowers and simple honest soap than cheaply scented candles. And just so you know my prejudices, I don't like them sweet and floral either. With a (very) few exceptions I like them spicy, rich, mysterious. I also learned from Jo Malone that you can create something new by burning two at once – amber and lavender, for instance, smell divine when burned together but there are lots of other combinations to try. Valentine Alexander, my make-up guru, always burns Diptyque's Figueur and Menthe Verte at the same time.

So here's my list of great scented candles. It's personal, idiosyncratic and very, very picky.

RIGAUD, the French candles that come in glass containers with a little metal saucer, are for me the all-time winner – subtle, sophisticated, classy. They remind me of those French apartments with an enfilade of elegant rooms, each one lightly perfumed, as well as those grand Park Avenue apartments with dark-red lacquered walls and toffee-varnished floors. Cypres, a light smell of wood and pines, is my favourite but there's also Cendre, Cythère and Tournesol. Find them in chic New York stores such as Bergdorf Goodman, or in little boutiques with taste, or in London at Thomas Goode, 19 South Audley Street, London W1K 2BN; 020 7499 2823; www.thomasgoode.co.uk.

LORENZO VILLORESI is a Florentine (of noble birth – what else?) who seems to spend his days like a mediaeval alchemist, sniffing, stirring and mixing potions and lotions in a Florentine eyrie. His scents are rich, mysterious, sensual and addictive. Rumour has it that they've been known to burn at Balmoral. He makes bespoke perfumes from the finest oils and essences and uses only natural fixes. I like best his Sandalwood and his Spezie but almost all of them are lovely. Best of all, make an appointment to go to his eyrie at 12/14 Via de' Bardi, 50125 in Florence (you'll have to ring first: +39 05 5234 1187) and sniff for yourself. Otherwise Fortnum & Mason (020 7734 8040) and Les Senteurs (71 Elizabeth Street, London W1; 020 7730 2322) stock his wares, as well as rather select boutiques around the world.

DIPTYQUE does gorgeous scents, something like fifty of them.

From Madonna (Figeur and Verveine) and Puff Daddy (Tuberose) to Nigella Lawson (Rose) and Elizabeth Hurley (Figeur), the range has many fans. I don't like them all but I'm mad about a few, most particularly Figeur. Don't be afraid to burn a couple of candles together. You can find Diptyque in many places: Space NK, Liberty and Selfridges.

ORMONDE JAYNE, a delectable little shop in the Royal Arcade, off Old Bond Street (020 7499 1100 and at www.ormondjayne.com), has a small but distinguished and growing cult following. Allegra Hicks is a great fan, as is Anoushka Hempel, who buys her candles in Pink Grapefruit by the fistful. Another customer, who heads up a posh luxury goods company in Old Bond Street, comes in every Saturday morning and buys four of her Green Tea candles (I can't quite make out whether he's got a lot of homes or a single house with a lot of rooms, but we have to hope he's got good fire insurance). Green Tea smells like a smoky Lapsang Souchong, very refined, very delicious, whilst Pink Grapefruit is crisper.

JO MALONE (www.jomalone.co.uk). It still takes a lot to beat her Amber and Sweet Orange scented candle and if you're feeling extravagant at Christmas you could burn a giant-sized one with four wicks. I love her Grapefruit, her Wild Fig and Cassis and her Pomegranate Noir. You can order from 020 7720 0202 and your candles will be delivered on the same day in London, and between two and five days later elsewhere, making them a terrific present. Jo Malone will also send goods abroad.

If you're giving a party it adds to the magic if you burn lots of little candles. Try something like PENHALIGON's miniature candles in fresh, green-smelling Lavandula.

TRUE GRACE (www.truegrace.co.uk). Its candles are made entirely from 100 per cent natural British wax (since petroleum is not a renewable resource) and come packaged in opaque white glass, shaped like a hatbox. They also come with boxes of long matches, handy for lighting candles when the wick has burned down low. As always, I go for the non-sweet end of the spectrum – Fig, Grapefruit or Jasmine Tea but lovers of things floral can find Hyacinth, Moroccan Rose, Tuberose and all the rest.

Remember to trim the wick each time before you light candles. Long wicks flop over and tend to disappear into the molten wax. Scented candles don't, I think, mix well with food, so keep them out of the dining room. And coloured candles (in my view) aren't great – keep them white, cream or black (which is quite sensual somehow).

Decluttering

Most people's response to having too much stuff is to think they need more cupboards. In fact the problem lies in having too much stuff. Get rid of some of it. The hard bit is finding the will to do it. Because nobody is going to die if you leave it for another day, it's awfully tempting to say, oh sod it, it can wait. If you're a sod-it sort of person, there are clutter counsellors (yes, really; even Madonna has been known to call on their services) to help put you right. There is also the more practical breed of person who will order files, stick photographs in albums, arrange your DVDs and get rid of the paper you don't need. It does, unfortunately, involve a bit of decluttering of the bank account but it's probably worth it.

I have a friend who was in such a bad way that she could scarcely find the kettle in the mornings. She'd screwed up the place with belongings, all of which had played some emotional role in her life. She called in Annya Ladakh of Clear Space (020 7233 3138 and at www.clear-space.co.uk), who certainly caused her to shed some tears (she is rather sentimental, my friend; she's had several marriages and many *affaires du coeur* and everything reminded her of somebody), but who also got her sorted.

This kind of service might seem as if it were geared to the idle rich but Annya says it's mostly used by busy professional women who find themselves overwhelmed by conflicting demands. They're just people in a muddle. Some of them were living amidst such clutter that they were ashamed to ask friends home. Annya brings along catalogues from companies such as Cotswold, The Holding Company and Lakeland (Lakeland, in my view, is a hero company, going from strength to strength), all of which have terrific storage systems, and she helps her clients find the right one to store the things that they do need to keep. She charges £50 an hour but needs a minimum of four hours if she's to be of any help.

Sometimes it's just a matter of being shown how to make proper files, when to throw out old chequebooks (it's certainly not worth keeping them for more than five years), or getting help with organising photographs into albums. If you work at home, or are suddenly changing from an office life to a home-based working life, she'll help you set up an efficient home office.

Hire Intelligence (020 8487 9450 and at www.hire intelligence.co.uk) is another organisation offering to help. 'Many people,' said one of its founders (who has now sold the company on), 'just don't seem to know how much paper-work to keep and how much to throw out. We'll come in, look at your files, help work out a proper system for you and then put it all in order. Usually it shouldn't take more than two or three days to sort somebody's paperwork.'

Hire Intelligence staff will declutter a house but they aren't interior designers, so if help is needed in smartening up the house for, say, a sale or just to cheer up its owners, they will call in other experts. They can sort out books, clear garages and attics, and charge £40 an hour (plus VAT) or £270 for a seven-and-a-half-hour day.

Philippa Muggridge of Pro-Organize (020 7378 9460) charges a daily fee of £240 or £35 an hour (but she doesn't do fewer than three hours) and she is a dab hand at paperwork: 'I've cleared out children's playrooms, put all the Lego and the puzzles together and classified their toys. I sort files, tidy up recipe books, sort photograph albums – whatever needs doing.'

The Clutter Clinic (07834 338 568 and at www.clutter clinic.co.uk) will send somebody to sort out your house. An initial consultation is £40, hands-on clearing up is £50 an hour and a six-hour clutter-clearing session can be booked for £275. If you're thinking of selling your house and need help to make it look more ordered, they'll come and do that, too.

If you've got young children or a baby, it's worth knowing about Fara Kids – check it out at www.faracharityshops.org. This is where mothers have a sort of exchange system going where they buy and sell things like high chairs, prams, cots, tricycles and the like. They buy when they need them and sell when they've finished with them. The profits go to a children's orphanage in Romania.

Small Things that Help

1. Try to keep untidiness at bay by doing a little as you go. Once things get really out of hand and a major effort is required, it becomes too dispiriting.
2. If you have children, get some attractive boxes (wicker ones are particularly nice) that fit under shelves. It makes it easy to sweep toys into them in one easy movement.
3. Small baskets or attractive trays and boxes can be used to order cosmetics and jewellery.
4. Jewellery can be stored decoratively. I've seen a wall covered with decorative hooks round which necklaces,

bracelets and the like were draped.

5. If you can keep surfaces clear, it helps to provide an aura of calm.

Do it Yourself

> Life's too precious to spend time searching for things. Dawna Walter

It goes without saying that if you can face sorting your files and office on your own, it'll be a lot cheaper. You could start, though, by buying Dawna Walter's book *Life Laundry: How to De-Junk Your Life* (£8.99) and scouring it for tips. She always maintains that nobody, except the extremely leisured, can afford the time to be disorganised or to have too much clutter. If you can lay your hand on what you need the minute you need it, she believes you can save several hours a week.

MUJI for files and storage. It doesn't have a large selection but what it has is brilliant. There are elegant, transparent boxes of almost every size and shape (great for organising cosmetics, too) as well as transparent files that cost very little.

ARGOS is fabulous for inexpensive storage. If you're really short of space, think about its shoe roller boxes, which are on castors and will hold up to eight pairs of shoes, and which can be slotted away under the bed.

THE HOLDING COMPANY's *raison d'être* is providing storage solutions and it has them to fit almost every aesthetic: steely, baskety, pastel. Telephone 020 8445 2888 for a catalogue or go to www.theholdingcompany.co.uk.

WWW.ORGANISEMYHOME.COM is a wonderful source of storage advice and products, including lots of storage kits.

LAKELAND (01539 488 100 and at www.lakeland.co.uk) and COTSWOLD (www.cotswoldco.com and 01252 391 401), both of which offer lots of inexpensive storage solutions and are recommended by Annya Ladakh.

ANY JUNK: Charity shops will take good things but not chipped china, dodgy clothes, broken toys and bric-a-brac. For a fee, Any Junk will come and take all your discarded junk away. Go to www.anyjunk.co.uk or call 0800 0431 007.

AUCTIONING4U (www.auctioning4u.co.uk and 0870 061 0000) will sell your unwanted things on eBay – for a fee.

SIMPLY SOLD (020 7624 0110 and www.simplysold.co.uk) will sell for you the stuff that isn't good enough for the grown-up auction houses but is too good to take to the tip. They'll value your things and then get their buyers and dealers to get you as good a price as possible.

YOUR LOCAL COUNCIL will often take away unwanted junk for a small fee. Larger branches of many supermarkets, including Sainsbury in the Cromwell Road, have big bins where you can dump your rejected shoes, books, clothing and other cast-offs. For clearing up the mess in your garden, for example, look in the Yellow Pages under removals and you'll find masses of companies ranging from grand outfits to a man with a van.

WWW.UK.FREECYCLE.ORG is the website of an organisation dedicated to recycling or giving away unwanted goods so that they don't go to waste. You can give your own unwanted stuff away as well as find things you may need.

THE BIG YELLOW STORAGE COMPANY (0800 783 4949 and at www.bigyellow.co.uk). And finally, if you're really unable to 'let go' or own, say, family stuff you really shouldn't 'let go', there is always a storage company which will store it for you.

Remember: tidiness matters but only to a degree. It's not more important than having time for your family, playing with your children, cooking lovely meals or reading a good book. Comfort yourself with the fact that it was Le Corbusier, that great rationalist and minimalist, who admitted that order isn't everything: 'Life always has the last word.' Remember, too, the poet Andrew Marvell's words: 'The grave's a fine and private place. But none, I think, do there embrace.' Think of that as you gaze at the mess and you'll feel a whole lot better.

Cheap Chic

Unless you have a feeling for that secret knowledge that modest things can be more beautiful than anything expensive, you will never have style. Andrée Putman

The problem with furnishing on a shoestring is that to do it brilliantly requires immense ingenuity. Take the New York restaurant owner who put hand-sanded acrylic mirror, a quarter of an inch thick, on the floor of his restaurant at a cost of just £4 a square foot – whoever would have thought of that? (In case you're interested, it's available from Industrial Plastic Supply in New York (+1 212 226 2010.) Otherwise it takes time, energy and taste buds that are more than usually alert. Details of all the places listed below can be found on p. 308. Pick up, say, the Next Directory (which I find I'm doing more and more frequently) and, in amongst stuff that you wouldn't give houseroom to, you will find some gems. Pass over the sickly bedding with beaded stars and the faux-naif patchworks, and home in on the slinky bath fittings: fashionably shaped pedestal basins in glass or plain white ceramic at a fraction of the prices to be found in swanky bathroom shops. Check out the chrome fittings – avoid the curlicues and go for the plain shelves and towel holders, and you could save yourself a fortune. Lighting too.

Next Directory won't solve all your lighting problems but it will deal with a few. After a trip to the posh lighting shops and some mental arthmetic I came over all faint. Turn to its lighting section and in amongst some horrors there can be found the simplest uplighter, perfect for landings, for very little. Look out, too, for well-priced bedroom furniture, painted white with simple wooden handles, and some ready-made, plain, tab-headed curtains in simple cottons or silks (www.next.co.uk).

If, like my son and his wife after they bought a farmhouse in the Cévennes, you have to kit out large numbers of beds (at least twelve in their case) in a hurry it's worth looking at the catalogue of the French mail order company, La Redoute (www.laredoute.co.uk). It has plain sheets in pure cotton in a range of mouth-watering colours (including white, pale blue, almond green, chartreuse green, sand and ivory) at absurdly low prices. Whilst Ikea can probably beat its prices, Ikea doesn't do what La Redoute does: take orders by phone and deliver to the door.

Other well-priced lighting comes from Habitat and from BhS (for some reason it has always had a little line in amazing lighting), and Ikea, if you can face the schlep, is good on inexpensive lighting. Ikea is also brilliant on inexpensive shelving, bookcases and the like.

If you're looking for crockery you could scarcely do better than Habitat (it is particularly good in the sales), which has some thankfully plain white and blue china at very good prices. Otherwise go to Leon Jaeggi, supplier to the catering trade, where I've just bought simple white catering crockery (almost childproof) in bulk for the French farmhouse. Churchill (made for the Churchill Hotel) plates start at £1.85, cereal bowls are £2.61, soup bowls, £2.20. Plain wine glasses start at £7.66 a dozen (yes, that's right, a dozen), while Louisiana Rock Glass is £41.04 for thirty-six nine-ounce glasses. And there are all manner of plain white porcelain soufflé and baking dishes at equally beguiling prices. For something a little prettier – some charming pale aqua-green bowls, for instance – Muji is pretty good, too.

For fabrics, there's Ian Mankin – his ginghams start at £3.25 a metre and jolly nice, too, for a farmhouse or a child's room. His classic tickings range in price between £11 and £15 a metre, whilst plain calico (which I've used to great effect to provide covers for some quite grand dining chairs) is £3.80 a metre and heavy canvas (great for curtains and upholstery) is £7.50 a metre. It's much better, when it comes to things like curtains, to be generous with less expensive fabrics (oceans of calico or canvas can look wonderful, and you can add borders to make them look bespoke) than to be mean with expensive ones. Curtains should always trail a bit on to the floor.

Just Fabrics in Burford sells at knock-down prices fabrics which it has tracked down from mills in this country and abroad – lining material starts at £2.95 a metre and there's nothing over £30 a metre. Try to find out when the great annual sale takes place of Colefax & Fowler, Jane Churchill and Manuel Canovas fabric (as well as wallpaper and decorative accessories), because there are great bargains to be had for those interested in the plusher end of the furnishing spectrum.

Otherwise take a day trip to Southall, if you aren't lucky enough to live there, and scour the Indian shops for saris. Now that houses are starting to be softened up again, saris, draped over curtain rings, make ravishingly pretty curtains. (Before I redid our drawing room, which is now curtainless, our curtains were made from twelve white-on-white appliquéd bedspreads bought for £10 each in Udaipur.)

Serious bargain hunters shouldn't leave home without *The Good Deal Directory 2007*. It is a fabulous source of information but you can also check everything out online at www.gooddealdirectory.co.uk. Its editor, Noelle Walsh, just to show what can be done, furnished a whole three-bedroom house in 2004 with nothing but pieces from factory outlets and you can see the result online at www.gooddealhouse.com. The directory is filled with more information than you'll ever be able to use but in particular it gives details of the Marks & Spencer warehouse where excess stock, customers' cancelled orders and the like can all be bought at knock-down prices. But some of its main lines are also very inexpensive – glass at £1 a time, for instance, or good 100 per cent cotton sheets for about £65 for a double duvet. The address for its warehouse is Unit 1, Waltham Hall Industrial Estate, Bambers Green, Essex CM22 6PF (take the right-hand turning at the last roundabout before Stansted airport car park).

If you're tempted by The Conran Shop's offerings but find the prices beyond you, put your name down for the occasional sales held at their Merton warehouse by ringing 020 7559 1140.

In North Yorkshire, old and antique furniture from Holland, China and Poland at very good prices can be found at Simply Dutch, a 20,000-square-foot, warehouse-style shop at Leeming Bar, offering tables, chairs, dressers, sixteen-foot dinosaurs, Mexican chimneys and bronze fountains. At Maison du Monde in London, there's indoor and outdoor furniture from Thailand, Morocco and India: swings, benches, bullock cart seats, mosaic tables and lots, lots more.

Worth checking out: B&Q and MFI for inexpensive but simple, streamlined kitchens. You need a good eye and you also need to know how to customise them – often it's just a question of changing handles and work surfaces. House of Fraser's own Linea home line, though still on the small side, has some quite cool things, particularly in bedlinens, and the prices are good. Try also Debenhams' Designers' line of home accessories (though it is not so good for the bigger things) and dear old Peter Jones, which when I was last in there had a humdinger of a chic charcoal-grey woollen throw for just £29. As previously mentioned, BhS recently launched the Kelly Hoppen range of furniture and it's surprisingly large – proper chests of drawers, chairs and sofas – and very good value.

As I write, what is known as 'brown furniture' is going for

rock-bottom prices. The mood is for the new, the edgy, the avant-garde. It's the loft-living set and the hedge-fund guys who've set the pace and they all want new, new, new. This means that those who like antique furniture can buy it at wonderful prices. Country auctions are a good source of inexpensive pieces. Check the local papers where you live as most areas have an auction house not too far away. Antique shops are obviously good sources if you have a good eye but they take energy and persistence. I love snooping around the Golborne Road in London's North Kensington where there is a whole series of good shops selling inexpensive French country furniture, mirrors, fireplaces and other decorative pieces. I once found four Charlotte Perriand steel and leather chairs for just £400 in a shop in the Golborne Road. (Charlotte Perriand was a wonderful designer and design fundis will know she used to work with Le Corbusier.)

And don't forget the sales. A white basin is a white basin and it's no less desirable because it's being sold off at a cheaper price. I've already mentioned that we always replace our Riedel glasses (rather expensive, beautifully austere, unadorned wine glasses) in the Harrods sale. Soap is another good thing to buy.

When it comes to floors, remember that there's scarcely anything nicer than painted floorboards (even old ones can be renovated with some sanding and the flaws are part of their charm), whilst seagrass matting is relatively inexpensive and very attractive. Instead of Persian rugs or hand-woven silks think of using a rug of seagrass matting edged with a wide border in chocolate (or some other neutral colour).

Cheap collections of things – even chandeliers or furniture – can be given a bit of pizzazz by painting them chalky white. I've seen touristy African masks transformed by painting a group of them in chalky white; they immediately looked intriguing and chic.

* Instead of throwing out furniture because it looks shabby, think of recycling it. Give it new life by painting it matt black or chalky grey-white, or lacquer the surface in deep vermilion, black or scarlet. Sofas or chairs that look old can be given a bit of new life by a great throw, which is much cheaper than reupholstering.

If you're short of money, though, the real pitfall to avoid is buying anything you don't really, really love. I know, I know, sometimes it is unavoidable. I remember well moving into our first London terraced house when we were very poor (we were about to produce a baby and had just taken on what for us was a vast mortgage) and all of a sudden we needed carpeting for four floors plus the stairs, as well as – if I remember correctly – something like twenty-seven light fittings. We bought cord carpeting and Japanese paper lights. They were just about all right but I never liked either much and so, in due course, we replaced the paper lights and the carpeting for something better. In other words the money we first spent was really wasted. If we'd bought slowly one by one things we really loved, we wouldn't have had to replace anything at all.

Common things, everyday things are the most important things. Margaret Visser

If you are short of money, take comfort from the thought that throwing money at the problem doesn't always result in a nicer, more interesting house. On the contrary, very often this can make a house look cold and over-designed, too perfect. Those who are short of money have to make their houses more personal, hunt for bargains, improvise a bit, but this gives character and individuality. And money was never, anyway, any guarantee of taste.

Room Doctors

Just as I'm a fan of personal shoppers – they can winkle out a whole new side of one's personality or show one ways of dressing that one hadn't thought of – so I'm rather a fan of getting professional advice on the interiors front. The thing about professionals is that they do what they do all the time. They've dealt with a million narrow passageways, kitchen-dining rooms or first-floor, L-shaped drawing rooms, and have sussed out how to make them work. Those of us who move house occasionally and have other jobs don't get enough practice at solving the practical problems. Getting it wrong on the interiors front (moving the wrong wall, for instance; making a silly decision about where to put

USEFUL ADDRESSES

The Good Deal Directory – usual cost is £9.99 (plus £2.50 p+p) (01367 860 016).

Ian Mankin, 10G Regent's Park Road, London NW1 8UR (020 7722 0997 and at www.ianmankin.com).

Just Fabrics, Burford Antiques Centre, Cheltenham Road, Burford, Oxon (01993 823 391 and at www.justfabrics.co.uk).

La Redoute (0844 842 2222 or at www.laredoute.co.uk).

Leon Jaeggi & Sons, 77 Shaftesbury Avenue, London W1D 5DU (020 7434 4545).

Maison du Monde, 273–279 The High Street, Acton, London W3 9BT (020 8993 5559 and at www.maisondumonde.com).

Next Directory (0845 600 7000).

Simply Dutch, Darton House, Bedale Road, Leeming Bar, North Yorkshire DL7 9AS (01677 427 800).

the cloakroom or the kitchen; not plotting the lighting scheme soon enough) is a very expensive business. I've never been able to afford the whole pukka expensive interior design service but I have found that buying in bits of expertise pays off hands down.

In the last five years we've been redoing our house floor by floor as it had got very shabby and out of date. Just as we were about to embark on trying to do the drawing room, I heard from a friend about Christopher Prain and Chanond Purananda, who run an interior design service (for details of how to contact them, see below). For a small commission on the expenditure they agreed not only to come up with ideas (which we would obviously have to approve) but – brilliantly – organise it all. I loved their ideas – they had 'got' my slightly boho, eclectic tastes perfectly – and once that was agreed they organised the removal men (because we had to empty the room completely if the builders were to meet the two-week deadline that we'd given them) and the sending of the discarded pieces to Christie's.

They brought to my attention fabrics, furniture and ideas that I hadn't thought of or known about. Chanond suggested a brilliant deep apple-green paint (Moxa from The Paint & Paper Library) for the inside of the bookshelves. I would never, ever have come up with that myself and yet I love it. It's very, very glamorous. They suggested a subtle wallpaper from Knowles & Christou as well its Lulu cabinet with delicately pretty painted glass fronts to house the TV. Everybody falls in love with it. They found an antique iron cot at Alfie's Antiques Market (see p. 86) and filled it with velvet-covered upholstery, which has turned it into a small sofa. Together we trawled Alfie's and found a wonderful 1930s photographer's light and, from Babylon in the Fulham Road (alas, now gone), a nicely shabby French 1930s leather armchair. The other light, by Flos, came from Aram (see p. 312), as did the small Eileen Gray table. The antique Venetian mirror they found at B & T Antiques. They sourced the perfect rugs – one from Christine van der Hurd, which she just happened to have in stock, and one, in deep olive green with delicate purple swirls, which was specially woven in Nepal, from Veedon Fleece. They organised a very beautiful screen, which is printed with fine copies of a hand-engraved map done by John Rocque and published in 1746 (see it on www.motco.com), and it's set into a black-lacquered frame. I think it's wonderful.

Working with professional designers has reaffirmed my belief that not only does it ease the whole burden (they made sure that finishes were right, that builders turned up on time; they helped make decisions about light switches and door handles), *but* even more importantly they widened the scope, offering ideas and solutions that I'd never have had on my own.

Yes, it did cost more than we'd envisaged but on the other hand it is infinitely more exciting than our modest plan would have left it. Given that we hadn't done anything for twenty years, it seems like money well spent.

Christopher Chanond Designs is at 66A Tachbrook Street,

London SWIV 2NA (020 7630 1155 and at www.christopher chanond.com). They will give advice by the hour (£100 an hour) or will do the design work for you but let you find your own builder and project manage it yourself. Alternatively, they can do this on your behalf, in which case they charge 10 per cent of the cost of the project. If they just source suitable items, they take a small handling charge on the furniture and goods they buy, but this is at trade cost and they don't charge the customer the full retail price so there's always a saving for the clients.

You can also get design advice from Laura Ashley (whose home collection is filled with little gems in my view – they're not avant-garde or edgy but they are charming and very usable).

Most kitchen companies will design kitchens for no charge.

Alfie's Antique Market, 13–25 Church Street, London NW8 8DT (020 7233 6066 and at www.alfiesantiques.com) and its sister market, Gray's, 58 Davies Street, London WIK 5A8 (020 7629 7304 and at www.graysantiques.com), both have personal shoppers to help track down the things you'd like. Since, I feel, it has some of the best selection of charming, decorative antiques in London (particularly if you're looking for a suitably shabby armchair or a stunning light), this could be well worth doing. It's by appointment only – telephone 020 7725 9601.

Favourite Shops

Here is a list of my favourite shops, the ones I snoop around when in need of something new or just to be inspired. I have to apologise for the fact that most of them are in London but that is where I live and so it's the place I know best. Several have websites, though, so you can access their products wherever you are.

Cutting Edge and Contemporary

ARAM, 110 Drury Lane, London WC2B 5SG (020 7240 3933 and at www.aram.co.uk). The place for the grand twentieth-century classics – Shiro Kuramata, Eileen Gray (whom Zeev Aram rediscovered and for which Aram is the official licensee), Breuer and many more, but there are lots of funky, avant-garde pieces as well.

MINT, 70 Wigmore Street, London W1U 2SF (020 7224 4406 and at www.mintshop.co.uk). This is tiny but is on every design aficionado's list of regular places to drop into. You might find some delicate handmade ceramics from an innovative new designer, some glorious rococo transparent resin mirrors, a mad chandelier, some papier-mâché Chinese urns or some classic French pottery, not to mention Maarten Baas's wonderfully edgy smoked furniture. (His technique is to take existing pieces and 'burn' them – yes, really – and lest you think this is a joke let me tell you that the renowned Li Edelkoort got him to burn her grand piano.)

SCP, 135–139 Curtain Road, London EC2 3BX (020 7739 1869 and at www.scp.co.uk). It's a trek to get there (though there is the website) but on the plus side you get a bird's-eye view of a great deal of contemporary design in this huge warehouse-cum-shop. SCP not only manufactures pieces by the new generation of British designers such as Matthew Hilton, Jasper Morrison and Terence Woodgate, but mixes in mid-twentieth-century classics by Eames, Eileen Gray and Verner Panton. Lots of small classics, too – Carl Rotter glasses, William Wagenfeld's see-through teapot, Alessi and the like.

THE CONRAN SHOP, Michelin House, 81 Fulham Road, London SW3 6RD (0207 589 7401 and at www.conranshop.co.uk). The first stop for those checking out what's latest, new and hot. It's expensive but keeps one up to speed. The mix has been livened up in recent times with some vintage finds – a Victorian shirt cabinet from an old shop, French farmhouse tables – placed next to a wildly cutting-edge glass table with curvy scarlet legs. Great for presents: toys for the boys, gadgets, tableware, design books, delicious smellies and food.

TWENTYTWENTYONE, 274 Upper Street, London N1 2UA and 18c River Street, London EC1R (020 7288 1996 and at www.twentytwentyone.com). *The* shops for fine re-editions of the great twentieth-century classics – Breuer's Wassily chair, the Barcelona, Le Grand Confort, the Corbusier chaise-longue, Eileen Gray *et al.* But also lots of fun small things from watches to lighting to kitchenware.

More Gallery than Shop

DAVID GILL, 60 Fulham Road, London SW3 6HH (020 7589 5946) and 2 Loughborough Street, London SE11 5RP (020 7793 1100). Gill is part shopkeeper, part gallery owner, part collector and curator. He specialises in twentieth-century decorative objects and mixes grand classic designs with very avant-garde work by our finest artists and craftsmen. He's been responsible for introducing a host of designers to the British – from Garouste and Bonetti (when they were a working partnership) to Oriel Harwood. Very expensive but absolutely fascinating.

EGG, 36–37 Kinnerton Street, London SW1X 8ES (020 7235 9315). Run by Maureen Doherty, a former assistant to Issey Miyake who is credited with having an eye that is amongst the best and most fastidious in London. She mainly sells clothes but in an adjoining gallery there's usually a small exhibition of wonderfully refined and elegant work by one or other of the ceramicists, silversmiths or other fine craftspeople that Maureen has unearthed. When you know that this is a shop that Giorgio Armani, Donna Karan, Ralph Lauren, Yohjo Yamamoto and others of their ilk always keep an eye on, you can see why it is worth a visit.

FLOW, 1–5 Needham Road, London W11 2RP (020 7243 0782). Up in the wilder reaches of Notting Hill, this gallery has avant-garde jewellery (perhaps some roses made from felt or strange bits of cut glass), toys from African craft co-operatives, limited edition prints and small decorative objects such as vases or sculptures. Always worth looking in on.

OGGETTI, 135 Fulham Road, London SW3 6RT (020 7581 8088). The nearest thing that London has to New York's Murray Moss in that Oggetti specialises in great design from almost any era. You will find Carl Rotter glasses next to beautiful wooden toys from Switzerland, a great leather-encased tape measure next to some exquisite Alvar Aalto glass. No furniture – more the smaller things that tell the world you know your 'design'.

RABIH HAGE, 69–71 Sloane Avenue, London SW3 3DH (020 7823 8288 and at www.rabih-hage.com). The place to see radical design. There's always a fascinating exhibition – the last one was on recycled furniture, whilst others have homed in on weirdly beautiful lights by Gaetano Pesce that look more like invertebrates than lamps. Hage has a fine eye and it is the place for really original pieces.

THEMES & VARIATIONS, 231 Westbourne Grove, London W11 25E (020 7727 5531 and at www.themesandvariations.com). A large and airy gallery-cum-shop with lights-cum-sculpture and pieces by Fornasetti. In all an eclectic mix of original, beautiful things that are halfway between functional items and art.

VESSEL, 114 Kensington Park Road, London W11 2PW (020 7727 8001 and at www.vesselgallery.com). This has very innovative ceramics, featuring designs by Hella Jongerius, Ted Muehling, Marcel Wanders and other darlings of the avant-garde design world. Always beautiful, always interesting.

WILLER, 12 Holland Street, London W8 4LT (020 7937 3518). Run by Rebecca Willer, a woman of enormous taste and design erudition. A small shop, specialising in selling exquisite accessories – Sabattini's re-editions of great classic designs, such as Charles Rennie Mackintosh's striking silver candlesticks or his fantastic Willow bowl, glass by Massimo Micheluzzi, Han Dynasty cocoon jars. Also some small pieces of furniture, such as Paul Kjaerholm and Noguchi stools.

Quirky Specialists

ABIGAIL AHERNE, 137 Upper Street, Islington, London N1 1QP (020 7354 8181). A delicious shop whose owner just seems to buy what takes her fancy. Her style is what you might call boho–eclectic: flocked anglepoise lights, gorgeous rugs, quirky accessories.

AFTER NOAH, shops at 261 King's Road, London SW3 5EL (020 7351 2610), and 121 Upper Street, London N1 1QP (020 7359 4281 and at www.afternoah.com). A good source of old classics, from old American hospital furniture to classic lights. Usually lots of anglepoise lights, old enamelware, school desks, Shaker-style children's chairs, old cupboards –

what is commonly known as eclectic but great for a good rummage.

B & T ANTIQUES, 47 Ledbury Road, London W11 2AA (020 7229 7001). Glamour is the name of the game here – Venetian and Art Deco mirrors, plus other authentic pieces, some mirrored, some not, from the Art Deco period. Bernadette Lewis, who runs it, has a good feel for diverting pieces that could make a modern interior and you might find a steel chair from a French factory sitting side by side with a sleek 1920s desk.

NICOLE FARHI LIVING, 17 Clifford Street, London W15 2VE (020 7494 9051). If you can't get to the Paris flea markets, Nicole Farhi does it for you – at a price. A wonderfully enchanting mix of French flea market finds: worn leather chairs, library steps, eglomise glass-topped tables, exquisite ceramics, deliciously scented candles, huge glass bell jars and anything else that takes the very clever eye of the buyer.

LABOUR AND WAIT, 18 Cheshire Street, London E2 6EH (020 7729 6253 and at www.labourandwait.co.uk). A cult shop that goes in for sturdy brooms and brushes, enamelware, tinware, all the old-fashioned household equipment that our grandmothers were supposed to have used, brown paper, sturdy string and rope, old-fashioned glass.

STORY, 4 Wilkes Street, London, E1 6QE (020 7377 0313). Ann Shore is one of the most stylish people I know and her shop is filled with whatever happens to have taken her fancy recently. But you can be certain of one thing: it will be unbelievably cool and stylish.

Great for Antiques

GUINEVERE ANTIQUES, 574–580 King's Road, London SW6 2DY (020 7736 2917 and at www.guinevere.co.uk). One of the most beautiful antique shops in London – but *very* expensive. Beautiful old Tang clay figures, fine old French linen, antique silver, crystal glasses. Whatever is beautiful, whether from China, French provincial chateaux, Italian villas and palazzos or the grand old houses of England, the Guinevere buyers pick out the very best.

JUDY GREENWOOD, 657–659 Fulham Road, London SW6 5PY (020 7736 6037 and at www.judygreenwoodantiques.co.uk). She specialises in French provincial charm, laid on thick. For anything from a magic little chandelier or a range of old enamel kitchen tins to a great big kitchen dresser.

Department Store

LIBERTY, Regent Street, London W1B 5TR (020 7734 1234). A wonderfully eclectic collection of furniture with some fine old vintage pieces – some very old (an amazingly shabby eighteenth-century chair, for instance), some mid-twentieth-century classics and some spanking new and exciting modern pieces, such as the very experimental work of the newly launched co-operative Established and Sons. Liberty also has the only outlet in the UK for the designs of Svensk Tenn, the famous Swedish purveyors of Josef Franck's vibrant fabrics and small pieces of furniture.

America

CRATE & BARREL (www.crateandbarrel.com), I always look in on this website, which has a high standard of design, fantastically desirable pieces and lots of small things such as china, candlesticks, glass and so on to bring home.

POTTERY BARN (www.potterybarn.com), brilliant for a vast range of inexpensive cutlery in every mood and style, as well as inexpensive huge plain white heavy linen catering tablecloths, candlesticks and linen.

WILLIAMS SONOMA (www.williams-sonoma.com), the best cook's shop in the world.

All three of these shops have branches all over the States. Bloomingdale's linen department, as I've already pointed out, is a joy. After that I head down to SoHo where Murray Moss's eponymous emporium, at 150 Greene Street, is a design Mecca (www.mossonline.com) and where in the surrounding streets there are always new funky, design-led stores to check out.

Paris

Paris is no longer as cheap as it was, but if you're furnishing from scratch or just looking for a few very decorative pieces, it's fun to go and do it there. Go on a Friday (many shops in Paris are closed on Mondays), stay in a small left-bank hotel (saving your euros for the temptations that lie ahead) and then plan your days like a military campaign.

Keep a day for the left bank and a wander around the rue Jacob and the place St Sulpice, another day for the Marais, and at least a morning for the great unmissable treat of a good rummage around the flea market at the Porte de Clignancourt.

The Left Bank

MODÉNATURE, 3 rue Jacob, Paris 75006. Modénature sells calm and simple modern furniture that treads an attractive path between the monastically plain and the highly decorative – in other words it is eminently usable and fits as easily and beautifully into the country drawing room as the dockside loft. All the furniture is designed by the interior architect Henry Becq and is made mainly out of poplar or ash, which he either leaves natural or tints black or white. It's the place to go for clean-lined bookcases, elegant tables, simple and comfortable chairs and sofas, as well as a range of cream or white pottery, bowls and lamps, and some wonderfully comfortable and clean-lined leather chairs.

BLANC D'IVOIRE, 104 rue du Bac, Paris 75007. It's featured in every French design magazine and is chock full of Gallic charm – more *bastide* than *château*. Think Provence rather than the Loire. This is the place for romantic home furnishings in a modern mood – gauzy tablecloths and bedspreads made from hand-embroidered organdie, cream and beige quilted bedspreads, steel-grey silk cushions, simple lamps of wood or metal, clean-lined bedside tables in ebonised wood and a host of props that are easy enough to take home. Look for cushions in quilted cream or white as well as some gentle, faded florals and some quilts in velvet or satin that reflect the new glamour coming into the modish interior. It's the place, too, for subtly aged armoires, or handsome refectory tables. The props, in other words, for the life we wish we had.

MICHÈLE ARAGON, 21 rue Jacob, Paris 75006. Michèle Aragon's shop could come straight out of a classic old French movie. Here are all the ingredients for *la vie du château*, from antique red and white linen cloths, monogrammed sheets and tablecloths, sweetly floral quilts to old green majolica, crystal glasses and anything else that a grand chatelaine might no longer have a need for. It's a wonderful place to rummage in and the stock is different every time you visit, but what is constant is the taste behind it all – the eye that loves the old, the finely worked, that goes for a certain sort of sophisticated rustic Gallic charm. Allow plenty of time to browse.

Also in the area and not to be missed: OLARIO at 30 rue Jacob for pretty French accessories including the wonderful delicate cream tableware made by Astier de Villatte. CATHERINE MEMMI (very austere, impeccably refined and very expensive furniture, linens and a small range of clothing) at 32/34 rue Saint Sulpice, and MAISON DE FAMILLE (huge glass lanterns, inexpensive glass, great welcoming dining tables, side tables and characterful lamps) at 29 rue Saint Sulpice. CHRISTIAN LIAIGRE, 61 rue de Varenne, the undisputed leader of the minimalist set – lots of dark, streamlined furniture with not a decorative twirl in sight. JULIE PRISCA, at 46 rue du Bac, has bleached oak and ebonised tables, white linen-covered sofas, and lots of metalwork (chairs, mirrors, accessories) as well as lacquerware and a host of desirable small objects. Don't forget MURIEL GRATEAU, 37 rue de Beaune, Paris 75007. Design fundis around the world make little pilgrimages to Muriel Grateau where they find delicious ceramics, table linens, cutlery, glass and what she calls 'the things that are personal and so close to the user – all the little things that finish off the look of an interior'. Catherine Deneuve and Calvin Klein are both said to be fans. As a matter of interest she has also moved into jewellery now, which is fabulously strong and sculptural.

The Marais

CARAVANE, 6 rue Pavée, Paris 75004. Founded by one of Paris's best-known interior stylists, Françoise Dorget, who used to be the stylistic spirit behind Etamine, the wallpaper and fabric house, Caravane offers a beguiling mix of things new and old – the sort of exotic collection a sophisticated, travelled voyager might collect. It has a big North African (particularly Moroccan) influence tempered by a northern refinement – a sort of Ali Baba meets loft-style living.

VILLA MARAIS, 40 rue des Francs-Bourgeois, Paris 75003. Very quirky indeed with a mix of the contemporary (mostly of the kitsch variety) and the antique – it's called eclectic. Chandeliers vulgar enough to boggle the eye jostle side by side with delicate Fortuny lights; a wonderfully decorated old German antique chest sits beside a deep lacquered cupboard from China. It's a good place to browse for the strange, the unorthodox, the one-off present. Also in the area and not to be missed: Village Saint-Paul is much closer to the centre of Paris than the flea markets of Clignancourt and consists of a cluster of antique shops grouped in a haphazard way round the old streets and courtyards off the rue Saint-Paul and the rue Charlemagne. There are both inexpensive *brocantes* (the less expensive, junkier end of the market) and pukka *antiquaires* (expensive objects of some intrinsic worth), all of which provide inexpensive entertainment even if they don't always deliver up the unmissable bargain.

How to Do the Paris Puces

On Fridays the market is reserved for official dealers, and Saturdays and Sundays are for amateur trawlers like us. There's no need to get there too early. Dress for comfort, take cash if you can for the smaller things (though most stalls do take credit cards) and get on the Metro to Porte de Clignancourt. There are easily spotted kiosks where you can get maps of the market place. Give the cheap market stalls a miss and head straight for the rue des Rosiers.

The market you want first, if you're after charming pieces of furniture and accessories for the house and garden, is Marché Paul Bert and the things to look out for are wonderful old fireplaces, painted provincial furniture, old armoires, mirrors, chandeliers (there's something about French ones that gives a bit of oomph to almost any interior), bits and pieces of architectural salvage (particularly good for those with large gardens), old lights, and a hundred and one other things to perk up a room. If you're looking for a dining table, the Marché Paul Bert is a good place to find one of those charming old fruit-wood farmhouse tables or something originally made for the garden or conservatory in wrought iron and marble.

The Marché Vernaison is filled with mostly rather smaller stands, all specialising in something, whether it be pictures, tapestries, faded toile de jouy or military memorabilia. Linen fetishists should home in on Janine Giovannoni, Stand 141, at the corner of Allées 3 and 7, who has a cache of the sort of linen one wishes one's grandmother had kept. Serpette has biggish furniture, including a stand selling a vast quantity of leather chairs.

Go to Marché Biron for good solid bourgeois furniture, if that's your taste – great big ornate sideboards and highly embellished chests, as well as tapestries that would suit an ancestral wall.

Scouring these three markets can be done in a day and all still seem to have plenty of those beguiling French pieces that are such an essential part of the Notting Hill boho or the pale French provincial look. Just don't be too disappointed by the prices – bargains are thin on the ground.

How do you get it all home? *Pas de problème.* Hedley's Humpers, right on the rue de Rosiers in the Marché Paul Bert, will ship it for you.

Have a steaming cup of coffee and a good croissant at the Petit Landais at 96 rue de Rosiers and a big bowl of mussels for lunch at Le Petit Navire, on the corner of the rue Paul Bert and rue de Rosiers.

But a word of warning: shopping in the Marché aux Puces is still fun, and you can still find charming decorative pieces, but cheap it isn't.

A FEW GOOD WEBSITES

www.fabulousandfrench.co.uk offers all the main ingredients of the French provincial look.

www.thefrenchhouse.net has a very small range of furniture but a large range of enchanting French accessories, from linens to cutlery and garden furniture.

www.hiddenart.com has lots of craft-made items – everything from glass to small tables, cushions or bowls.

www.europebynet.com and **www.intirium.com** both sell good modern furniture at good prices. For some inexplicable reason the very same design by the same manufacturer is much cheaper in Europe than it is in the UK. Both of these sites ship to the UK.

The Great Outdoors

I'm no horticulturist. I've spent all my life living in cities and, if I'm not in a city, I try to go to wild, uncultivated wildernesses. Spending hours a week, let alone half a lifetime, in the cold, damp outdoors bent over flowerbeds, as serious garden-lovers do, is not my idea of a good time. *But* I do have two tiny bits of outdoor space: a pocket handkerchief of a garden at the back of the house and a minute roof terrace high up at the back of the house.

They are both a lesson in how to conjure up a little bit of magic in a very small space. Stephen Woodhams (s.woodhams @btinternet.com), who has now left his company (Woodhams Landscape Limited; 020 8964 9818; www.woodhams.co.uk) and set up on his own, designed both of them for me.

Personally, I think there are two approaches to having a small space and I've seen both work beautifully. One is to make it a wild, mad, overgrown plot, the walls suffused with climbing roses, clematis, jasmine, ivy and any other plant you can force upwards and sideways. The ground is then covered with pots and urns, each sprouting its own glorious assortment of blooms, to create a wonderfully romantic, flower-filled garden. Add some rustic curvy wrought-iron furniture for eating out of doors and you might feel as if you're in a country garden dell. I've known several hugely successful very small London gardens that have brought off this look brilliantly.

The other approach – the one Stephen produced for us

for our little patch – is more architectural and relies on some theatrical panache. Our backgarden sports just four huge (and I mean *huge*) white flowerpots – they must be about six feet high and about three and a half feet wide; we had to hire a crane to swing them over the roof. They give the garden a touch of magic that nothing small and pint-sized could ever have given it. (In white fibreglass, they cost £355 a time, plus delivery.) One has a giant yucca that we'd nurtured for years indoors and is now thriving outdoors. The other three, the ones visible from the kitchen window, each have a large bay tree in the centre, which is underplanted according to the season: bulbs in winter to bring us pleasure in the spring, busy lizzies in one colour (pure white one year, deep pink another) in the summer. If we wanted to be really trendy we could underplant with lettuces or cabbages – all tightly packed – as Stephen did for one of his exhibitions last year. The upkeep is minimal, which suits us just fine. He gave us lighting inset into the steps leading to the basement and in the pots themselves, so at night the uplighters illuminate the trees – magic. I found a beautifully sturdy and plain rectangular table and chairs from Habitat that were very inexpensive and are a perfect soft greyish-greenish colour that blends in beautifully with the soft greys of the English sky. And that's it.

Up on our tiny roof garden, Stephen's vision was to take what he (truthfully) called a 'nothing area' and make it magical. He wanted to maximise the planting and yet take up minimal floor space. He had to be careful with the weight on the roof (we've 'done' burst pipes; we don't want to 'do' collapsed roofs), so he decided that one of the two huge planters that he planned would be made to measure to fill in a strange oblong gap along one side wall where a protrusion in the wall below could take most of the weight. The other planter was also made to measure to fit a space between the railing and the stairs and it, too, was to be bolted to the wall to take the weight off the roof.

The bigger of the two planters has something like a metre's worth of planting, whilst the smaller has about three-quarters of a metre's worth. 'Most people,' says Stephen, 'make the mistake of having planters that are too small and then they're surprised that their plants die. If you want big lush plants you need big lush planters.' Ours are each nearly three feet deep, with one third of the depth taken up with drainage (using clay granules) and two-thirds with lightweight compost.

The planters are painted battleship grey, which, according to Stephen, is a great background for plants and which gives the terrace a suitably urban, slightly hip, industrial feel. They're stuffed with plants, devised to give a mixture of seasonal effects, and they both look glorious already. Two of the climbers are evergreen (*Garrya elliptica* will have silvery grey catkins come the winter and it's next to a trachelospermum that has heavenly, sweet-scented flowers from May through to September). There are purple thistles, a vigorous *Solanum jasminoides* (which will give lots of white flowers from June until September), an olive tree, some wonderful silvery-grey grasses, a fantastic Chinese bamboo, and lots of other things with long botanical names. We both decided it would be nice to plant a clematis – one very pale blue, one deep burgundy – at the outer end of each planter so that they could, in time, cover the railings.

At the edge of the front of the terrace are three huge, oversized, cylindrical, lightweight, galvanised-steel containers topped with balls of boxwood topiary. As Stephen put it, 'You need something over-scaled, architectural, gutsy and sculptural – after all, you're in Kensington, not suburbia.' He was right. They're splendid.

Once again lighting makes the garden wonderful on a summer night. 'It's not Blackpool,' said Stephen, 'you don't want floodlights, just something gentle and magical.' There's an extra plug so that one can read up there at night if one feels like it. The irrigation system is completely automatic and computerised so that we can go away for weeks (we should be so lucky) and not come back to horticultural devastation.

I dithered about the furniture, being temporarily beguiled by the Provençal charm of Grange's wrought-iron *lit de repos*: I had had visions of lounging about reading novels on it but it didn't suit the persona that the terrace had acquired, which needed something sleek and urban. So what we have now is a couple of black Verner Panton moulded resin chairs and a small stool as a table – the space is *very* small.

Our terrace must be like thousands of others that lie at the back of urban terraced houses – at about twelve feet by eight feet it is probably smaller than most – but it has amazed me to discover that such a small patch can give so much joy. Even the vista from the stairs gives pleasure. On a summer evening we can sit up there, enjoying the cool breeze and the view of what Stephen Woodhams calls 'the borrowed landscape' (all the other trees and gardens belonging to others).

Some Favourite Addresses

NINE ELMS market is a brilliant place to look for urns, pots, windowboxes and vases, at amazingly good prices and with lots of choice. Not to mention plants and flowers, of course.

LE PRINCE JARDINIER, 37 rue de Valois, Paris 75001, has some deliciously old-fashioned, traditional gardening implements, including watering cans, beautiful little tags for the garden, wonderful aprons and the like.

R. K. ALLISTON (www.rkalliston.com) has lovely classic planters, pots, string, pruning scissors, hand cream, candles and all those traditional gardening things.

MARSTON & LANGINGER, 192 Ebury Street, London SW1W 8UP and at www.marston-and-langinger.com, is quite simply a delightful shop, filled with really pretty charming things, not just for gardens but also for conservatories, patios and roof terraces. There are lovely pressed-glass plates and sundae dishes, as well as candles, flowers and wrought-iron planters. Also dramatic hurricane lamps and candle-holders for that indispensable aid to magic out of doors – candles.

SARAH RAVEN'S CUTTING GARDEN (www.thecuttinggarden.com) has become a bit of a cult source for all sorts of gardening delights, mostly for serious horticulturalists but it's also a great place for gardening presents. She sells parasols and thick cotton rag rugs as well as those old-fashioned gardeny and picnicky things that are hard to find – enamel bowls, weighted tablecloths, glass wasp traps, tin jugs, flower arranging and gardening gloves.

FRANCES HILARY'S HORTICULTURAL GIFTS BY POST (0870 120 2299 and at www.franceshilary.com) sells hammocks, night lights, garden trugs and all the appurtenances the well-appointed gardener needs.

WWW.CROCUS.CO.UK delivers plants for pots, windowboxes or indoors and has a huge variety at great prices.

WWW.GREENINTERIORS.CO.UK has some chic steel-grey cylindrical fibreglass containers – very urban, very sleek.

WWW.HENANDHAMMOCK.CO.UK is the website for those who hate waste. It sells planters (actually rather wonderful) made from recycled tyres, glass lanterns made in Vietnam from recycled glass, and teak furniture made from recycled teak, as well as an extremely chic panama hat made, as all the best ones are, in Ecuador.

THE CONRAN SHOP (www.theconranshop.co.uk) sells the

world's most delightful sunshade – a fantastically pretty green (or cream) leafy, lacy parasol topped by a little bird – that is the brainchild of that wonderful Dutch design collective called Droog.

Food glorious food

Eating Well

Have the courage to serve the most homely dish provided it is perfect of its kind. Edouard de Pomiane

I see no point in eating bad food. It gives no pleasure, no proper nutrition and makes you fat. I love eating. I love wine. And real, proper food lies at the heart of one's domestic and social life. To sit at a table filled with friends and family, all enjoying the food I've provided and some decent wine, is one of life's great pleasures and – think about it – it doesn't, on the scale of things, cost a fortune.

Families that sit around tables enjoying Sunday lunches and evening suppers that have been properly (by which I don't mean elaborately) cooked and served tend to be closer and warmer than those who sit perched in front of the television set with fast food or take-aways, not talking, not communicating. Families gathered round a table build up memories of intimacy and warmth that last throughout one's life. My children still remember the change in our eating habits when, after a small induction into the French way of life (via a holiday at the Club Mediterranée), I decided we, too, would eat with our children in the evening instead of giving them early supper and then having dinner by ourselves later. They remember that the food was revolutionised (for a few heady months we had a wonderful girl from Avignon doing the cooking) and the end of the day was transformed as they spent some real time with their parents. They have each decided in their turn to do it with their own children as soon as they are old enough. Did you know that some 20 per cent of homes in this country don't have a table at which the whole family can sit and eat, and that one in five families never eats together? This seems to me deeply sad and something that over the years must wear away at the fabric of family life.

It's over dinner and lunch tables that all over the world we entertain our friends. By indulging in that age-old ritual of breaking bread together and drinking wine, we bond as families, as friends. So I have no truck with people who go to no trouble at all. I understand that we're busy and some of us are busier than others but it's never been easier to serve decent food with less trouble. I do know that cooking does take a certain amount of time. As a seriously distinguished writer put it to me one day, 'The thing is that when you're cooking there are all sorts of other things you're *not* doing.' In other words, it's not that cooking isn't pleasurable – it is, immensely – *but* if you've got a deadline to deliver, an operation to perform or a brief to master, you can't cook at the same time. *So* this chapter is not for those of you who are expert cooks and love nothing more than setting to in the kitchen. It's for those like me who love good food, don't want to eat rubbish and want to see their friends and families, but don't have the sort of time they'd like in which to do it all.

For just as Shirley Conran always claimed that life was

too short to stuff a mushroom, I think that life is too short to eat junk or to serve up lousy food. Anyway, these days there's no excuse. Waitrose's Ocado (www.ocado.com) is a wonder of the Western world. Marks & Spencer deserves a halo for the difference it's made to the working woman's life. Good meat, fish, fruit and vegetables can be bought online. Farmers' markets take fresh, gutsy and homemade food to almost every corner of Britain, even to central London, and bring to the experience of shopping in person something of the élan we all learned to admire in the French.

I grew up in South Africa at a time when food, in spite of the amazing quality of the natural ingredients, was mostly what you might call abysmal. It was Elizabeth David's sensuous prose that awoke in me a love of food, not to mention a deep desire to live in France. If you belong to the younger generation and haven't read her books, it's time you did. One heavenly summer in France my perception of food, of its cultural and geographical roots, of its life-giving daily pleasures, was awakened. We'd taken a villa in La Baule in Brittany, and with a three-year-old in one hand and a new baby in the other, and Elizabeth David's paperback *French Provincial Cooking* by my side, I embarked on a culinary educational journey. As the children slept in the searing afternoon heat, I would read Elizabeth David under the shady trees. By the time they awoke I knew what I was going to cook and we'd head for the butcher, the fishmonger, the market. Every day I made a different dish. One day it was pork chops spiked with juniper berries baked in stock or white wine between layers of onions and potatoes. On another it was paupiettes de veau or a richly aromatic boeuf en daube. I learned that a simple omelette properly done, a green salad, some cheese and a piece of perfectly ripe fruit are better than many a formulaic fancy restaurant meal. Elizabeth David was also fanatical about eating seasonally. That way the food had real flavour, the fruit was properly ripe and nothing needed complicated treatment.

Some of that sounds a bit old-fashioned, now that so many of us have so little time, but though many of her dishes take a long time to cook they don't take much time to prepare. Take a classic braised rolled loin of veal. If you've bought it from a good butcher, all you need to do is to soften an onion, a carrot, some leeks, if you can be bothered, will help, brown the veal all over, add white wine and herbs, bung it in a slow oven for two to three hours and there you have the basis of a delicious meal. I'm rather a fan of petits pois (and I even like the French tinned or bottled petits pois) and will add them about ten minutes from the end to cook in the hot juices.

These days old-fashioned dishes are coming back. When Tom Parker Bowles married Sara Buys, the wedding feast consisted of oysters and champagne to start with, his own fantastic recipe for cottage pie (the recipe is given on p. 365) to follow, and a pudding that I now cannot remember. I just know it was fabulous, so much more satisfying than itsy-bitsy fancy things of heaven-knows-what.

Fish pies, lasagnes and moussakas, risottos, roast chicken: all these are heart-warming dishes that, if carefully made from fine ingredients (a chicken that has lived a decent life, been able to run around and has not been fed on its relations, for instance), are always comforting. You can always jazz them up a bit for guests: add shellfish or salmon to the fish pie, plus some cream and dill to its sauce; add truffles or porcini to the risotto; tuck some tarragon into the chicken, swirl some white wine round the roasting juices and add some crème fraîche to make a sauce.

Accompany these with crisp fresh mixed salad greens drizzled with a good virgin olive oil, a dash of balsamic vinegar and some herbs, and you can just follow up with cheese and fruit whilst leaving your guests feeling well looked after.

These days, though, you can get away without cooking if you know how to shop (I'm not addressing here that ever-increasing crowd who call in the caterers: lovely if you can afford it but most of us can't). It's all about sourcing. You need to track down the freshest of herbs if you don't grow your own (herbs do wonders for any dish), and know where to get the organic salmon, the fresh crab, the Stinking

Bishop cheese, the proper ceps and porcini, the fine virgin olive oil, the walnut oil and great bread. You need to cook seasonally when flavours are at their freshest and most intense. There are also plenty of suppliers who can now be sourced online and will deliver. Some of the addresses can be found at the end of this chapter.

I've had some of the best meals of my life in the houses of friends who don't really cook but take trouble over sourcing the very best. One friend dishes up wonderful food in her country house in Dorset and not until the weekend is over do you realise that very little cooking has gone on. Saturday lunch is usually a vast dish of fresh crab, bought (ready cooked) first thing in the morning from a fishmonger in Bridport. It's served with a dish of garlicky mayonnaise (Waitrose and Marks & Spencer both sell proper mayonnaise in the summer months; and you can easily add your own garlic), a huge bowl of green leaves, some sliced tomatoes with basil, and new potatoes, all from the garden, scattered with herbs. Sunday lunch is a socking great sirloin or fillet of beef cooked to perfection (all crispy on the outside, rosy pink on the inside) by the husband on the barbecue outside. It comes with baby carrots still with their tops on, tiny peas and more new potatoes. It's followed by great cheese and strawberries from the garden dipped in balsamic vinegar in the summer or something like poached pears in winter. All accompanied by delicious wines. Not cheap, I know, but it does save the cook getting frazzled.

Another friend, the writer and journalist Victoria Mather,

always serves up heavenly food but it is simple in the extreme. It could be gulls' eggs to start with, asparagus in season or smoked salmon (from the Hebridean Smokehouse), or a big plate of lovely charcuterie. She'll follow it with a fillet of beef ('I only ever cook it for twenty minutes') and prefers salads to vegetables ('Saves that last-minute frazzle and getting your face all red'), though she will do new potatoes. She's lucky in that she has a really good butcher nearby but she gets her vegetables (seasonal, of course) from New Covent Garden and they're delivered to the door by Mash (020 7720 9191).

For an after-theatre supper when it all has to be ready in a flash, she'll do a Spanish tortilla (eggs with potato and onion) or scrambled eggs and smoked salmon topped with red caviar (but she serves the scrambled eggs cold) and follows it up with a tarte tatin from a good patisserie. Really good bangers and mash are another favourite – but the bangers come from a farmers' market or a really good butcher, and the potatoes (Maris Pipers) are put through a ricer. She, like me, is a fan of A. N. Wilson's fantastic way with shoulder of lamb, a really comforting winter dish. He puts the meat into a good ovenproof dish, covers it with two large tins of haricot beans and their liquid, two chopped onions, ten shallots, six tomatoes, some tomato purée and enough white wine to cover. He tucks in some bay leaves and rosemary, and then puts it in a low oven for four (yes, four) hours. It goes down a particular treat with children. But do take care to cut away as much fat as you can before you cook it, as otherwise it can tend to be a little on the greasy side.

* If you're going to keep it simple, then you must be wildly, madly generous. Great platters of fresh foods – good cheeses, salads, chunky slices of rare beef, fat pink prawns, charcuterie – look wonderfully welcoming and hospitable.

Presentation is also vitally important. Herbs sprinkled over things can do wonders – for the look as well as the taste. Use attractive dishes and make the food look fantastic. You should aim for only the best and freshest of ingredients. Smoked salmon, for instance, is still a delicious treat but only if it is the best – that nasty, pink, oily farmed stuff isn't worth eating, in my view. And it should be offered with really good bread, now available almost everywhere. Buy the smoked salmon from somewhere like Inverawe (www.inverawe.co.uk) or the Hebridean Smokehouse (www.hebrideansmokehouse.com), where the fish is organically farmed (in wide-open tidal pens) and they smoke it themselves. Chicken should be organic and free-range, it goes without saying. Get your beef, pork, bacon and their like from the best sources (the addresses are on p. 368) and there are now growing numbers of dedicated farmers who farm named breeds in humane ways without pesticides or chemicals.

When it comes to wanting to feed our friends, our wise mentor Edouard de Pomiane believed that 'For a successful dinner there should never be more than eight people. One should prepare *only one good dish.*' In other words, for the other two courses (usually, presumably, the starter and the third course) *faites simple* (by which you will have gathered by now that I do not mean slapdash). Now that we have good *traiteurs*, delicatessens and patisseries, you can easily top and tail the meal with something bought. There's also no need any more to stick to the structure of the three-course meal. I sometimes like doing something more Middle Eastern and have lots of dips (Marks & Spencer and most delicatessens do very good hummus, aubergine purées and tzatziki) and grilled vegetables (aubergines, red peppers, roasted onions), which can also be found in good delicatessens, followed by something simple and grilled, like crispy chicken dressed with herbs and lemon juice.

I also sometimes do a great big tureen of aromatic fish soup, dead easy to do. Then I jazz up some fresh mayonnaise with chilli and garlic to serve as a sort of *rouille*, offer a herby green salad and gorgeous bread, followed by cheese and fruit, and it always goes down a wow. If I'm really, really pushed for time and need to produce a supper for sixteen – or even a smarter dinner for six – I've learned ways to doll up the best supermarket food. It may not be up to the finest home-made but it's better than not seeing your friends or making excuses not to welcome visitors. For a buffet supper for sixteen when I had endless deadlines on the go, I've taken packets of Marks & Spencer mushroom risotto, decanted them into a vast baking dish (which makes it look home-made) and heated them up in the oven, remembering to double or triple up on the heating times. I've then sautéed some wild mushrooms (I always keep packs of dried procini on hand) in a mix of butter and oil, which I stirred in, adding a tiny bit of truffle oil and showered it with chopped parsley, and then served it with bowls of freshly grated Parmesan. At least three people asked me for the recipe.

I mostly avoid pasta, not because I don't like it (I *love* it) but because it's fattening (all those carbs). If that doesn't worry you, you can whip up endlessly delicious fast-food dishes using fresh pasta (it takes only three minutes to cook) and many of the bottled sauces you can buy are terrific. I first came across fresh pesto when it was served to us by Italian friends in a beach hut near San Remo – mixed in with fresh spaghetti and proper Parmesan, it was a revelation. But to my mind the best pasta dish of all is the tagliarini al bosco from the River Café's first cookery book. It's a creamy herby asparagus pasta dish that is probably my husband's favourite dish in the world (though not especially fast, it's not difficult).

Marks & Spencer (no E numbers, stabilisers, preservatives, artificial colours, flavourings or sweeteners) does a pretty good chicken and parma ham parcel, all nicely skewered with a sprig of rosemary, as well as a pretty decent beef wellington and a very nice big piece of salmon with chopped spring onion, red pepper and a soy sauce topping. Add a green salad, or a green vegetable, and either new potatoes (Jersey Royals, if in season) or mashed (Maris Pipers again). I'm addicted to mashing potatoes with olive oil – it's better for the arteries and I prefer the taste.

If you're really, really stuck on a dank Sunday evening (as once happened to me when some friends I'd forgotten I'd asked rang at about 4 p.m. just as we were clunked out on the sofa after rather too jolly a lunch to say they were going to be a little late for dinner), you'll have to turn to the store cupboard. Keep certain things always in store: tins of tomatoes; carnaroli rice for risottos; good chicken and fish stock in the freezer (buy from Waitrose if you haven't made your own or if you're near Harvey Nichols, get the utterly fabulous stocks and jus from More than Gourmet, www.morethangourmet.com); also Baxter's potted shrimps in the larger sizes, which freeze well; proper yellow-fin tuna preserved in oil in bottles (Waitrose again); dried mushrooms; olives; ceps; some good tapenade. Fortnum & Mason have a brilliant line called Chefs-d'Oeuvre, which really consists of what it calls 'accessories' – that is, pommes purées with truffles, saffron butter, flavoured butters and sauces. Now that you can access them online (www.fortnumandmason.com) and they'll deliver, they're well worth keeping in the store cupboard. Have really good ice-cream in the freezer: Hill Station, Ben & Jerry's, Green & Black's Organic, or Fresh Daisy to name just a few. It's worth trying out a few local takeaway services to see if anybody does it well. Londoners can be rescued by Rôtisserie Jules (www.rotisseriejules.com), which will deliver a ready-roasted organic chicken with pommes dauphinoise, green beans and a salad. Gordon Ramsay it isn't but it's fresh, healthy and very nice, thank you, when you're in a jam. Raoul's in Maida Vale (020 7289 6649) cooks freshly everyday things like osso buco, wood-pigeon breasts, Puy lentils, slow-cooked lamb shanks and lots, lots more. The three Ottolenghis (Notting Hill, Kensington and Islington: www.ottolenghi.co.uk) are all fabulous for delicious take-away food. The Grocer on Elgin (020 7221 3844) is fantastic for Londoners in a panic, but it is very expensive. It sells vacuum-packed portions of home-made soups, confit of duck (particularly good), interesting risottos (we had duck and red wine), all with no preservatives or nasty E numbers and made by individual suppliers. Just take them home, open up and follow the instructions. It now also sells online (www.thegroceron.com).

If you're going to dish up takeaways (and provided you choose good ones and serve them so that they look good, why on earth not? My mantra, as you may already have gathered, being that it's better to compromise than not to see your friends because you can't find the time to do it all perfectly), there are three golden rules: keep the lighting glamorously low (candles, candles, candles); hide the evidence (packets); and garnish, garnish, garnish.

You can finish with one great gorgeous cheese (*not* a dinky little selection with assorted cheese biscuits, please), like a huge mound of sharp Cheddar; a great big Camembert, unpasteurised for the best flavour (try wrapping it in puff pastry – Dorset Pastry is the best as it has no cheap hydrogenated fats – and baking it at 220°C, 425°F or Gas Mark 7 for twenty minutes and serving with a frisée salad); or one of the heavenly English cheeses now being made; a generous wodge of fresh Parmesan; a great big Stilton at Christmas or a Stinking Bishop in season, which you dip into with spoons and serve with a crisp green salad. They are all so much more appealing than weeny bits and pieces. Charles Martell makes Stinking Bishop on his farm near Dymock in Gloucesterhire (01531 890 637), though since it featured in a recent Wallace & Gromit episode he has been flooded with orders. Charles Martell also saved the breed of Old Gloucester cows and uses their unpasteurised milk to make a mild, buttery Single Gloucester (from April to December). Alternatively, it's hard to beat a perfectly ripe pear and a piece of Taleggio as a fine way to end a meal.

For pudding, most Londoners live near a good patisserie these days, but even supermarkets are offering up really good puddings. I don't like all of those at Marks & Spencer but its tarte au citron is admirably sharp (a nice accompaniment in the summer to lots of berries) and its individual open apple tarts, straight from the bakery on the premises, are terrific. If they don't have them, you can order them. Marks has also now started selling cold individual lemon soufflés and créme brûlées in white porcelain pots, which means they can be transported straight from fridge to table. Gü is a brand worth checking out (sold by Waitrose) especially any of its many chocolate puds (very seductive), which come in delicious little pots that you could produce in any company. I also love Gü's lemon curd pots, which I serve with raspberries when in season. Now there's a Fru, which does delicious fruity puddings. Its hot lemon soufflés come all ready to cook for just twenty-five minutes in respectable small glass pots. The Serious Food Company (www.serious food.co.uk) is a recent arrival on my radar and does proper fruit crumbles with chunky bits of fruit in nice china pots that can go from oven to table. Greek yoghurt topped with honey and toasted almonds or walnuts takes some beating.

Nigel Slater's *Real Fast Food* is a classic for those who want proper fast food, what he calls 'fresh food, bright flavours and relaxed eating'. None of the dishes takes more than thirty minutes to cook and most are exactly the sort of fresh, robust modern food that most of us want to eat today. Here, though, I'm parting with some of my own favourite quick dishes. Some are really obvious but it's useful sometimes to be reminded of them. All of these I produce quite often and I hope they'll give you some ideas. That said, I do think that being better organised would mean one could do all those long, slow-cooked dishes that Elizabeth David wrote about so evocatively. They often take very little time to prepare and are less likely to frazzle the nerves since they need less precision in their cooking times and usually no last-minute attention. You just need to put them in the oven ahead of time (which may sometimes mean cooking the previous night so that you can just reheat the following evening) and then let them simmer away, slowly allowing the flavours to mingle and work their magic.

Ten Dead Easy Starters

1. MELON SOUP. Whizz together one large ripe orange-fleshed melon, half a cucumber, 2 teaspoons of red wine vinegar and some salt and pepper. Slowly add some olive oil to the mixture to emulsify. Chill and serve.

2. CHILLED GREEN PEA SOUP. Soften a chopped onion in a little oil, add 500 grams of peas (fresh or frozen), some fresh mint and 20 fluid ounces of chicken stock. Cook for 5 minutes. Add salt and pepper, and purée. Serve cold with a little crème fraiche stirred into it and some chopped chives.

3. A GREAT PLATTER overflowing with the freshest of prawns from a fishmonger (or, better still, if you've time, cook your own in a big pan with some ginger and garlic) and a huge bowl of mayonnaise – home-made if you have time, otherwise buy it from stores (including Waitrose and Marks & Spencer) or delicatessens. Serve with fresh

crusty bread and some farmhouse butter.

4. PARMA HAM or, better still, San Daniele ham (from Marks & Spencer) or the Spanish pata negra ham (if you can find it; try www.brindisa.com), curled over roasted red onions on a bed of rocket. Sprinkle with toasted pine nuts and drizzle with olive oil. Or air-cured ham and fresh figs (after washing the figs, open them up into quarters). Or Bresaola with proper buffalo ricotta from a good delicatessen, a base of rocket, a trickle of best olive oil and shards of fresh Parmesan.

5. FIG AND MOZZARELLA SALAD. In the summer months, make a base of peppery rocket and on top put a combination of ripe figs, quartered, ripe nectarines and chunks of proper buffalo mozzarella. Swirl over good olive oil and some balsamic vinegar.

6. ASPARAGUS. You can serve it lots of ways. Either simple: hot (with melted butter and Parmesan cheese or hollandaise sauce from Waitrose) or cold (with a French vinaigrette). Or wrap it in Parma ham and grill until browned.

7. CONSOMMÉ, good tinned jellied (it must be from the fridge so that it is properly jellied; Campbell's is the best brand, I've found). Serve with sour cream and the cheapskate's caviar (black fish roe eggs), topped with chopped chives.

8. MORECAMBE BAY POTTED SHRIMPS. If you can't get hold of them locally, you can buy them direct from James Baxter & Sons (01524 410 910). Serve with brown bread and lemons.

9. BEETROOT SALAD. Juliennes (this is important: don't on any account cut them into rounds, which reminds me of school and desperate bleeding salads) of beetroot (*not* the ones doused in vinegar; freshly cooked versions are now available in supermarkets if you don't have time to cook your own), mixed with crumbled Roquefort cheese and topped with walnut pieces. Combine with a walnut oil dressing and lots of parsley. Serve on a base of rocket.

10. CHICKEN LIVER SALAD. Toss some chicken livers in butter until crisp outside but still a bit pink inside. Slide onto a mixture of peppery rocket, crisp torn cos lettuce and other green leaves. Deglaze the pan with some vinegar, scrape up all the juicy bits and pour over the leaves. This works nicely with lardons as well.

Ten Easy Main Courses

1. ROAST CHICKEN. It must be free-range organic (buy it from www.sheepdrove.com). Stuff it with a lemon cut in half and masses of tarragon, dribble over olive oil and roast. When cooked, lift out, add white wine to the juices,

swirl in cream and it makes a heavenly sauce. If you want to upgrade the meal do the same thing with guinea fowl. Serve with a crisp green salad and new potatoes.

2. ROAST FILLET OF BEEF (or grouse or pheasant in season). Timing is all. Brown it all over so you get a crispy outside and then roast at a high temperature (200°C, 400°F or Gas Mark 6) for 10 minutes per 500 grams. Serve in chunky slices with crème fraiche spiked with fresh horseradish or lots of mustard, herby new potatoes and a green salad. I also like to serve it accompanied by little branches of slow-roasted small tomatoes on the vine (but you need a separate oven to do that).

3. PORK FILLET. Cut into rounds, fry until brown on either side and cooked through. Swirl a little white wine in the juices, add cream and lashing of mustard. Serve with noodles or mashed potato. If you have time, mushrooms make a nice addition to the sauce.

4. SCALLOPS. Fry some bacon in a sturdy frying pan. Add fresh scallops (dry them on kitchen paper first) until crisp one side, then turn over to cook the other side. Add some shrimps and prawns, a little white wine (it must bubble), some cream and lots of herbs. This takes no more than 5 or 6 minutes. Serve either on a mound of rice, or a bed of watercress, mâché and rocket. Or do the Kensington Place trick and serve on a bed of puréed green peas.

5. RACK OF LAMB. (Marks & Spencer sells them beautifully trimmed and butchered – I never bother with the paper hats.) Rub with olive oil and rosemary and roast for 25 minutes in a hot oven (200°C, 400°F or gas mark 6) over a bed of halved onions, bottled artichoke hearts and parboiled halved potatoes. This is fabulously easy. Sprinkle with loads of parsley and other herbs.

6. STEAK. Buy the best fillet steaks. Sear in a mixture of olive oil and butter. How long depends upon how rare you like them. When done, remove from the pan, add some red wine (let it bubble), lots of mustard and crème fraiche. You can make it more elaborate by cooking a little onion and some mushrooms in some butter first. Remove from the pan and add to the sauce when the steaks are cooked. Serve with heaps of mashed potato (I like it with olive oil but you may prefer butter) and a green salad.

7. FISH. This is tricky to time but if you're just a small group (no more than four), trout with almonds is dead simple. Dip the trout in flour, and then fry in a mixture of butter and oil. When it has crisped on the outside and just turned opaque on the inside, remove it from the pan, deglaze it with some white wine, add a little more butter and some blanched almonds, and cook until brown. Pour the juices over the trout, add lots of lemon juice and parsley and serve with whatever you like (new potatoes and baby green peas or beans are lovely).

Alternatively, go for a whole fish (sea bass is prohibitively expensive, but you can doll up a fresh side of haddock with herbs and lemon juice), which you simply sprinkle with olive oil, add fennel and fresh dill, and then bake – but you must check your timings so that you don't overcook it.

8. COD. You can bake cod (fry it skin-side down first to give it a crisp surface, then bake until cooked), serve it on a bed of lentils (which makes a change from potatoes) and give it a lift with a salsa verde sauce. (Whizz in a blender a mass of parsley, mint, basil, some capers and cornichons, anchovies if you like them – I don't – and olive oil until you have a lumpy, emulsified sauce.)

9. PORK CHOPS. If you get these from a proper butcher, they make great quick easy food (from a supermarket they tend to be tough). Simply brown them on either side in a small amount of hot oil and butter. When brown add one whole head of chicory, halved, per chop. Brown the chicory on both sides. Then season, add a glass of white wine, cover and fry gently until cooked – about 15 minutes. Remove from the pan when done. Stir a little more butter into the juices and pour over the chops. Serve with new potatoes or noodles and a salad. This can also be done with chicken pieces.

10. SALMON. You can do lots of things with small salmon steaks. Simply fry them crisply in a combination of

butter and oil (the oil helps stop the butter burning), and when they are done, deglaze the pan with some white wine, adding lots of dill, lemon juice and some crème fraiche. Alternatively, try something more Eastern and bake with a topping of chopped spring onions and finely chopped chilli, ginger and garlic. When done, serve with a sauce made quickly from more chopped ginger, honey and soy sauce all mixed together. Serve with green vegetables, new potatoes and a salad.

Ten Easy Puds

1. A SIMPLE BOWL OF MIXED BERRIES with crème fraiche or try strawberries in balsamic vinegar. If you have time (it needs to drain for a few hours or, better still, overnight), make coeurs à la crème as an accompaniment. Line heart-shaped white china moulds that have holes in the bottom with muslin and put in a mixture (all whipped together) of cream, yoghurt and some unsalted cream cheese, chill and allow to drain. When firm, turn out the little heart-shaped mounds. Lovely with crunchy sugar. If you're short of time, serve with fromage blanc.
2. STUFFED PEACHES. Crush amaretti and stuff into the hollow of stoned, halved peaches, spoon over some honey and grill, or put in a low oven for 20 minutes. Serve with chilled cream.

3. COFFEE DELIGHT. Make a pint of strong, fabulous real coffee. When hot, add one packet of gelatine and stir until it's properly dissolved. Pour into a glass bowl to set. When firm, cover it first with a layer of whipped cream (or a mixture of yoghurt and cream, or just crème fraiche) and crumble lots of amaretti over the top.

4. FRUIT AND CHEESE. One summer in the Dordogne, when on holiday with friends, after the children were all safely in bed, our nightly treat was a perfect peach, some sharp unsalted creamy cheese (Petit Suisse will also do nicely) and a glass of Monbazillac. I still think there's nothing more delicious though these days I'd take a bit more care over the quality of the pudding wine.

5. BOODLES PUDDING is dead easy. Soak a plain sponge cake (with no cream or jam in the middle) in *fresh* orange or grapefruit juice (both can be bought in a supermarket) and, when the juice is absorbed, mix in some whipped cream.

6. COLD ORANGE SOUFFLÉ. Elizabeth David's wonderful recipe from *A Book of Mediterranean Food*. Soak ½ oz of gelatine in one pint of fresh orange juice. Add 2 table-spoons of sugar. Heat and when nearly boiling pour over 2 well-beaten egg yolks. Combine thoroughly. When cool, mix in the stiffly beaten whites of the 2 eggs. Chill.

7. PEARS BAKED IN WINE. Peel but leave the stalks on. Add

3 oz of sugar per pound of pears and either sweet white wine or red wine, mixed with water. Cook slowly in a low oven (100–150°C, 200–300°F), one hour is enough if they're ripe, or up to three hours if they're hard.

8. POACHED FRUIT IN MUSCAT. Quinces are the most delicious but aren't always in season. Otherwise peaches are brilliant, too, but are more delicate and need a shorter cooking time. Whenever I see quinces in the shops I grab them because they aren't easy to get hold of. I cook them very, very slowly in a low oven (something like 2 to 2½ hours) in Muscat or Sauterne, with a little added sugar and some spices to cut the sweetness – cinnamon, bay leaves, cloves and cardamom. Dissolve the sugar, bring the wine to the boil, then put in the fruit. Serve when cool. Ambrosia.

9. BAKED BANANAS. Cut them in half. Add some butter, brown sugar, orange or lemon juice, nutmeg, cinnamon and some honey. Bake for 30 minutes.

10. ICE-CREAM. Most supermarkets have a good range made from proper ingredients like cream and eggs. You can add all sorts of toppings, ginger in syrup is my favourite, but defrosted berries, honey and chopped walnuts, crushed meringues and melted chocolate all work well.

A Word about Chocolate

We're trained from girlhood to think it's *not* allowed. Not everyone knows this but pure cocoa has no cholesterol-raising ingredients at all. Real chocolate is low in sugar and has lots of vitamins, whilst cocoa butter lowers blood cholesterol levels. And there's more good news: really good chocolate increases the levels of serotonin in the brain (serotonin is what makes us feel happy) and it also contains phenylethylamine, which is very similar to the chemicals released in our bodies when we fall in love. There – chocolate's allowed after all and doesn't that feel better?

So on a cold winter's night you can now go for a guilt-free cup of brilliant hot chocolate. Pierre Marcolini of 6 Lancer Square, Kensington, London W8 4EH (020 7795 6611 and at www.marcolini.be) sells flakes of purest 100 per cent dark chocolate. Stir slowly into heated milk (skimmed to keep it guilt-free) and never let it boil. This is as different from the sugary, saturated-fat-infused commercial versions as Château Lafite is from supermarket plonk and it comes in very chic black tins.

Other terrific brand names to look for are La Maison du Chocolat, 45–46 Piccadilly, London W1J 0DS (020 7287 8500 and at www.lamaisonduchocolat.co.uk), which sells chocolate beans for making hot chocolate (£10.99 for 300 grams), and Rococo, 321 King's Road, London SW3 5EP (020 7352 5857 and at www.rococo chocolates.com), which has an Artisan Hot Chocolate flavoured with cinnamon, nutmeg or black pepper (£10.75 for 250 grams).

Some Ideas on Drinks

I'm not going to embark on a discourse about wine here, largely because I'm not an expert (I tend to buy quite a lot from a wine merchant called Swig, www.swig.co.uk, because they send me the most beguiling emails that make every wine sound unmissable; I just click the mouse and the wine arrives, is usually terrific and some time later I notice the bank account is down rather more than I'd remembered) and partly because all newspapers dispense good advice regularly. However, I do wish more people would go to a bit more trouble over non-alcoholic alternatives. I love wine but can't drink too much of it without getting a hangover. Here are a few non-alcoholic suggestions:

THE BEST TOMATO JUICE is made from puréed and sieved fresh sweet tomatoes, seasoned and spiced. I first tasted it in Spain and thought I'd gone to heaven. I assume they peeled and deseeded the tomatoes first. Big Tom Spiced Tomato Juice is a new brand that is the next best thing. No additives, no preservatives, it's £2.29 for a biggish bottle and you can get it in Sainsbury's and Waitrose. Great for Bloody Marys as well as Virgin ones.

FUNKIN PURÉES are made from fresh white peaches, strawberries, passion fruit and raspberries, and they make brilliant smoothies, can be poured over ice-cream or can make instant Bellinis (add the peach to your favourite champagne or prosecco). They come in very groovy packaging and are £3.95 a pack from Harvey Nichols, Selfridges or www.funkin.co.uk.

RIPE PURÉED MELONS make a deliciously refreshing drink that can be lightened with a little iced soda water and zipped up with some fresh ginger or mint.

THORNCROFT CORDIALS (01642 791 792 and at www.thorncroftdrinks.co.uk) makes traditional plant-based cordials: elderflower, pink ginger, nettle and rosehip.

ROCKS ORGANIC (01189 342 344 and at www.rocksorganic.com) does additive- and preservative-free lime, ginger, elderflower, summer fruit and blackcurrant cordials.

Farmers' Markets

There are over 500 farmers' markets in the country today. If you haven't already discovered them, the easiest way to do so is to tap into www.farmersmarkets.net and you'll be able to track down the one closest to where you live. Authentic farmers' markets consist of small stallholders, each of whom sells only things he or she has grown or raised personally. Many of them have expanded into producing dishes – soups, cakes, puddings, pies and the like, all of which have to be home-made, and whilst the ingredients are nearly always (one assumes) authentic, the quality of the finished product is variable. Trial and error at your local market will lead you to the suppliers whose wares you like. But some of the breads, home-made cheeses, cakes, soups and pâtés are truly delicious.

The daddy of them all is Daylesford Organic in Daylesford, Gloucestershire, Lady Bamford's wonderful organic farm shop, which set the whole of south-west England alight when it opened a few years ago, selling perfectly hung and butchered organically raised meat, home-made cheeses, dairy products, fruit and vegetables from the Bamfords' own farms as well as a delicious selection of home-made breads, cakes, biscuits, soups and other dishes. Now Londoners can get the products more easily as there's a branch at 30 Pimlico Road, London SW1W 8LJ, and everybody else can shop online at www.daylesfordorganic.com.

In London there is Borough Market down by London Bridge, which has transformed shopping for serious foodies, but there are many, many other farmers' markets dotted all over London from Blackheath to Ealing.

Paris Markets

Even if you're not planning on doing any cooking, it's well worth browsing the best food markets. You can always come back with some cheese, sausages or ceps. These are my favourites:

Marché Richard-Lenoir, just by the Place de la Bastille, is one the liveliest markets in Paris and it's open on a Sunday.

There's always a great selection of mushrooms.

Rue Cler in the 7th arrondissement has a wonderful villagey atmosphere where French housewives often shop for Sunday lunch on their way home from church.

Rue Mouffetard in the 5th arrondissement is another charming little market for those who live in the neighbourhood.

For picnics you can, of course, patronise Fauchon and Hediard, the twin grand food stores, but for a picnic *de luxe* on the hoof, I think you couldn't do better than Flo Prestige, 42 Place du Marché-Saint-Honoré. Here you can pick up charcuterie, foie gras, breads (in small portions or large), cheeses, *une douceur* for afterwards, wine and anything else you might need.

New York Food

Don't miss out on Whole Foods markets – there are several dotted around the city (check the addresses on the internet), with the latest being below the Mandarin Hotel at Columbus Circle, and they are a wonder to behold. Never will you have seen so many varieties of shrimp, bean, bread, cheese or anything else. They pride themselves on quality and abundance. Go, look and wonder.

Tom Parker Bowles' Chilli Cottage Pie

Serves 4

3 tbsps olive oil
3 Thai chillis, finely chopped (deseeded and deveined for less heat)
2 medium red onions, coarsely chopped
450g organic beef mince
1 tsp tomato purée
1 can Sainsbury's beef and sherry consommé
3 tbsps Worcestershire sauce
a few shakes Tabasco
4 medium sized Maris Piper potatoes
generous lump of unsalted butter
splash of milk
freshly ground black pepper and salt

Heat the olive oil and sweat the chillies to infuse in the oil for 2–3 minutes. Add the onions and cook over a low heat until soft and brown (about 5 minutes). Turn up the heat a little and add the mince in handfuls, stirring into the onion. When all the onion and beef is mixed together and browned, add the tomato purée and stir to combine. After 1 minute, pour in the consommé. Add the Worcester sauce and Tabasco, and stir again. Turn the heat down to a simmer and reduce for about 30 minutes. Keep tasting. In the meantime, peel the potatoes and throw into a large pan of cold, salted water. Bring to the boil and simmer until soft. Drain and put back into the pan over the heat (to dry off any excess water). Add the butter, a splash of milk, and mash. Turn the mince into a shallow overproof baking dish and cover with the potato. Dot the potato with chunks of butter, season with salt and pepper, and bake in a preheated oven (at 190°C, 375°F or Gas Mark 5) for 25 minutes. Serve with peas or small broad beans, drenched in butter.

Picnics

> No climate in the world is less propitious to picnics than the climate of England, yet with a recklessness which is almost sublime, the English rush out of doors to eat a meal on every possible and impossible occasion.
>
> Georgina Battiscombe in *English Picnics*

I love picnics but there are, of course, picnics and picnics. There are the ones on top of a snowy mountain in the middle of a hundred square kilometres of wilderness (yes, really, when heli-skiing in British Columbia) when the hot soup and even hotter chilli con carne, served out of huge thermoses, were just perfect. There are the ones huddled by dunes, sheltering from the wind in what passes for a British summer, when some hot soup was what one longed for and stodgy sandwiches were what one got. There are rustic ones in France (our son has a house in the Cévennes, surrounded by woods and hills, and picnics are a big feature of time spent there) when one knows why La France Profonde is such a beguiling place – the fresh baguettes, the cheeses, tomatoes, olives, farm-made pâtés, good charcuterie, ripe peaches and grapes, and wine are better than anybody could wish for. For British country outings (point-to-points and country fairs, not to mention visits to the seaside), sturdier food is needed. A game or chicken pie, if one can find a good local supplier, is perfect (see www.foodfullstop.com), while Fortnum & Mason's new online shop does wonderful pies (www.fortnumandmason.com), and drinks like home-made ginger beer and lemonade are ideal. It's great to end with some sharp cheese and a very fruity fruitcake (Fortnum & Mason's Gamekeeper's Fruitcake is perfect). For wintry picnics (on Scottish moors or Gloucestershire walks), hot soups are wonderfully restorative and things like stews and goulashes can be kept beautifully hot in a thermos. I'm not a sandwich fan – for me they're dull and never hit the spot.

And now, since we have finally got to the top of the Glyndebourne list and love Grange Park and Garsington opera almost as much, we indulge in grander picnics where a little more effort is needed.

Here is what I've learned about picnics. Without staff, bringing the fantasy of the perfect picnic to life is too burdensome even to try. When you read the details of the grand picnics that feature in novels or old-fashioned memoirs, there are always hordes of staff, huge barons of

MORE USEFUL, ADDRESSES AND WEBSITES

Mash of 31–32 New Covent Garden Market, Nine Elms, London SW8 (tel: 020 7720 9191), will deliver in the London area fruit, flowers and vegetables from the market.

Swaddles Organic (tel: 0845 456 1768 and at www.swaddles.co.uk) not only sells organic meats, fish and vegetables but also a selection of pretty good ready-made dishes (lasagnes, fish pies, boeuf stroganoff, fish cakes, that sort of thing). It also sells chicken carcasses (£1.90 a time) if you're up for making your own stock.

www.valvonacrolla.com is Edinburgh's most famous delicatessen but it also sells online things like San Daniele ham as well as bottarga (divine dried tuna eggs), which is fabulous grated over fresh pasta, dressed simply with a good olive oil.

www.esperya.com is a brilliant Italian food supplier that sells, amongst other things, carnaroli rice for risottos, fresh buffalo mozzarella from Campania, ravioli stuffed with goats cheese, charcuterie – you get the full Italian picture.

www.blackface.co.uk sells products from Weatherall Farms in Dumfries: lamb, mutton, haggis, Iron Age pork (a cross between a Tamworth sow and a wild boar), oven-ready grouse, partridge, bronze turkeys and venison direct from the heather hills of Scotland.

www.northumbria-larder.co.uk sells grass-fed Aberdeen Angus beef – steaks, mince, joints, sausages – reared by the MacPherson's of Well-Hung and Tender.

www.dukeshillham.co.uk sells fabulous ham. Some prefer the Wiltshire ham, others the Shropshire black ham. You choose.

www.1001huiles.fr for great vinegar and olive oil. To whet the appetite before dinner, serve chunks of Parmigiano Reggiano on a plate and gently drip their balsamic vinegar on to each piece.

www.martins-seafresh.co.uk for fresh shellfish and fish.

www.french-truffle.com for black truffles.

www.hebrideansmokehouse.com for peat-smoked sea trout and salmon (very smoky and an acquired taste but I love it).

www.arbroath-smokie.co.uk for proper Arbroath smokies, which make the simplest and most divine fish pâté in the world. (Whizz in a food processor the smokies, some crème fraiche, lemon juice, pepper, dill and parsley, and serve with toast.)

www.foodfullstop.com has been set up by three young chefs who love food. It sells everything good – from organic fruit and veg to rare-breed meats, speciality cheeses, preserves and pâtés. A good source of oysters, things like pheasant and partridge pie, fresh dressed crab and lots of English cheeses.

www.organicassistant.com helps you find organic foods (and anything else organic come to that).

beef, elaborate mousses and a host fancy dishes. The grand picnic that one conjures up in one's imagination would involve wicker baskets (a devil to carry), a beautiful linen cloth, a fine rug (even a faded Persian one?), flickering candles, china, crystal, and wonderful food and drink, but all this involves much carrying to and fro, which becomes tiresome if the car isn't close to the picnic site – which in one sense defeats the point of the truly rustic picnic, which is to be far from roads and cars. If you happen to have a country house, on a summer evening you could replicate something like this at the end of your very own garden – a magic thing to do and not impossible without staff.

Otherwise I tone down my expectations. For Glyndebourne, where the car park isn't too far from the picnic grounds, I have a routine that involves a folding table and chairs that fit in the car boot (bought from the Glyndebourne shop and a present from our son), an antique French linen cloth and linen napkins (extravagant, as we always get red wine on them, but worth it), and proper china and glass, but for any other sort of picnic I adopt a much more casual approach. I don't take a table and chairs but instead we sit on a waterproof rug with handles (from R. K. Alliston, www.rkalliston.com) I also love those traditional old plaid Welsh blankets called Carthenni, which you can buy from Athene English of the Great English Outdoors (01497 821 205). Then there's the cooler for the drinks. We start with champagne and move on to whatever wines my husband has chosen (though not too much because everybody has to drive home again afterwards).

In France, where long walks nearly always precede the picnic, all the children (even the four-year-olds) have light inexpensive picnic backpacks that include little plates, knives, forks and glasses, so that they can carry their own stuff whilst the adults hump the heavier things.

I have in my time done more elaborate picnics – strips of chicken marinated and then grilled, things wrapped in pastry, multi-layered confections of eggs and vegetables – but these days I find simpler food works best. I keep away from anything that could melt (obviously) or anything with a runny sauce, but on a really hot day I do like cold soups (a thermos keeps them cold very efficiently) and hot ones on cold days.

So here are some of the foods that have worked for us when we're in more elaborate mode.

CHILLED PEA OR WATERCRESS SOUP OR VICHYSOISSE from a thermos are very English and very summery. Morecambe Bay potted shrimps with brown bread and lemons. Smoked trout or smoked eel with some horseradish sauce and lemon juice, and thinly sliced buttered brown bread. A selection of crudités with dips from Marks & Spencer (hummus, tzatziki, aubergine purée), though I decant them into little china pots to make them look prettier. Asparagus with vinaigrette and some shards of Parmesan (also from M&S), packed separately. Parma ham and figs (easier to cope with – and in my view nicer – than dealing with cutting up a melon and its seeds). Freshly cooked prawns and some mayonnaise (a reminder: Waitrose and Marks & Spencer sell good versions). Marks & Spencer's classic quiches are delicious, particularly when warm.

COLD FILLET OF BEEF – all crusty on the outside and pink on the inside, cut into nice thick slices and served with a creamy horseradish sauce.

COLD CHICKEN, but only if organic and cooked the same morning with lashings of tarragon. Bought ready-cooked and cold from a supermarket is, in my view, a waste of money.

COLD PINK RACK OF LAMB – ideally cooked the same morning – with mint jelly or a spicy chutney is perfect.

SALMON is somehow more predictable so I don't do it but most people love it. Salmon trout is more delicate and good served with a herby, green mayonnaise.

With the above I serve new potatoes, cooked and tossed whilst still warm in a vinaigrette with lots of herbs, chopped spring onions and chives, plus some baby tomatoes spiked with basil. Sometimes I vary the salads with a combination of peas, broad beans and feta cheese, or a combination of peas and mangetout, or green beans perked up with toasted almonds and some small chopped tomatoes.

Afterwards we have a great big slab of cheese and some oatcakes (taking bread, a breadknife and butter is a complication too far), followed by fresh berries of some kind with crème fraiche, or a perfect tarte from a patisserie.

And I agree, as always, with Elizabeth David when she writes (in *Summer Cooking*) that she likes to end with a 'slab of the driest, bitterest chocolate available'. Green & Black's Organic is perfect.

And, finally, don't forget the corkscrew – or a bag to house the rubbish.

Perfect Presents

The Pleasure of Giving

If it were not for the presents, an elopement would be preferable.

George Ade (1866–1944), *Forty Modern Fables*

Few of us *need* presents but life without them would, I think, be a rather greyer matter. The instinct to give, to express one's esteem, love, affection, seems to lie deep in the human psyche. In the earliest societies the gods had to be placated with offerings. Later it was the turn of chiefs. In the poorest countries of the world people present each other with songs or flowers, little home-made bits and pieces, to indicate that they love them, think of them, admire them. Most of us love giving presents and I can't think how we've come to the sort of state we're in in the Western world where come Christmas time they seem to be a source of such angst and resentment. If you told somebody in a poverty-stricken village in India or Africa that there were people with money and resources who yet found the buying and the choosing of presents so stressful that it kept them awake at night, and that newspapers run hosts of articles on the subject every year, I do believe they'd conclude that we'd taken leave of our senses. And perhaps we have.

Perhaps it's time to remind ourselves how lucky we are that we have money and a plethora of fabulous shops and delicious things to choose from – and, even more importantly, that we have people in our lives that we love and care about to give them to. We're short of time, I grant you, and that's a problem, but there are ways round it. One way is to pick up delightful things when we come upon them all through the year so as not to have do it all in the run-up to Christmas. For instance, I always look out for special things when I'm travelling. Every time I'm in Africa I come back with African artefacts, with gorgeous wooden salad spoons or bowls, so that I've got something to give that isn't standard department store fare. In India I come back with textiles, with boxes of bangles, with Indian silverware, and anything else that takes my fancy and that I know can't be got in Europe. That way I've always got something interesting and unusual ready for the occasion when a present needs to be found.

Anyway, I love presents – I love giving them and I love getting them, though I'm usually too pressed for time to be as imaginative as I'd like to be. But it is easily observed that good presents don't need to be expensive. Recently a friend wrote and delivered a most delightful love poem for his wife's fiftieth birthday. I dare say there were a couple of more solid manifestations of his love for her as well (history does not relate), but it was the poem, read out to the assembled friends, that made her night. Another husband secretly learned to conduct a piece of music that was meaningful to him and his wife, and then conducted a small group of musicians at a party to celebrate her birthday.

One of the happiest Christmases we ever had was when

our children were both at university. We rented a shooting lodge in Scotland, invited an assortment of their and our friends, and decreed that nobody was allowed to spend more than £15 on a present. It tested our ingenuity but, my goodness, we had fun – and the presents were terrific, too. I seem to remember some delicious fine olive oil, second-hand books featured largely, as did enchanting little objects found in antique shops, as well as a fantastic collection of small stationery gadgets for my home office.

The most perfect presents, of course, are those that are so particularly appropriate to the person, their life and needs, that they offer little general guidance for the rest of us. For example, the book that is perfectly chosen because it relates to something personal (the Christmas after we'd all been to Pompeii our daughter gave us Pliny the Younger's memoirs with its vivid first-person description of Vesuvius erupting – perfect) isn't quite so apt for anybody else. I think back to the presents that have given me most pleasure: the huge Chinese pots that my husband noted I'd admired when we'd passed a shop and later bought as a surprise; the bracelets (one of chunky semi-precious stones, the other of twisted lime-green resin) that he just *knew* were 'me'; the little piece of embroidery my daughter did for me even though she was in the middle of intensely important exams; the Edmund de Waal series of pots that my son and daughter recently gave me as a joint birthday surprise; the special pictures my father sometimes used to give me. They're all so particular to me that it's hard to recommend them with any certainty of their being right for anybody else. So, too, the brilliant vase, bought because it will lend colour and splendour to a particular room that one knows well, wouldn't go down quite so well in a totally different room with a very different aesthetic. People with hobbies – the photographer, the football fanatic, the hill walker, the tennis player, the stamp collector, the cook, the golfer – seem at first sight the easiest of all to buy things for, but the more one looks into it, the more one realises that the more intense the relationship with the hobby, the more precision matters. The keen photographer will know precisely which lens his kit is missing and something just a little bit like it won't do at all.

But as I've been giving and receiving presents for more years than I'm going to own up to, I've both given and received my share of duds. I've also had presents of such generosity and perfection that it makes me feel happy all over just thinking about them. So here are some ideas garnered from my experience of giving and receiving over the years.

For the New Mother

A NIGHT AWAY at Olga Polizzi's ravishingly situated Endsleigh House Hotel (www.hotelendsleigh.com) in the middle of 180 acres of Devon countryside where they can sleep until noon. Or Whatley Manor (www.whatleymanor.com), where there's a private cinema and a divine spa. Or any other country house that you think would soothe and pamper.

TICKETS TO THE OPERA OR THE THEATRE, paired with a night at somewhere divinely glamorous like Claridge's (if they're traditionalists) or the Soho Hotel (if they like to think they're still just a little hip), would so restore their spirits. *Plus* the babysitter.

ONE OF ANYA HINDMARCH'S BE A BAG BAGS with a picture of her baby on it. The bags are great and having a picture of the new baby makes it special (020 7838 9111 and at www.beabag.com).

BRORA'S CASHMERE FOR BABIES (www.brora.co.uk) or something from THE WHITE COMPANY (www.thewhitecompany.co.uk), which has lots of delicious things for babies – from cashmere blankets to cute little towelling robes.

THE GIGI BY STORKSAK – the best baby holdall in the world, according to many a new mother. Rumour has it that both Angelina Jolie and Gwyneth Paltrow have been spotted carrying one. It's really a handbag with shoulder straps and two outer pockets for all the things that Mummy needs, and a big inner pocket for all the baby stuff, with a nappy-changing pad and pockets for bottles, creams and all the rest. About £140 from www.totsplanet.co.uk, a great website with lots of other ideas for mums and babies.

SAMSONITE POP-UP TRAVEL BUBBLE COT – it folds down into

a small round parcel, weighing less than three kilos, but pops up to form a cot or safe playpen for any baby that isn't yet walking. About £50.

THE MILASONG HOLDALL-CUM-SUITCASE called La Malice – it's brilliant for the travelling mother. It comes in three parts, on a hanger and it zips together. One section holds toys, one food, one clothes, and you simply unzip the whole thing and hang it on its hanger. You don't have to unpack or (therefore) repack and you zip it back up again when the time comes to leave. Only, so far as I can discover, available from Pure Baby, 208 Fulham Road, London SW10 9PJ, conveniently right opposite the Chelsea & Westminster Hospital (020 7751 5544 and at www.milasong.com).

DELICIOUS OILS AND LOTIONS – there are so many it's hard to choose but give a generous selection of the sort of pampering bathtime pleasures that a new mother wouldn't usually buy for herself.

A HALF-DAY AT A SPA or an appointment for a masseur, manicurist, etc., to come to the house.

A GOOD NIGHT'S SLEEP – if you're a godmother or grandmother, a month's maternity nurse is a fantastic present to give. Otherwise a single good night's sleep (from Night Nannies, 020 7731 6168) gives some relief.

COUVERTURE at 310 King's Road, London SW3 5VH (020 7795 1200), has lots of delectable tiny things –

slippers, baby bracelets, vintage hand-embroidered Heidi cardigans with pompom ties, cute striped polo tops and masses of desirable baby linens.

BUY TIME (0870 486 2624 and at www.buy-time.co.uk). Give help in units of time – one hour, two hours.

If you can handle shopping from QVC, the shopping channel, it has some fun things to buy. It is particularly good on girly things like great gobstopper rings for just £39 (clearly fake, or what it calls a simulated imperial topaz and pavé ring with sterling silver – but who cares?), a gorgeous 'gold' bracelet consisting of lots of discs for £87, and pretty turquoise and gold-plated earrings for £40.

For The Christening

I think there's something inherently different about a christening present. It shouldn't be ephemeral; rather it should be bought with the notion that it will be meaningful all through the child's life. And it's nicest of all if there is some real connection between the person and the presents. For instance, one of my daughter's children's godfathers – a keen fisherman – gave one of her sons a fishing rod, with the unspoken promise that he'll take him fishing later, and through the years no doubt flies and other fishing paraphernalia will also follow. It's why, of course, traditional gifts like the Common Prayer Book, Shakespeare, Dickens and their like often appear

– they're part of the background to every cultured home.

Girls are easy: little strings of tiny pearls or coral. An antique piece of jewellery or an enchanting small precious box for her to keep things in later on. Something from Tiffany, which does a great line in little silver items that aren't very expensive and come with their own beautiful boxes – silver charms, spoons, mugs, eggcups.

If you're a godparent and years of present-giving loom ahead, I think it's lovely to start a collection of something. You could do that very traditional thing and start laying down wine. Berry Brothers offer a great service on this front (www.bbr.com). It does, of course, mean that the young years should be enlivened with something else (inexpensive) come Christmas and birthdays – it's too much to expect a six-year-old to be thrilled at the prospect of waiting until he is eighteen to enjoy his present. But when he does become eighteen, what a thrill!

In the past I've given collections of books – the great classics, beautifully bound to make them special, and you can add to them as the years go by. The complete set of Everyman would be a great present. Its core 300 titles represent the heart of Western literature, a platoon of living and dead writers that no other publisher can match. Rushdie, Nabokov, Dickens . . .

Something that might give a great deal of pleasure in years to come: wonderful binoculars, with the implicit promise of doing something special in later years, like going on safari.

I've also given some lovely beaten silver mugs from Nepal from William Welstead (william@williamwelstead.com), one at the christening and then one each Christmas, accompanied by something cheap and cheerful on the day. You could start a collection of almost anything – precious glasses, silver, lithographs: the scope is endless.

For Anniversaries and Big 'O' Birthdays

Anniversaries and big 'O' birthdays are often the time when husbands and wives, fathers, mothers and siblings give each other classic presents: a really good watch, a special camera, a fine string of pearls, a fantastic ring or brooch, some gorgeous cufflinks, the sort of things that get handed down through the generations.

But here are a few other suggestions:

The complete set of books published by Persephone. This is an enchanting small house that publishes neglected fiction, diaries, cookery books and short stories, all by women writers and written mainly for women, but they are all fabulous. They don't aim to be too highbrow but neither are they overtly commercial. What they do aim to do is to give real pleasure and so would provide hours and hours of delight. The website is www.persephonebooks.co.uk, but visit the charming little bookshop in Bloomsbury if you can, at 59 Lamb's Conduit Street, London WC1N 3NB; 020 7242 9292.

55MAX (020 7625 3774 and at www.55max.com) will take personal photographs and turn them into art in some way. Holiday or family photographs can be framed, set in perspex, 'painted' on to canvas or turned into a brilliant découpage. All the grandchildren could be photographed and turned into some art form.

Otherwise it's a good opportunity to buy something one-off and totally special, or even to commission a customised picture, piece of jewellery or silver. A fantastic black and white photograph (of the beloved, or of children, grandchildren – even a dog or horse) is a less expensive option than a portrait. You can commission an interesting piece of jewellery from Wint & Kidd (www.wintandkidd.com) in London's Notting Hill (you choose your diamonds and then they devise a setting of your choice) or from Mappin & Webb, Asprey *et al*. If your tastes run more to the avant-garde the Goldsmiths' Company has an online site that leads you directly into the workshops of some two hundred different craftspeople. Check out the styles you like at www.whoswhoingoldandsilver.com.

* For a portrait, contact the Royal Society of Portrait Painters, 17 Carlton House Terrace, London SW1Y 5DB (020 7930 6844 and at www.therp.co.uk), and choose the artist you like.

There are specialist galleries and craft shops up and down the country that are well worth looking at because they sell things you won't find in the average high street shop or department store. A few of my favourites are Flow, 1–5 Needham Road, London W11 2RP, which has avant-garde tastes and beautiful things, and Contemporary Applied Art at 2 Percy Street, London W1T 1DD (www.caa.org.uk), which always has masses of one-off things – almost all hotly desirable, in glass, ceramics, jewellery, textiles.

Maureen Doherty of Egg has a brilliant eye and her small craft gallery at 36–37 Kinnerton Street, London SW1X 8ES, often has beautiful, special things, including silver work by William Welstead (see p. 385), and she also has some lovely unpolished diamond necklaces (not expensive).

Commission a special binding for a favourite book. Get a first edition, if you can, and then consult www.designerbookbinders.org.uk for a bookbinder to customise it. The website has details of individual bookbinders with small pictures to give you some idea of each craftsman's style as well as sensible advice.

The Thank-you Present

I've been musing on the matter of what constitutes the perfect weekend house (or staying in a country villa or yacht) present. Unless we're like Uncle Matthew in Nancy Mitford's *Love in a Cold Climate,* who never liked to go anywhere (least of all, of course, abroad), we none of us want – do we? – to be like the man who was invited to most of the grand houses of England – just once. Though whether it was due to something he said or the presents he took isn't clear. If we are lucky to be invited to share our friends' country cottages, tennis courts, swimming pools and herbaceous borders, clearly we cannot arrive empty-handed.

Take your hostess or host luxurious versions of everyday things – a new or particularly lovely version of bath oils and gorgeous soaps. The Conran Shop has a fabulous selection but there are smaller niche names, such as Jo Woods' Organic range, Ren's wonderful Moroccan Rose Otto or Lavender bath oil, Designers' Guild soaps, or almost anything from the Farmacia di Maria Santa Novella.

Softly padded exquisite hangers – Colefax & Fowler and Laura Ashley both do lovely ones. A beautiful pair of pillowcases, antique if possible and only in white.

A single perfect silver jam spoon, butter knife, horn spoon for caviar, honey spoon or big serving spoon or salad servers, from a specialist craft shop or maker, or from an antique shop.

Other things that have gone down well: the latest hardback biography or must-read novel; a luscious gardening tome (if they're into gardening); a beautiful (antique or wonderfully carved modern) doorstop.

Food treats: a whole Cheddar from Daylesford Organic, a big chunk of proper Parmesan, a jar of saffron, bottarga (that fabulous dried tuna's roe that is ambrosia folded into pasta), a bottle of truffle oil, olive oils and balsamic vinegars with a special provenance. A great knife, a beautifully packaged game. Chocolates, but only if they're really good; a box of Cadbury's Black Magic won't do. Truffles from Sally Clark in Kensington Church Street, or Rococo, or one of the small artisanal chocolate houses popping up everywhere would be fantastic. A magnum of fine wine (much nicer, says my friend with the smart Scottish shooting lodge, than supermarket champagne) from Justerini & Brooks or Berry Brothers (www.bbr.com). Addresses of good foodie websites are all to be found in Chapter 6, (see p. 368).

Gardening presents – if they have gardens – obviously need to suit the garden and the gardeners, but Throw & Grow Wild Flowers have a tub of mixed seeds for wild flowers to attract butterflies, bees and birds. At £24.50 for enough to cover ten square metres.

The most imaginative present I ever heard of was that of an expert gardener who took to a less horticulturally gifted friend fifty rare and precious tulip bulbs and *planted them all herself*. Antonia Fraser was once on the receiving end (though no doubt not from a house guest) of a rose hedge: 'a daily renewed present', as she put it.

A friend who owns a house in France said that one of the nicest presents she was ever given was a beautifully bound album filled with photographs of the holiday that they'd all shared, which arrived a week of two after the visit.

Authentic gardening trugs, a linen tool bag, oilskin kneelers, brilliantly sturdy glass storm lanterns, string-in-a-tin, mini-boules or a croquet set all make good presents and can be found at R. K. Alliston (www.rkalliston.com).

The Wedding Present

Trickier and trickier . . . These days so many couples are getting married so much later by which time they've got not one, but *two* sets of all the things once found on traditional wedding lists. That doesn't mean to say that there isn't scope for beautiful, upgraded versions of some of the useful household accoutrements – really ravishing serving spoons, silver, glass, linen, candlesticks and all the rest. But taste and lifestyle have such an important part to play that it's hard to give one-size-fits-all advice. If we're lucky, the bride and groom will guide us. When Lady Sarah Chatto, Princess Margaret's daughter, got married, I seem to remember she asked for nothing but books. That would send one scurrying off to find special editions or perhaps sourcing a complete set of a beautiful edition of something like Dickens or an author you know the couple particularly love.

I think that on the whole, unless you are very close to the

couple and really understand their taste, it's best to give what I call taste-neutral presents, or to consult the wedding list if there is one, which will at least give you some idea of where their tastes lie. The quirky candlesticks that you absolutely love may clash, not just with their own inclinations but with the candlesticks and the house they already have. If they're really close – like your children, a godchild or a best friend – then something special, chosen with care from an antique shop, a small interior design shop like some of those listed in Chapter 5, or a special craft shop, makes a terrific present as they won't have anything else like it. For those less close to the happy couple, my advice is to keep it more neutral.

More Ideas

A FANTASTIC CASE OF FINE WINE. Either your local wine merchant or somebody like Berry Brothers (www.bbr.com) will give good advice, and will also store the wine if the couple haven't got anywhere to keep it until it's ready to drink.

THE BEST FOOD MIXER – say, the original Waring mixer (*if* they haven't got one and *if* you know they're cooks). From John Lewis – quite brilliant.

HIS AND HERS PLAIN WHITE TOWELLING ROBES from the White Company (www.thewhitecompany.com).

Gorgeous THICK WHITE TOWELS from John Lewis. Or some

great beach towels – Missoni's at Selfridges are fabulous.

A fantastic SET OF KITCHEN KNIVES *plus* a sharpener, from Divertimenti (www.divertimenti.co.uk).

A really fine LEATHER PHOTOGRAPH ALBUM OR VISITORS' BOOK, from Smythson (www.smythson.com).

A set of amazing SAUCEPANS, from Alessi, 22 Brook Street, London W1K 5DF.

Carl Rotter WATER GLASSES in jewel colours from Oggetti, 135 Fulham Road, London SW3 6RT (020 7581 8088).

Some ANTIQUE GLASSES – a pair, or a set of six or eight, for water, wine or champagne.

A great ESPRESSO MACHINE – a Gaggia (nice and plain and classic) for choice.

For Him

Bamford & Son, 31 Sloane Square, London SW1W 8AQ (020 7881 8010 and at www.bamfordandsons.com), has to be one of the most irresistible shops in the world for men. It doesn't go in for gimmicks and flashy eye-catching touches but instead homes in on all those absolutely classic things that most of the men I know love – soft-as-butter cashmere scarves, light-as-a-feather cashmere jackets, relaxed leather jackets, deep grey flannel trousers, gorgeous leather gloves and satchels – but gives them all a relaxed and modern twist.

It also has fabulous toys for the boys. Look no further than the divine tiny (three-inch) digital camera, which comes with all the newfangled technology (SD memory cards, white balance, fast shutter speeds, two-megapixel sensors and LCD monitors) but looks exactly like a miniature old-fashioned Rolleiflex Twin Reflex camera. It also has a brilliant OQO Mini Computer Notebook, which, since it is £1,795, is probably mainly of interest to the City bonus crowd. It's easily portable (it weights about 398 grams) and has 'Wifi, Bluetooth, 30gb shock-mounted HDD and an easy docking solution'. It means you can send and read e-mails, you can listen to music on a train or watch a movie on a plane. It also has a proper keyboard concealed under a slide-out screen.

A VINTAGE WATCH can be bought from the Vintage Watch Company, 24 Burlington Arcade, London W1J 0EA (020 7499 2032 and at www.vintagewatchcompany.com).

MOLESKIN NOTEBOOKS, the ones allegedly used by Bruce Chatwin and Ernest Hemingway, from Modo e Modo, make a terrific small present. Get the authentic article from Selfridges or from www.npw.co.uk.

PERSONALISE THE SELECTION FOR HIS IPOD if he hasn't got around to doing it himself . . . with sentimental songs for an anniversary.

TICKETS TO MEDIUM RARE CABARET with dinner (020 8735 3520 and at www.mediumrare.tv).

A DVD OF THE ASHES series.

A MASSEUR to come to the house and give ten massages (this was my last birthday present to my husband and he loved it).

TRANSPARENT SHOWERPROOF SPEAKERS so he can sing along as he soaps (from Muji).

CLOTHES. These are always tricky, but I haven't known too many men who don't love shirts by Emmett (380 King's Road, London SW3 5U2; 020 7351 7529; www.emmettlondon.com), cashmere socks (for winter treats) and soft-as-butter napa gloves from Ralph Lauren (1 New Bond Street, London W15 3LU; 020 7535 4600; www.ralphlauren.co.uk), ties by Richard James (29 Savile Row, London W15 2EY; 020 7434 0605; www.richardjames.co.uk), fine-gauge silky knits by John Smedley (25 Brook Street, London W1K 5DG; 020 7495 2222) and cashmere sweaters from Asprey (167 New Bond Street, London W15 4AY; 020 7493 6767; www.asprey.com). Not to mention an original Belstaff jacket.

For Kids

Some of the best presents for children that I've found take imagination. For instance, for one grandson's birthday we bought him a rucksack and filled it with survival aids: a two-way walkie-talkie, a small torch, a small multi-purpose knife, a water bottle, a book on edible plants and flowers, and so on, all bought from a selection of camping shops, like Snow + Rock or Black's Camping. He keeps it in his family's farmhouse in France and takes it with him when they go for all-day walks. My mother gave my daughter when she was small a tiny, colourful chest of drawers, each drawer tissue-lined and with some treat inside it – a small bracelet, some coloured pencils and so on.

The Natural History Museum is a great source of presents with lots of books, puzzles and kits based on dinosaurs, skeletons to put together, scientific experiments to do. In fact most museums – the British Museum, for instance, has wonderful books and puzzles – are great for interesting presents.

Harrods has a fantastic department of antiquities, including amazing fossils, which small boys in particular seem to love.

There are lovely small children's shops tucked away all over the country, which those of you who live near them know all about. But for those who don't fancy the nightmare that a visit to Hamley's or Harrods entails, wonderful though their departments are (the traffic, the lack of parking, the crowds: the full disaster), it's worth knowing that there are lots of great online websites where all you have to do is browse, sit back and your chosen item will be sent to you.

WEBSITES FOR KIDS' PRESENTS

www.hawkin.com is great for stocking fillers. It has a section called 'pocket money' where kids can go for inexpensive small presents and there are splendid quirky ideas, such as 'Adopt a Reindeer' or 'An Acre on Mars' (I'm not entirely sure how that would go down at Christmas, though) as well lots of stuff for parties.

www.letterbox.co.uk (telephone 0870 600 7878 for a catalogue if you prefer to browse through paper) has a wonderful selection of toys for all ages. It's not particularly cheap, but its selection is terrific and it's worth paying a bit extra to make sure the toys you're giving don't fall apart.

www.english-heritage.org.uk, the English Heritage online shop, has a children's gifts section and, since one of my grandsons is quite astonishingly interested in weaponry, it provides a great source of presents for him.

www.the-green-apple.co.uk has quirky ideas for eco-conscious presents for children – things like a cardboard rocket, a doll's house and a castle, as well as dominoes made from bamboo, skittles and the like.

www.carouseltoyshop.co.uk sells all those little plastic figures that children love – pirates, fairy-tale characters, scary knights, all of which they'll sell individually and not just in expensive groups.

www.pedlars.co.uk has some nice quirky ideas.

For Miscellaneous Birthdays and Anniversaries

A sundial or sculpture for the garden from Gaze Burvill, www.gazeburvill.com.

For Londoners, tickets for Intelligence Squared Debates, from www.intelligencesquared.com.

Daylesford Organic hampers from www.daylesfordorganic.com.

A first edition of a favourite novel, such as *Oranges Are Not the Only Fruit* by Jeanette Winterson, from Simon Finch (53 Maddox Street, London W1S 2PN; 020 7499 0974; www.simonfinch.com). Price depends upon condition.

Now that smoothies are what the health-conscious set are drinking, a Kitchenaid ultra power blender from Peter Jones or John Lewis.

Ready-planted bulbs in vintage receptacles from the new Wild at Heart (020 7727 3095 and at www.wildatheart.com).

Talking Books, great for long car journeys or for those whose eyes are no longer what they were, from www.talkingbooks.co.uk.

Floradora's bejewelled 1930s sepia photographs of glam girls (07970 619 277).

Hazlitz Bespoke Stationery, Ready to Write collection, from www.hazlitz.com.

A few fashiony ideas for a young girl: a leather filofax, a funky watch (by Dolce & Gabbana), beatnik tights, a Nails Inc. manicure kit and Chanel lipgloss.

Tickets for ice skating at Somerset House, from £22.

Silk pyjamas from Carine Gilson, 12 Lowndes Street, London SW1X 9EX (020 7823 1177 and at www.carine gilson.com).

Antiques from one of my favourite (if expensive) antique shops, Guinevere, 574–580 King's Road, London SW6 2DY (020 7736 2917 and at www.guinevere.co.uk). One perfect antique Blanc de China rice bowl or a large temple jar.

Almost anything from Lady Bamford's new enterprise: Bamford, 169 Draycott Avenue, London SW3 3AJ (020 7589 8729). A beautiful kaftan, in fine-as-fine chiffon, hand-embroidered. White peony tea (£4 for 50 grams) or the pure white Elixir porcelain from Japan with the simple lines that have all the calm tranquillity of a Buddhist temple.

Cute customised cashmere sweaters. Jeanetta Rowan-Hamilton takes old cashmere sweaters (much better quality than new ones, she says) and gives them new life by adding lace, buttons, frills, embroidery – they're quirky and delicious (0207 584 3030 and at www.nettlescashmere.com).

Gorgeous Indian jackets (mostly for women) are imported

by Sara Stewart, 22 Redesdale Road, London SW3, but you must telephone first for an appointment (020 7351 5375 or mobile 07798 711 600).

FOR A YOUNG BOY

Movie Unlimited card from UGC Cinemas (www.cineworld.co.uk) at £10.99 a month.

Table football from £500 (020 7739 8700 and at www.cafe kick.co.uk).

Foldaway hammock from www.pedlars.co.uk.

A globe light from www.pedlars.co.uk.

Joe Brown T-shirts from www.joebrown.co.uk.

Pepe jeans.

***The Apprentice* boxed set of DVDs** and board game.

***Little Britain* DVD**.

Games: air hockey table, or a Batman pinball or a Laser FX Bowling Arcade Game or an Aluminium Cabinet and Silver Comet Darts Set (Peter Jones).

Travel speakers for his iPod and a pack of six iPod socks.

For Those Awkward People Who Have Everything

Giving presents used to be a doddle. A new handbag, cashmere socks, a brilliant little gadget, a fine new saucepan, some fabulous scent, if carefully matched to the nearest and dearest, could usually be guaranteed to bring a smile to the face and a thank-you letter in the post. These days, though, giving presents is infinitely more taxing. Most of us, even those of us who are far from rich, have way too much stuff. We can identify with David Collins, the interior designer, when he said, 'I really can't wear another pair of shoes or carry another bag.'

What all this boils down to is that we need to think harder, plan more and add a huge dollop of imagination into the mix. Not easy. So here are a few suggestions for as to what might go down well for those who really have no need of another pair of socks, a coffret of lotions and potions, or even a 'must-have' handbag or designer suit. Some of them are expensive (aimed at that annoying fellow who 'has everything'), but not all – and if you're prepared to do the work yourself (sort the iPod, make the memory box, cook the special meal), then they can be relatively cheap.

And if you're really stuck you could do what my husband did for a recent big birthday of my own (I think he'd surveyed the house and the wardrobe and given up on the whole notion of any more 'things'). He arranged instead for the scattered immediate family to be together for the whole day and organised a series of not very expensive treats (a trip up the London Eye, lunch in a Chinese restaurant, a visit to a cinema followed by a special tea). It couldn't have been nicer.

1. MEMORY BOXES. Jeannine Saba of Lost for Words 020 7262 2292 and at www.lostforwordsonline.com runs what she calls a personalised story-telling service. She listens to the story the giver wants to tell and asks for lots of clues – newspaper clippings, theatre tickets, opera programmes, photographs, drawings, paintings, all of which she puts together to create a totally personal memory book. She needs something like sixty or seventy different items and comes up with a rough draft for approval before going ahead. She does these usually for very special birthdays, for anniversaries, for corporate events and even for funerals (a wonderful thing, it seems to me, for, say, grandchildren after a grandparent dies). Albums with something like sixty to seventy different bits of memorabilia cost from about £450 but she can also do little gift booklets, which would be terrific to hand out at special parties (the minimum order is ten for £350), or party crackers, each of which will contain a teeny personalised booklet (£175 for a set of four).

2. FRAME THE ALBUM COVERS. For a music lover – particularly a fan of pop music – get the best old album covers framed. Gives a wonderful chart of the musical history of the recipient.

3. OLD SCHOOL PHOTOGRAPHS. Gillman and Soame will print for you a copy of most old school photographs from their archive if you email them the school and the year (www.gscovp.co.uk).

4. SORT THE IPOD. For the technophobe who wants to load his iPod and doesn't know how, www.audiosushi.net will do it for you. It will put together a specially customised playlist of music *and*, for £75, give an hour's personal tuition in how to download music and manage the programme. For £130 they'll devise an eighty-minute playlist, put the music on your iPod or on your Mp3 player.

   Glamorous DJ Alessandra Nerdrum (020 8964 7604 or email at alessandra@musicguru.info; www.music guru.co.uk) is another techno-whizz who will sort the music out. After an initial consultation of £150 (to help suss tastes), she'll create a soundtrack to match the life, charging about £20 to download two hours, worth of songs.

5. HORTICULTURE. An avenue of trees, a sea of daffodils, a hedge of roses: presents to last for ever. A tree-lined avenue of ten flame-shaped hornbeams (*Carpinus betulus*) would be £4,000. A five-acre sea of daffodils could be done for £8,000. A five-acre rolled 'instant' summer-flowering meadow would be £27,000, whilst a five-metre run of pleached magnolias could be done for £2,500 and a hedge of hybrid tea rose bushes (*Rosa* 'Black Baccarat') for £450. Your very own award-winning Chelsea flower

show garden would be £250,000. All from Woodhams Landscape (020 7730 3353 and at www.woodhams.co.uk). Remember, you don't have to get the professionals in. Do the planning yourself and it's not only more meaningful, but also much less expensive.

6. A SPECIAL DAY OUT. Fly by jet to Venice for a private after-hours tour of St Mark's Basilica. Go by gondola to a private candlelit palace, be serenaded by world-class opera singers, and have dinner prepared by a top Italian chef: from £8,500 per person.

   Three nights in Florence. Stay at the Ferragamo family private palace on the Arno. *Day One*: dine at Enoteca Pinchiorri with a set *menu degustazione* for two people at one of the best restaurants in Italy with outstanding food and a fantastic wine list. *Day Two*: a tailor from Ermenegildo Zegna, one of Italy's top menswear brands, will send a tailor to your penthouse suite to offer its made-to-measure service (the suit is included in the price). A private visit with a guide to the Vasari Corridor, running from the Uffizi to the Pitti Palace, over the Ponte Vecchio, with an unrivalled collection of portraits. *Day Three*: a convertible Alfa Romeo Giulietta is delivered to the hotel for a drive through the rolling Tuscan countryside to the Cappezine estate, home of Avignonesi, one of the finest vineyards in Italy. There's a private tour of the cellars and vineyards, then a four-course lunch and wine-tasting in the loggia overlooking the hill town of

Montepulciano. *Day Four*: a hot-air balloon ride taking off at dawn from the olive groves of Montisi. A champagne breakfast greets you on touchdown. A Mercedes with private driver takes you to and from the airport or the station. From £4,500 per person.

Both available from Bellini Travel (020 7602 7602 and at www.bellinitravel.com).

7. A PAIR OF SWANS, for the must-have lake. Mute swans are hard to come by (requiring a licence and lots of paperwork) but Bruce Howell, a waterfowl breeder, sells them (01362 668 303). It's easier to buy a pair of black swans for £200 or Trumpeter swans from £500–£600 a pair. Hoopers are £350 a pair and Black Necks £350 a pair.

   Anglia Wildfowl will deliver the birds and offer to buy back any cygnets the following year. Call Nick Willis on 07752 160 009 (www.angliawildfowl.co.uk). Swans are not always a safe present, however, as they have been known to abscond to other more favourable lakes.

   If the lake is missing, Woodhams (see p. 403) will make a ten-metre one for £32,000.

8. THE SPECIAL BOOK. For a first wedding anniversary a doting husband found a first edition of *Rebecca* by Daphne du Maurier (a favourite of his wife), arranged for Joan Fontaine (who starred in the film) to sign it and then got it specially bound. A wife found a first edition of *The Compleat Angler* (for £50,000 plus) for a

fishing-mad husband. If you want to find a first edition book, start at www.abebooks.com, a Canadian-run site that began as a book exchange and now carries stocklists for rare book collectors and sellers around the world. Bertram Rota, which stocks modern first edition books from 1890, will conduct more complicated searches for books (020 7836 0723 and at www.bertram rota.co.uk).

Maggs Bros Rare Books (www.maggs.com) has a large collection of first edition books. Simon Finch (who recently sold a Shakespeare first folio edition for £1.2 million) is another dealer in rare books (020 7499 0974 and at www.simonfinch.com).

9. COMMISSION A SYMPHONY. Follow in the footsteps of Mervyn King, governor of the Bank of England, and Sir Nicholas Goodison, ex-chairman of the Stock Exchange. King contacted the London Symphony Orchestra and, with six friends, commissioned a symphony. It cost them £18,000 over three years (£3,000 per head), but they had creative control over the project and worked with players from the orchestra. A cheaper alternative is offered by the Birmingham Contemporary Music Group: as a Sound Investor for £100, you can buy a share in a symphony or you can buy the entire symphony for from £10,000. When it is ready, you get to attend rehearsals, go to the première, meet the composer and get a signed copy of the score (www.bcmg.org.uk).

10. COMMISSION A PORTRAIT. Anna Wimbledon, aged

thirty, a lauded portrait artist who has been well reviewed in *The Times* and nominated for various prizes, will do nine-inch-square portraits on blocks for £5,000, up to a full-length portrait, which might come to £15,000 plus VAT. There is a waiting list for her work but there are plenty of other artists to call on. Telephone Francis Kyle Gallery on 020 7499 6870 (www.franciskylegallery.com).

11. HAND-MADE MODEL OF A HOUSE. David Linley will create a model of your humble cottage, fine rectory, beautiful manor house or very grand castle. (Castle Howard, done as a present for Simon Howard, its owner, is just one of his many commissions.) From around £25,000. It can be entirely decorative or made into the form of a humidor, jewellery or pencil case (020 7730 7300 and at www.davidlinley.com).

12. A SPECIAL DAY WITH A SPORTING, LITERARY OR CULINARY HERO. Play a game of tennis with John McEnroe or a round of golf with Greg Norman. The cost of the game depends upon the star.

    Organise a day at Wimbledon – either playing doubles with an ex-Great Britain Davis Cup player, lunch and tour of the grounds, or a centre court ticket and champagne lunch during the 2007 Championships. From £1,000. Have lunch at a top restaurant with a literary figure such as Martin Amis, Margaret Atwood, Zadie Smith or Roddy Doyle, from £5,000.

    A famous chef to cook at home: Raymond Blanc,

Anthony Worrall-Thompson, Ainsley Harriott, Rick Stein and many others. The price depends on who the chef is. From around £15,000.

Quintessentially will organise any of the above once you join. Membership costs £750 (0870 850 8585 and at www.quintessentially.com).

13. A DAY WITH A PERSONAL SHOPPER. Choose from Paris, New York, Delhi or Bombay. Whisk him or her there by private jet.

In Paris, Susan Tabak's your woman. She's best of friends with some of the capital's sassiest dressers (Nathalie Rykiel, Loulou de la Falaise, Marie-Hélène de Taillac, to name but three). From £760 a day (+1 212 404 8398 and at www.parispersonalshopper.com).

In Bombay, Greaves Travel can fix for Monica Vaziralli to find you the finest pashminas, best-value diamonds, sumptuous silks and off-beat antiques. A three-day package, flying out on Thursday night, arriving back at 7 a.m. on Monday with two days with a private shopper and a luxury car, is £999. Fly her or him first class and it'll be rather more (0207 487 9111).

In New York, stay at the Mandarin Oriental and book four hours with a personal shopper at Bergdorf Goodman. From £627.

Plants and Flowers

A bunch of flowers every week of the year must be one of the best presents ever – expensive but memorable. Scented roses can be delivered every month from the Real Flower Company (0870 403 6548 and at www.realflowers.co.uk) at £365 for a year's worth. www.foreverflowering.com is a wonderful website delivering fresh flowers, brilliantly arranged, all over the UK. www.crocus.co.uk is a terrific site for horticultural presents – gorgeous huge orchids for indoors, flowering trees, orange trees.

John Lewis gets better by the day. You can now order very nice flowers – possibly not up to the delicious standards of an Ercole Moroni or a Rob van Helden, but pretty good all the same – from John Lewis twenty-four hours a day. Tap into www.johnlewis.com or call 08456 049 049 between 7 a.m. and midnight.

Special Florists

Paris

CHRISTIAN TORTU is the most famous Parisian florist, at 6 Carrefour de l'Odéon, 75006 Paris (+33 1 43 26 02 56).

London

We're spoiled for choice. Choose from WILD AT HEART (020 7727 3095); ERCOLE MORONI at McQueen's (020 7251 5505); ORLANDO HAMILTON (020 8962 8944), and Rob van Helden (020 7720 6774 and at www.partyflowers-london.co.uk).

New York

TAKASHIMAYA FLORAL BOUTIQUE, 693 Madison Avenue (+1 212 350 0111); WILD POPPY, 159 East 92nd Street (+1 212 717 5757); ELIZABETH RYAN, 411 East 9th Street (+1 212 995 1111); and SPRUCE, 222 8th Avenue (+1 212 929 9252).

Charitable Presents

Amongst the very well-heeled set and the not-so-young crowd, it is now quite the norm to ask either for no presents or to suggest a charity for guests to donate to instead. When Jamie Oliver married Jools, for instance, they asked for guests to donate something to the Stroke Association in memory of Jools's father. Many people have their own favourite charities and sometimes a specific one is named. Otherwise, choose one that means something special to the couple getting married.

Or give to eco charities like Earthroots (www.earthroots.org) and get a great gift for your budding animal lover.

Adopt a Wolf for just £29 (www.anglianwolf.com).

Through the World Wildlife Fund (www.wwf.org.uk), you can organise to adopt any number of endangered species – a tiger, gorilla, polar bear, panda.

It's also very fashionable these days to ask wedding guests to contribute to environmental charities, most particularly when they've been asked to fly hundreds of miles to the wedding itself. www.carbonneutral.com (which used to be called Future Forests) enables you to buy trees to reforest a big selection of projects.

Through the Woodland Trust (www.woodland-trust.org.uk) you can give as many trees as you like, for which you get a certificate plus a map showing the wood where your trees are planted.

Through Oxfam Unwrapped (www.oxfamunwrapped.com) plant fifty trees.

Robin Birley started www.envirotrade.com, which develops projects in Mozambique that encourage the local population to treasure their forests. You can buy carbon credits via the website.

Wrapping

I'm of the school of thought that thinks that wrapping matters. I'm entranced by lovely packaging and one of the

A FEW GOOD WEBSITES FOR PRESENTS

www.raptdirect.com (0870 160 7580). An offshoot of OKA, a charming provider of decorative pieces for the home, Rapt is a small mail-order or online operation that is geared specifically to the market for presents. Nothing dramatic, but the sort of pieces that would fit into most people's homes: big hurricane lights, small leather-covered tape measures, throws (nicely Eastern, with a touch of Paisley), Nailsea wine glasses, candlesticks – you get the picture.

www.reglisse.co.uk is run by Pascale Karam-Boemond, a chic Lebanese who lived in Paris for years, and she has things you won't find in most shops – Gaetano Pesce's amazing resin vases-cum-sculptures, jewellery by Philippe Ferrandis, who makes jewellery for many of the haute couture houses, ceramics from a Danish design duo, one of whom helped modernise the grand old house of Copenhagen China. She's got a great eye and great taste.

www.notonthehighstreet.com brings together a whole range of niche designers and craftspeople. Search for quirky bags and jewellery, for offbeat craft items and, one thing's for sure, you won't find them in any of the major department stores.

www.plumo.com is another enchanting little catalogue and online source of things you won't see anywhere else. It has a rather rustic, nostalgic air to it and is definitely not for city slickers, but if you're looking for a flower-spattered silk kimono, some embroidered handkerchiefs (oooh, that takes me back), some adorable little pagoda lanterns or some pressed glass cakestands, then Plumo will come up trumps.

great joys of visiting Japan is the sheer aesthetic refinement of it all. A single apple is wrapped and then delivered to its buyer with all the care and love that in the UK might be attached to buying jewels. Do I always manage, come Christmas time, to deliver up little works of wrapped art? Of course not. But, unless something is oversized (which, funnily enough, many children's presents tend to be, the bicycle, the doll's house, the football table) they at least get wrapped somehow. And I do have aspirations – one day, one Christmas, it's all going to be gorgeous. In the meantime, for those who are really pushed for time, more and more stores offer wrapping services, which, when you're lucky enough to have lots of people you care about to find presents for, is, one has to confess, an amazing boon.

For a particular birthday, you can go to town because there are just one or two presents to consider. Colour combinations, paper, ribbons and trimmings can all be customised and time taken. You could choose papers that are somehow specific – special newspapers or maps; or ordinary white paper with photographs printed digitally on them; a music score of a piece of music that is meaningful. Try customising the container, for instance, matching it to something imaginative: flowerpots for something horticultural, cake tins for something food-related – you get the idea. You can make the package seem special by adding little stars, flowers, beads.

Come Christmas, I usually adopt a streamlined approach. I have a colour scheme each year and everybody's present gets the same wrapping. Funnily enough, it works quite well because, when all the family is together and everything is piled up under the tree, it makes the groups easily identifiable. One ploy could be to use a different colour scheme for each family group, making it easier to distribute them.

I've used plain brown paper in the past, which can look wonderfully chic particularly if you use a nice wide black ribbon. I quite often use plain silver paper with gold ribbon or plain gold with silver ribbon. Both gold and silver, if plain, also look gorgeous with any jewel-coloured ribbon and make a happy background for stars and other stickers.

In India I sometimes fall in love with their gorgeous hand-made papers but they don't work very well for wrapping – they're too stiff and not malleable enough. But tissue paper works well and if, on Christmas Eve, you run out of paper, you can always use tinfoil, though it is a little on the fragile side. Newspaper is another useful emergency wrapping and it can be saved from looking tatty by folding the edges and using some wide black ribbon – very graphic.

Don't stint on buying paper, it's daft. If you buy too much, you can use it up during the year or at the following Christmas, but if you don't have enough on Christmas Eve you're stuck. Keep ribbons as they come in during the year and recycle them. These days you can buy cute boxes and bags that make good containers for presents.

Stock up on supplies if you ever go to India, most particularly in Delhi where you should go to Chandni Chowk, where they sell a myriad wonderful things for every kind of festivity for literally a few pence. I buy ribbons and all sorts of glittery bits and pieces – flowers, stars, beads, plastic drops, decorations – to bring home and put in the Christmas drawer.

Favourite Places to Buy Wrapping

UK

PAPERCHASE, 213–215 Tottenham Court Road, London WC2 7PS (www.paperchase.co.uk), has a fantastic selection of papers, labels, tags, boxes and bags.

TEMPTATION ALLEY, 359–361 Portobello Road, London W10 5SA (www.temptationalley.com), is a gem, filled with all sorts of decorative ideas from feathers, buttons, fabrics – you name it.

V. V. ROULEAUX must be one of my favourite shops of all time. It is filled with decorative inspiration – ribbons, bows, butterflies, flowers. Check it all out on www.vvrouleaux.com.

THE WRAPPING COMPANY, (01483 823 023 and at www.thewrappingco.com), has lots of cute bags for bottles, chic boxes for everything from a cashmere sweater to a pair of cufflinks, masses of tags and a vast variety of ribbons.

Italy

Italy has fabulous papers of all kinds, including beautiful

hand-marbled ones – a little expensive if you're doing lots of wrapping but lovely for a one-off treat.

Il PAPIRO, check www.ilpapirofirenze.it for branches. They are all over Italy with six branches in Florence and four in Venice.

New York

KATE'S PAPERIE, 561 Broadway, New York, and two other branches – check on www.katespaperie.com. Fabulous papers but special ribbons, too.

Tokyo

TOKYO KYUKYODO, 5–7–4, Ginza Chuo-ku, has a fantastic selection of Japanese paper products. Whether it's a little notebook, some writing paper, a cute bookmark, an address book or fanciful paper creations, they're all beautiful.

Fun and Games

Parties

The making of a successful party is like the baking of a wonderful soufflé – the ingredients and proportions must be weighed and measured by the hand of an artist – which should be taken out of the oven at exactly the psychological moment – and *served hot*. Elsa Maxwell

Elsa Maxwell was a legendary party giver in the 1930s, featuring regularly in magazines such as *Vogue* and all the newspapers society pages, but if one listened to her advice, nobody would ever dare give one. I don't believe it's *that* tricky myself. But I do go along with her when she says that no hostess (to use the vocabulary of her heyday) should take her own party so seriously that the guests end up being solemn about it as well. The best parties are gifts to your friends. The point of a party is to have fun. Most of us have been to the sort of party that is more of an ordeal than a pleasure – the sort where nobody introduces you to anybody and you mill about, having to make your way through a mêlée of heaving bodies and hoping desperately to catch the eye of somebody you know. It seems to be a formula that some people indulge in at New Year's Eve, where one's hosts keep one standing about with nothing more substantial than endless drink until midnight, when they finally produce something long after one is past it, and never introduce one to anybody.

Speaking personally, I've always loved best the sort of party where you eventually sit down – where there are perhaps drinks first and then a proper placement so you really do get to meet at least your neighbours properly. I love small dinner parties and anything where there is a possibility of genuine exchange. I also love the sort of parties that people are more prone to give around Christmas time when all the generations are mixed up and our hosts include both their children and their parents. Games are played with everybody mixing in and such parties often end the evening with carols around the piano. And then, of course, there is the grand party to mark an engagement, a wedding, an anniversary – the marquee, the placement, the band and the dancing. They can be wonderful, provided the hosts have done more than worry about the theme, the food and the decor, and have gone to the trouble of thinking who might like to sit next to whom, organising the table plans with real care.

I'm not particularly adventuresome myself since our house, being long and thin without one single room large enough for more than about twenty-five people, doesn't lend itself to parties but I've been to enough to know what works from the guests' point of view. I'm with Elsa Maxwell when she says: 'A good party should occur in one room only, and that room should always be too small.' (But only just too small; very much too small, which I've also experienced, doesn't work either because you can't circulate and you get trapped.)

The best parties have an entertaining mix of guests but I have this old-fashioned notion that parties are for your friends, so the idea (much promoted by professional party givers) of inviting famous people one doesn't know to jazz up the proceedings is, to my mind, bizarre. Beauties, eccentrics, creative people and great entertainers are all great additions to the mix – *if* you happen to have them in your circle. In my view, it's critical to try to think who might be pleased to meet one another, and to make sure you introduce people likely to get on. The really big sin in my book is merely to throw yourself into enjoying your own party while giving no thought as to how your guests are getting on (and, believe me, I've been to a few like that).

Brits used to give rather spartan parties but since the advent of proper party planners and fancy caterers, not to mention all that City money that has begun to swill around the country, the ante has been upped considerably. Wedding parties take place in Rome and Prague, in castles and on tropical islands, and the celebrations are meticulously planned over many days. (Did the Hurley/Nayar celebrations really take eight days?) I don't recall much in the way of hen parties, baby showers or Hallowe'en parties when I was growing up, but these days they're all the rage. Even children's parties have become a source of angst with tiny tots demanding to know what the entertainment is (in my day you made your own and Grandmother's Whispers was our idea of a great game), while goody bags on departure are, it seems, de rigueur. No wonder it's become a stressful matter.

Which is why if the party is going to be large and grand, there's nothing for it but to hand it over to the professionals. If you're strapped for cash or want to do it simply, you can buy in bits of help. You can hire simple marquees – just Google 'marquees for hire' and you're spoiled for choice. Prices vary hugely depending upon the grandeur and elaboration of the tent itself and of the decorations inside. If you live in the country you can often get local women to do some of the food whilst you rope in friends and family to do, say, the flowers and the puddings.

For dinner parties at home I often have some help. We have an open-plan kitchen and dining room, so there's no room for posh staff as there's no 'behind-the-scenes' to put them. There was a time when I knew of a wonderful girl who would cook the entire dinner party at her home and deliver it to me at six o'clock on the given day with precise instructions as to how to serve it and what needed heating, and with all the garnishes in sweet little containers. Alas, she's gone the way of such help and has got married, giving dinner parties of her own. But I still buy in odd bits of help. I quite often order the first and last courses from Ottolenghi (www.ottolenghi.co.uk) and do the main course myself.

Or you can hand over the party arrangements lock, stock and barrel. Party planners these days are increasingly inventive and they not only come up with themes but have all the props to bring the theme to life. I once saw the warehouse of John Robertson-Roxborough (of the caterers The

Admirable Crichton) and it was huge, so stuffed to the gills with varieties of glasses, flower containes, tablecloths, tables and a most of other paraphernalia, that you could see why he is able to conjure up so many different sorts of magic. As to themes, Ben Goldsmith had an ice-cavern for his twenty-first; Elton and David like to go in for kings and queens and their 'opulence' themes; Truman Capote famously had a black and white ball; Patty and Andy Wong every Chinese New Year ask their friends to dress up according to the particular theme of the ball; Philip Green had his famous toga party; one hedge-fund manager had a heaven and hell party (which sounds rather fun: guests could wander between the two).

I think seating plans matter hugely. It's an act of generosity and essential to a good party to try to match people who might like each other, fall in love with each other or just have a rattling good conversation. Some people like switching the seating plan halfway through a dinner, getting the men to move along a few paces. I rather like that, though to be sure sometimes you've just got going when it's time to move on. Husbands and wives or other couples should be on different tables at large parties but if they are at the same table do *not* seat them next to each other – they can do that at home and it isn't why they've come. Don't put best friends together either; they see each other all the time, too. At big seated dinners the host and hostess should make a point of visiting all the tables, checking that all is well and nobody seems left out.

Whom to put next to the host is a tricky question. You can choose the jolliest, most amusing person there, but I think it displays better manners to look after those who might know fewest people, who are very old or who have come the farthest distance. I remember being immensely touched at a very, very grand summer lunch party being put on the right hand of our host when there were many much more important people there. It showed exquisite manners, for he realised that my husband and I were less likely than most to know many people there (they were new friends of ours and it was the first time we had been invited to their house) and he did it (I assume) to make sure we were properly looked after. These are the sort of manners that come from an inner courtesy and elegance, and are what one hopes for in a perfect host.

* I think friends rather like being asked to help at a party. Some could pour drinks and make sure everybody's glass is full, and others introduce people who seem to be out on a limb or on their own.

Venue

Of course it depends on the party. Small ones – dinner parties, small birthday parties – are nicest at home. For anything bigger, and for people with country cottages or houses and lawns, the simplest solution is to hire a marquee. You might think about combining a couple of parties –

we've been to a friend's big 'o' or wedding anniversary party where either the night before or the night after, a child has its twenty-first birthday party. But there are all sorts of strange places for hire for parties, ranging from cellars and dungeons to clubs and castles. Most caterers have lists of suitable venues, but just in London alone some of the options are the Victoria & Albert Museum, the Orangery in Holland Park, the Chelsea Physic Garden, the Serpentine Gallery, and Leighton House in Kensington (020 7602 3316), not to mention some offbeat venues, such as the Admiralty Arch (020 7276 5200), which is a wonderful if bizarre venue for a largish dinner (it holds some thirty people). The list is endless, not to mention the large number of country houses, plus castles both small and large, that can be hired in almost every corner of the UK and abroad.

Atmosphere

Lighting is important. Anything too harsh spoils the atmosphere. At a big dinner, groups of small candles – what the Americans call votives – are wonderful. You can group them on tables, or on side tables, around the house. At night you can add lots of enchantment to the proceedings by lighting up the steps to the house on both sides. I've seen paper bags used as containers with tea-lights inside them. Lakeland has a version (01539 488 100 and at www.lakeland.co.uk) which is made of fire-retardant white paper with a pretty etched pattern in it that is illuminated once a tea-light is put inside. Put lights in the trees if you have them or hang lanterns (again from Lakeland and very inexpensive), or stick huge garden flares (from Habitat) in the ground to light up a drive or pathway. To lend magic to the garden there are now little battery-operated lights that need no electricity. Marks & Spencer has some, made from solid white and transparent acrylic that come in the shape of flowers, butterflies or dragonflies, as well as stars and flower-shaped lights, all of which change colour constantly and glitter away in the dark. Lakeland sells battery-operated hummingbirds that are mounted on black sticks so that they appear invisible at night. You simply stick them into flower-pots or into the earth so that the hummingbirds appear to hover. Should you happen to have a pond, a lake or a still river, you could add magic with floating waterlily lights that have an LED inside them so that the light changes as it glows (from Marks & Spencer). Habitat has strings of pretty lights that can be draped over mirrors or the edges of tables. They need to be plugged into an electrical socket but they add a lot of magic and come in various forms (flowers, stars, blossoms). You can also drape coiled lights in Muji's transparent cubes at Christmas.

For dinner parties, lots of candles are wonderful. Massed ranks of assorted candlesticks, hurricane lamps (Marks & Spencer have sold some nice generous ones for very little money), or candelabra all would look good.

Flowers are, of course, essential for the good party, and if you're doing a large party with caterers, you'll probably get the flowers done by a professional florist (find names and addresses in Chapter 5, p.285). If you're going to do the flowers yourself, try to make your arrangements as dramatic as possible. It's not the time for sweet little posies but for tall dramatic stems and branches in oversized containers. But for a smallish party at home you can buy lots of flowers inexpensively at markets. In London, Nine Elms (the old Covent market), a district of London between Battersea and Vauxhall, is an amazing place, not only for the flowers themselves but for every kind of container you might need for them. They're so cheap there that I always end up buying far more than I need. There are buckets of every sorts, huge vases in glass and ceramic – it sets the imagination going.

* If you're going to have flowers on a dinner table, remember to keep them either quite low or very high (I've seen huge tall thin vases with amazingly dramatic flowers emerging from the top) so that people can see each other across the table.

Instead of flowers you could have big bowls of aubergines and oranges. I've seen ornamental cabbages, displayed like this, especially those small purple ones, looking wonderful. Nigella Lawson, I once read, likes big bowls of lemons.

At Christmas there's nothing like lots of black roses in dark vases – not cheap, I know, but *very* sophisticated. Otherwise get masses of one thing. Bunches of asparagus fern look good and in winter huge branches (and I mean huge: it's the mimsy approach that spoils it all) of leaves can be immensely effective. Bowls of pine cones don't cost much and look and smell wonderful.

I personally like to keep the table fairly plain, with antique white linen cloths and big plain linen napkins, but I do think at Christmas or for children's parties or themed parties, you can go a bit wild. At Christmas I always bring out a huge tartan cloth that I sewed up from lengths bought at Peter Jones. It's a terrific background to a collection of red glass and pretty red and pink Ralph Lauren china.

And I love scented candles (though not in the dining room): a house should smell wonderful, too. There's a whole section on candles in Chapter 5, p. 290, but for parties my favourite smells of all time are Rigaud's Cypres and Lorenzo Villoresi's Spezie.

Invitations

For a grand party I like invitations plain and classy on nice card with a classic typeface and thick creamy envelopes with tissue lining in a colour of your choice. It's hard to beat Smythson's (020 7318 1515 and at www.smythson.com), but there's no getting away from the fact that they're very expensive (that's what comes of being the leader in your field). Leeming Brothers (www.leemingbrothers.co.uk), which sounds like a bank, I know, but they're actually excellent stationers, has developed a new technique that enables them to offer proper engraved invitations with that lovely raised type at very good prices (01962 738 492). If you're really skint you can design your own at the high street printing outlets – Kall-Kwik, for instance (www.kallkwick.co.uk).

But there's nothing to stop you having funky invitations, or thinking up a special theme, or getting an artist or graphic designer friend to do something particular to you – it's your party after all. If you're a techie you can probably create your own on the computer. One friend makes her own Christmas cards every year, printing them out on clear, crinkly paper, and somehow they manage to seem cooler than anything shop bought.

* Ideally invitations should go out at least six weeks before the event but for really serious parties (a big '0' birthday) when you really want all your favourite people to be there, send them out three, six or even twelve months ahead of time.

Some people ask calligraphists to write special invitations (for, say, a bar mitzvah or a wedding), which can look beautiful. I've known some people send a balloon through the post that you blow up to read the invitation printed on it. Others have sent cute little records with songs inviting people to parties or DVDs

And whilst we're on the subject of invitations, guests should answer promptly. Imagine the angst of not knowing how many people to cater for.

SOME USEFUL ADDRESSES

There are good caterers all over the country but here are a few I know to be good.

Absolute Taste, 14 Edgel Street, Wandsworth, London SW18 1SR (020 8870 5151 and at www.absolute taste.co.uk), does some really grand events (all those for the Grand Prix, for instance) and comes up with terrific ideas and 'themes' should you be short of ideas.

Fait Accompli: (020 7352 2777 or email afitzgibbons@faitaccompli.co.uk) can also handle really big events.

Rhubarb (020 8812 3200 and at www.rhubarb.net) is brilliant at parties and, at a Christmas ball I went to, gave the guests the most sublime pasta (perfumed with black truffles) that most of us had ever eaten.

By Word of Mouth (020 8871 9566 and at www.bywordofmouth.co.uk) is good for dinner parties.

Rachel Mount (020 8672 9333 and at www.rachelmount.com) does the most sublime cakes. She is really an artist manqué who happens to use cakes and icing as her medium. One of her cakes was on the cover of *Vogue*'s ninetieth birthday issue. She does brilliant cakes for the fashion set: a collection of ridiculous, vertiginously high-heeled shoes, handbags, magazine covers. For my daughter's wedding, she made a three-tiered cake with delicate decorations of exquisite blackberries, dog roses and other country flowers. Not cheap but enchanting.

www.partyparties.co.uk has a website with 101 ideas for different parties that you can consult if you're looking for a theme: vicars and tarts, safari, togas and lots, lots more.

www.cardamondesigns.com will design cards to order.

www.elegantice.co.uk will not only deliver huge packs of ice for cooling drinks but will also provide extraordinary ice sculptures. They leave me slightly cold (sorry) but it is apparently a newly trendy thing.

Music

Not, I have to say, my area of expertise (my almost total ignorance of pop is a great gap in my education and something I'm determined to put right). If you're going to have dancing, live bands are wonderful. There are small ones all over the country that are thrilled to perform for not very large sums – you don't have to have Robbie, J. Lo or any of the other mega-buck acts that hedge-fund managers seem to feel are essential for their jollifications. Otherwise track down a good DJ or ask your guests to bring along their favourite CDs. However, don't have the music so loud that nobody can hear anyone else speak. The wrong music can ruin a party so choose it very, very carefully. If you want people to dance, you need some catchy dance music – try the Nolans' 'I'm in the Mood for Dancing' followed by some of the great classic dance music of all time. Go to HMV in London's Oxford Street, which has personal shopping advisors who will guide you to the right music for you. Otherwise check in online at www.hmv.co.uk.

My young friends tell me that there are now wonderful compilations for good parties. They especially recommend the compilation from the Buddha Club in Paris and the Hotel Costes. Otherwise *After the Playboy Mansion* by Dmitri is, they tell me, loungy and cool. *Ultra-chilled 01* is sophisticated and likely to appeal to those over fifty. All can be bought over the internet from www.amazon.co.uk. These days there are people whom you can turn to for advice on how to fill the iPod (see p. 402): just give them the scenario (over-fifties who want to dance; under-thirties who want something edgy, blues, jazz, whatever).

If you're after something more cultural, the music schools have trios and quartets, as well as singers, who are only too pleased to be asked to perform for not very large sums of money.

In case you're as ignorant about pop music as I am and want advice on what the great all-time records are so that you don't waste your time with junk, this is the list drawn up for me by James Brown, creator of *Loaded* magazine, erstwhile editor of *GQ* magazine, founder and owner of *Jack* magazine, and currently editing *Quintessentially* magazine.

Rolling Stones: *Let it Bleed* and *Beggar's Banquet*
Lou Reed: *Transformer*
The Smiths: *Queen is Dead*
Marvin Gaye: *What's Going On*
Curtis Mayfield: *Superfly*
Bob Dylan: *Blonde on Blonde*
Michael Jackson: *Off the Wall*
Kate Bush: *Hounds of Love*
Patti Smith: *Horses*
Serge Gainsbourg: *Bonnie and Clyde*
Led Zeppelin: anything

Drink

If you're having a grand party with lots of people, you'll have to have somebody to help serve the drinks and then you can run more of an elaborate bar with fashionable mojitos and all the rest. If you're having a party at home and help is minimal, keep the drink simple. In Chapter 6 I mention trying to offer some really delicious non-alcoholic drinks. Water is great but not very festive (though you do need to have lots of it on hand for those who simply get thirsty and don't only want alcohol). Try to offer something better than that. I was at a book launch once on a summer evening where the two drinks on offer were a refreshing melon drink (see the recipe on p. 362) and champagne. Most people chose the melon drink.

Otherwise I usually stick to champagne but have things like whisky, vodka and gin as well as a good chilled white wine available for those who don't like champagne. Caterers tell me that you need to calculate for something like three-quarters of a bottle per person. Prosecco or some sparkling white wines are cheaper than champagne and some people actually prefer them. Some like Buck's Fizz (it's key not to add the orange juice – and it must be really fresh – until just before serving) whilst others like Kir Royale (champagne with a little cassis), though speaking personally, if it's good champagne (and I'm not talking Dom Perignon, Bollinger or Krug here: much too expensive for parties unless we're the City bonus set, but I am talking something a cut above the horrible cheap sweet champagnes), I prefer it plain. Cooling champagne in bulk can be a problem. Check out www.elegantice.co.uk, which will deliver it in bulk and then you can cool lots of bottles in the bath. If you're young and giving a party, you may find that at least half the guests prefer beer. Again use the bath to chill in quantity. If you're buying drink in bulk, most wine merchants will lend you enough glasses and they're usually of perfectly simple and acceptable design. They'll also supply ice in bulk.

As the evening wears on, offer lots of chances for non-alcoholic drinks: sparkling and still waters sprigged up with a little lemon, really refreshing home-made lemonade or ginger beer can be fabulous.

TWO EASY BUT SOPHISTICATED PARTY DRINKS

Simply pour a good iced vodka over crushed ice and add lots of gorgeous pink pomegranate seeds – looks fabulous, tastes good.

Mix equal quantities of gin and Campari, plus half as much sweet red vermouth, with plenty of ice in a shaker. Add a thin slice of curled fresh orange peel.

Dinner Parties

My favourite sort of party. I personally never have enough time to spend hours making my table look amazing. My tastes run to the classic look: white antique linen cloths, plain white linen napkins, a selection of non-matching china and glass, set off by two huge hurricane lamps holding great cream candles. Those of you who are better organised can be more creative, coming up with endless different tables. Sherrie Bodie and Jan Grinling, two charming – and, it has to be said, dextrous – women *d'un certain âge* and clearly *d'un certain* affluence, run occasional courses on the subject (07989 402 259 or 07836 689 603 for details). They call their courses 'Dare to Do it' and they're nothing if not inventive, for these who have the time and the inclination, they show you how to do it. They have their minds firmly on the pennies and they don't go in for too much fancy work.

Here are a few of their tips. Always have a big generous cloth. If you don't have linen or antique ones, or you want to change the colour scheme, they suggest you go to Southall or Indian markets for gorgeous saris, or metres of plain hessian, or curtain lining material (which they use under gauzy fabrics to give body and depth of colour).

They use things like decorative hairbands as napkin rings and they pin little things like flowers, or old brooches and bits of glitter, to the band to make them look glamorous.

They buy glass vases and bowls in assorted shapes from Ikea for anything between £3 and £5 each, or from John Lewis. They introduced me to Temptation Alley (www.temptation alley.com) in London's Portobello Road where you can get lots of wondrous props – anything from glitter and feathers to buttons and bows.

They create a lot of glamour with an all-black table. They start with a large black cloth (from Temptation Alley), which they cover in mirrored table mats. Then come crystal plates (expensively from William Yeoward but Ikea has some at about £3 each). They fill little shot glasses (from John Lewis) with silver almonds to reflect the light and suggest dotting the table with glass tea-lights with candles in them. Then around the table they scatter silver boxes, a collection of old decanter tops and other crystal bits and pieces – the idea being to catch and reflect as much light as possible. Napkins can be tied with black ribbon to finish the look.

They're very keen on centrepieces but they don't believe you always have to have flowers, lovely though they are. Try bowls of Christmas balls – either glass or silver, or a mixture of glass and silver, or fruits or vegetables. And don't forget candles – the most magical light of all (but they shouldn't be scented at a dinner table; keep them plain and creamy).

Food

I've already covered this in Chapter 6. Food matters hugely but, as I said then, whilst it doesn't have to be elaborate, you can't get away with taking no trouble at all. What's right depends so much upon the season, the occasion and the guests.

I'm not keen on itsy-bitsy canapés though that is clearly what you need to serve if you're just having a drinks party. Suffice it to say that trends in this area change quite fast. At one point there was a rash of little Italian bites (tiny squares of ravioli, exquisite morsels of parma ham and Parmesan); then there was the trend for miniature portions of proletarian food made posh – fish and chips, eggs and bacon, hamburgers and the like; whilst as I write, Eastern still seems the reigning mood with tempting mouthfuls of sushi or teriyaki being served on equally exquisite pieces of Zen-like porcelain. I think only professional caterers can manage these things. If you're doing drinks at home and are catering yourself, it's best to keep it simple. I don't know anybody (except vegetarians) who doesn't like really, really good sausages (Waitrose do organic chipolatas; all too often baby sausages seem made of indeterminate pink gunk) or spiced nuts (see box on p. 441 for recipe) or Marks & Spencer's wonderful cheese straws. Even plain hunks of real Parmesan are delicious, particularly if offered with a fragrant olive oil or balsamic vinegar to dip them into. Sometimes it's better to serve just a few rather more robust things – bruschetta with gravadlax and mustard sauce, say, and some chicken satay on cocktail sticks.

Dinner party food – particularly for those short of time – is covered pretty fully in Chapter 6.

Buffet food, I find, is great fun to do. Lots of it can be prepared a little in advance. Once again generosity is the key – a huge platter of something simple like mozzarella, tomato and avocado, scattered with masses of basil and a really good olive oil and balsamic vinegar, looks wonderfully colourful and inviting. Many of the first courses in Chapter 6 can be made in far larger quantities for buffets. Delia Smith's grilled vegetables with couscous (from *Delia Smith's Summer Collection*) makes a terrific dish for a buffet lunch or supper and looks brilliant too.

Some classic hot dishes make superb centrepieces. For Bonfire night there's nothing to beat a fantastic chilli con carne served with baked potatoes, or an aromatic boeuf en daube (again with baked potatoes), or even a wonderful chicken or lamb tagine (with couscous or baked potatoes).

Sometimes it's fun to do a themed meal. For my father's eightieth birthday I did a buffet supper for about fifty people that homed in on his South African origins. I made a cold curried fish dish (easy to do and much, much more delicious than it sounds – it disappeared in a trice), and followed up with two classic South African dishes: bobotie (a South African version of shepherd's pie in which the meat is slightly curried and mixed, when cooked, with a little bread soaked in milk, which may sound horrid but adds some creaminess to the texture, and then topped with a custard before being baked in the oven), served with a variety of chutneys (Daylesford's are fabulous, www.daylesfordorganic.com), plus a meat and fruit curry. Any South African cookbook will have these recipes for they are probably the best-known indigenous dishes, reflecting the influence of Malay cooking. To finish, we had sorbets (bought in) made from tropical fruits – mango, passion fruit, pawpaw, guava and the like. I can only say it went down a treat with some very sophisticated Londoners.

The idea can be adapted to almost any cuisine – Creole, typical American (baked chicken, cheesecake), French, Italian, Spanish or anything else.

In summer there are some classic French dishes that make a really good centrepiece to a buffet lunch or supper – in particular a grand aioli, which consists of a huge cold cooked fish (classically cod but, in these more eco-conscious times, a freshly baked haddock would be equally lovely), surrounded by some tender young cooked vegetables (baby carrots, beans, asparagus, fennel, new potatoes, cauliflower, artichokes) and a vast pot of garlicky aioli in the middle. Or the Italian dish, vitello tonnato – cold roasted veal sliced and served with a cold tuna fish sauce. I even happen to like a properly made coronation chicken (though not, please, with any pineapple anywhere near it), which is really just cooked chicken (best made with a boiling fowl from your butcher that has been gently poached), served in a lightly curried creamy sauce. And what's not to like about perfectly cooked chunky slices of pink fillet of beef with a creamy horseradish or tartare sauce?

Add fresh salads, some good cheeses and patisserie, and you're there, though those who love cooking puddings can, of course, go to town.

You don't have to conjure up something different every time. We have friends, for instance, who always give us roast lamb on Sundays, others who always serve osso bucco (as it happens, one of my favourites, particularly when served with a classic risotto Milanese). There's quite a lot to be said for perfecting one dish and being known for it. I have an American friend who makes the best cheesecake I know and I'd feel cheated if I turned up at her house and it wasn't on offer.

For serving I find that antique china platters, picked up in antique shops and at antique fairs over the years, make the perfect background for cold dishes and salads.

SPICED NUTS

200g mixed shelled nuts of your choice (almonds, hazelnuts, cashews, pistachios, pecans, etc.)
1 tbsp chopped fresh rosemary (discarding the stalks)
¼ tsp cayenne
1½ tsps brown sugar
1 tsp salt
½ tsp walnut or olive oil

Preheat the oven to 160°C, 325°F, Gas Mark 3. Mix all the ingredients together and spread out on a baking sheet. Bake for 10 minutes. Remove from the oven, stir, turning them over, and return to the oven to bake for another 10 minutes. Cool on the tray. When cold, store in an airtight container for up to a week.

Christmas

Christmas, unless you're so organised that you've bought your presents in the January sales or in September and have them all wrapped by October, is stressful for most of us, but especially for those with jobs and precious little help. Some things can't be delegated – such as getting your secretary to buy your husband's Christmas present – but many can. Help is out there and it comes in varying packages – some very expensive, some surprisingly reasonable. Here's a guide to just some of what is available.

Presents

I don't think buying gifts should be handed over lock, stock and barrel to somebody else (who else would know that your husband hates a certain shade of blue, or that the son and heir already has everything Bob Dylan ever wrote), but advice and suggestions are always useful (the stores usually know what the hot children's toys are), whilst wrapping, packing and delivery can all be safely delegated. If you need more ideas on presents there are lots to be found in Chapter 7.

Stores are realising more and more that personal service is the key to buying the punters' loyalty and so personal shoppers are on the increase. Selfridges, for instance, has a team of gift gurus. You can simply turn up at the information desk and ask for one, pose your questions (what's the best laptop case, what's the hot handbag) and you'll be directed to the right department. For more personal advice, book into their personal shopping service. Free gift wrapping is available all through the store *but*, though very attractive, it will announce its Selfridges' origins.

At Peter Jones you can simply hand over a list, giving as vivid a thumbnail sketch of the lucky recipients as you can, and leave it all to them. They'll shop, wrap and deliver, but personally I'd be wary of delegating quite so much. Better to take half a day (if you can) to crack the problem and ask either for the help of a personal shopper or a scanner, so that you can go round zapping the things you want to buy (so that you don't have to pick them up and carry them). When you've finished, you simply hand in the list and Peter Jones will collect them up, wrap (for £3 extra per item) and deliver them all.

Stockings are supposed to be fun and they usually are but oh, the stress. I remember well sitting up until one or two in the morning, wrapping every single satsuma and paperback personally. These days Sarah Standing will do bespoke children's stockings to order as well as women's stockings (there's nothing yet for men), and deliver them for a charge. Telephone her on 020 7730 9333 and discuss what you'd like. The price depends on the contents.

If your time in the boardroom doesn't leave enough time for wrapping or store visiting, there's an array of the new breed of lifestyle or concierge services that will do it for you. The downside is that you have to pay a membership fee and whilst they can nearly always solve most problems, the price isn't cheap. The upside is that you can describe exactly what it is you're after and leave it to them to track it down. These services are particularly useful if you're desperate because the ten-year-old has to have this year's hot present and all the shops have sold out, or there'll be tears beside the tree if you haven't found the right Chloé blouse.

QUINTESSENTIALLY (www.quintessentially.com), for instance, has an annual membership fee of £750 but that gives you access to a whole host of services. It now has a special department called Quintessentially Gifts, with a small army of personal shoppers who will do the shopping for you – for a fee. The first hour is free but after that the charge is £30 an hour. It can also organise tree delivery and collection, as well as send somebody to dress the tree.

CONCIERGE LONDON (020 7736 2244) offer a similar range of services but the annual membership fee is high – £5,000 – and you need to be proposed. Once you're a member it will do almost anything – buying and decorating the tree, sorting the presents, booking travel, finding a cook – for a fee of £30 an hour.

WWW.CUSHIONTHEIMPACT.CO.UK (020 7704 6922) doesn't charge an annual fee at all but is adept at finding people who will do whatever it is that's required (one of its long-standing clients refers to cushiontheimpact as 'his wife without the sex'.) Want somebody to shop for presents? Fine, they'll sort it. Want to give your husband an iPod and fill it with his favourite music? No problem, they'll get somebody to load the lot. They'll do your Christmas cards, organise a dinner party for eight or ten people, order the food, whatever you need. You can buy blocks of hours and use them as you like. Five hours' worth of labour costs £135, ten hours £250.

CONSIDER IT DONE (020 8742 8718 and at www.consider-it-done.co.uk) charges £295 (plus VAT) a month for eight hours' worth of services. If you need more hours you can buy them on an ad hoc basis. So if you're pushed only at Christmas you could buy what it calls its Now and Again package for £325 (plus VAT), which entitles you to eight hours of labour – they'll order the turkey, decorate the house or the tree, send off the Christmas cards or search for presents. You choose.

GILL MCCAFFERTY OF JUST2BUSY (01372 467 251 and at www.just2busy.net) will shop for presents, then wrap, send or deliver them. She'll also buy the tree and decorate it for you, as well as the house. Labour is about £20 an hour. Surrey and South-West London area only.

RACHEL MEDDOWES, who is an interiors and design editor, has wonderful taste and ideas. She will come up with imaginative suggestions and do all the shopping, for £250 for half a day (07770 511 969).

Trees and Decorations

If you've young children and choosing your very own tree together from the market is part of the fun, good. If not, get it delivered. Choose a Nordmann non-drop pine tree if you don't want to clog up the vacuum cleaner.

THE BRITISH CHRISTMAS TREE GROWERS ASSOCIATION (0131 664 1100 and at www.bctga.co.uk). Their website lists suppliers of British Christmas trees all over the country, from Land's End to John O'Groats.

TREES DIRECT (01588 680 280) will deliver trees all over the country and for an extra charge will provide simple decorations in the shape of little bows and ornaments.

JO BOGGON (020 8749 3399) will deliver a tree, ready-decorated, in Central London for £50 a foot, with white lights, icicles, glass and frosted balls, and lots of ribbons. Many other good florists will do this for a fee.

SELFRIDGES usually has what it calls a ready-designed tree, which means a package of tastefully chosen decorations, and it will deliver the tree plus all the non-breakable baubles and decorations, which you then have to attach yourself. They range in prices from £150 to £500 for a large-sized tree.

JOANNA WOOD, 48A Pimlico Road, London (020 7730 5064 and at 020 7730 5064), will buy and dress the tree (choose traditional or modern), adding lights and presents. She'll dress the house, too – everything from fireplaces to swags. Prices start at £300.

WWW.PINESANDNEEDLES.COM will deliver your tree, install it and decorate it, but only, sadly, for those who live within the M25.

WWW.TENBURY-MISTLETOE.CO.UK will deliver boxes of mistletoe.

Christmas Food

The trick here is not to aim at perfection. Culinary pyrotechnics are not essential at Christmas and if you're a budding Tom Aikens you can leave the fancy cooking for another time. Order ahead the very best organic turkey (or baron of beef, goose, whatever your family fancies), ham and smoked salmon from companies such as Swaddles (www.swaddles.co.uk) or Inverawe (www.inverawe.co.uk), and then do the rest of it the easy way. Fine cheeses can be ordered from www.nealsyard dairy.co.uk and great cakes from wwww.megrivers.com, whilst if you want a lighter change from the standard plum pud you could try the Carved Angels' very own version of an Eliza Acton pudding (www.thecarvedangel.com). You can order everything online, if you can master the technology – remember that Ocado (www.ocado.com) is the busy woman's patron saint – or go to the best food store near you. Buy ready-prepared Brussels sprouts, potatoes ready to roast (unless you have your own patent recipe), ready-prepared roasted parsnips (Waitrose), white sauce, pudding, brandy butter and all the rest from the good stores (Marks & Spencer now has a policy of not including hydrogenated fats or using GM foods). Save your time and keep your nerves in good shape so that you can enjoy your family and friends. Add cream to the white sauce, a tad more brandy to the brandy butter, masses of herbs to the vegetables, sprinkle some nutmeg on the Brussels sprouts and toss them with caramelised canned chestnuts, and you're there.

If even the shopping is beyond you, www.banquet-in-a-box.co.uk (0800 197 9510) will deliver every single thing that makes up the traditional Christmas meal. (Stuffings, baby sausages, carrots, Brussels sprouts, potatoes, white sauce, brandy butter, crackers, goose fat, roasting tin and instruction sheet are all included, as well as, naturally, the star turns.) It has two packages: £395 for six to eight people, and £595 for enough for ten to twelve people.

And don't forget . . .

. . . the loo. When hosting parties, always have lovely soaps and good hand lotions available, as well as small piles of nice old-fashioned plain linen or huckaback hand towels.

Good Manners

Manners are an age-old condition of the civilized mind, in order to have a system of behaviour which prevents human contact from sliding into chaos and old night. The primitive peoples of Africa that I have known have wonderful manners and the most courteous and orderly forms of debate. One of the most significant things for me in Dante's great journey down into Hell and up into Heaven was that in Hell there was an absence of good manners; when he emerged and arrived in Purgatory he was amazed how grace and courtesy between the spirits he encountered were already present, and increased with a breathtaking and inspiring acceleration as he neared paradise.

A Walk with a White Bushman, Laurens van der Post

Good manners, in my book, real manners, the sort that are about an inner grace, have nothing to do with where you put the soup spoons or whether you say 'toilet' or 'loo'. Real manners are about considering other people. Certain formalities exist to smooth the path and give us guidelines, but at the end of the day the matter is very simple: well-mannered people are never rude to others, or hurtful, and never do anything that makes other people feel awkward or small.

I well remember being at a party when a male guest had inadvertently got the dress code wrong and turned up in a turtlenecked sweater when everybody else was in suits. He was welcomed in by his host and introduced all round. Some ten minutes later the host appeared – wearing a turtlenecked sweater. Now that's what I call real manners, where the host wanted immediately to make a guest feel at home.

Then I remember being at a lunch given by the mayor of Avignon. The first course consisted of lovely fat spears of white asparagus served with hollandaise sauce. I picked mine up in my fingers, but it wasn't until I'd eaten the first one that I looked around and saw that everybody else was eating them with a knife and fork. Scarlet with embarrassment, I turned to my host and explained that in England everybody eats asparagus with their fingers. My host had an immediate response. '*Tout le monde les mange avec la bouche* [Everyone eats them with their mouth]' was his sweet reply. *That is* what I call real manners.

So whilst saying 'please' and 'thank you' matter up to a point, true manners, really graceful behaviour, means never being unkind, and never doing or saying anything to make anybody else feel small. It involves putting others at ease at all times and considering their feelings.

I must say that I'm not much enamoured of what sometimes passes for manners in so-called sophisticated and socially elevated circles. I observe – regularly – at so-called smart parties the kind of rudenesses that an African in a rural village would be ashamed of. It isn't, in my view, decent behaviour to blank people to whom you have been introduced several times but who you deem to be somehow uninteresting or beneath you. No African in his traditional society would ever do this. Acknowledging the existence of another human is a critical form of showing respect – and kindness. Yet this happens every day at grand gatherings.

At dinner parties, if you're lucky enough to be invited to them and you accept, then it seems to me that you should sing for your supper, which includes taking an interest in your neighbour. I have sat through many a dinner party where I have taken a deep interest in the intricacies of my (male) neighbour's work/life/hobbies but have not had a single enquiry as to the nature of my own concerns, the implicit attitude being that they couldn't possibly be of such absorbing interest as his. I've never quite known how to deal with this but a friend, to whom it happened recently, listened dutifully for a long time, punctuated the monologue with suitable questions and finally, exasperated, turned to her neighbour and said: 'Since there is clearly not a single thing of interest that I can tell you about myself, I will bid you goodnight' – and with that she turned on her heel. I'm sure the neighbour to this day will not have the smallest clue as to why she behaved as she did.

I myself am rather guilty on the punctuality front but I mind about it, think it's rude and berate myself continually for not always being on time. Being late implies that the other person's time is of less value than your own. For meetings and in one's social life, I think it's important to turn up when you've said you would, most particularly when it's a formal dinner and precise numbers matter. Unless you really are ill, it's seriously bad manners to cancel on the day. Dinners in cities tend to start on the late side but arrive no more than twenty minutes after the time you were asked for and don't overstay your welcome.

I think how you dress matters when it comes to dinner and party invitations. OK, if you're very young and you're all gathering around for supper in somebody's flat, dress codes are entirely superfluous. Or rather, you'll know what they are and you'll probably have the right pair of jeans in your wardrobe as well as the au courant pair of trainers. You'll know exactly how *déshabillé* it is currently fashionable to be and how much glamming up is part of the scene. And anyway it's just as much a cause of embarrassment to over-dress – to turn up as if you're expecting a banquet when your friends had scrambled egg in mind – as to underdress.

Invitations these days usually specify some kind of sartorial code. It may vary from casual glamour (rather a bummer, that one) to black tie, white tie, informal or 'festive' (even more of a bummer). If you're stumped, it's best to be quite straightforward and simply ring up and ask. What is unforgivable, in my view, is for the hostess to so arrange things that all her guests turn up looking ridiculous (having been asked to dress 'gypsy' or 'decadent' or 'over the top') whilst she swans around, elegantly and minimally chic. I well remember being invited on a very small and privileged press trip and told to bring just jeans and casual wear, only to find my tall, slim and beautiful minder had packed a different glam outfit for every single evening. That is very poor manners in my view.

I think there's nothing better than a hand-written thank-you letter to follow up a dinner, lunch or opera invitation and the sooner you write it, the better. The longer you leave it, the more time it takes because you have to make it more fulsome, more eloquent and probably include a bunch of flowers to boot. I'm not much enamoured of thank-yous by email – a growing modern habit – unless it be for something like a casual girly lunch. I like taking small presents to dinner parties and bigger ones when you are asked to stay overnight, for weekends or holidays (see Chapter 7).

How to Deal with Some Modern Dilemmas

Q. You're on a low-GI (no starch, no sugar) or a wheat-free diet and you're invited round to a friend's house for dinner. Do you expect them to tailor their meal to your needs or just hope for the best?

A. If it's a diet for serious health reasons (allergies, cholesterol, diabetes), ring well in advance and explain. Women today understand these things. Otherwise eat your way round the plate as best you can. Do *not* ring up with peculiar requests an hour before dinner begins.

Q. You've just put away the pudding plates and are serving up the coffee when a couple of your guests start offering a line of cocaine. Can you ask them to stop?

A. Certainly. They're the ones breaching the rules.

Q. Most people hate smoking these days. A guest in your house lights up. Can you ask them not to smoke?

A. My own view is that tobacco isn't illegal (like cocaine) and if you've asked a smoker to your house, then you should grin and bear it. A host's duty is to make his guests' stay enjoyable and comfortable.

Q. We're getting married and we've got most of the things

we need for the house. Is it OK to ask wedding guests for money?

A. No, it's not. If you've got all you need, ask guests to make a contribution to charity. Otherwise ask for something that nobody ever has too much of – wine or books, to name but two.

Q. We often go out to dinner with other couples but, as I never drink, I feel we're always paying more than our share of the bill. Is there any way round this?

A. Only by dining alone. There's something indescribably small and mean about people splitting hairs over the cost of shared meals.

Q. Should a woman always pay her share of bills on a date?

A. If it's a first date and he's asked you out as well as chosen the restaurant/theatre/opera, I should let him pay. After that you can offer to pay your share. Once you're going steady you're presumably up for sharing bills. If you're richer than him, you should sometimes treat him entirely.

Q. Is it OK to send invitations out by email?

A. If it's an impromptu informal barbecue on a Sunday or a sudden invitation to a theatre, yes. If it's a proper party, no – send a stiffy some six weeks at least before the big event.

Q. I always get stuck at parties with the most boring man on the planet. How do I get rid of him politely?

A. You take him over to meet somebody else and introduce him, saying, 'I want to introduce you two to each other,' and then you move quickly away. If your or his glass is empty, you use that as an excuse to ask for a refill and quietly move over to another group while he fetches it. When he returns you're deep in conversation with somebody else.

Q. Is it OK to break off a relationship by email or text message?
A. You're seriously asking? No, no, no. It's cowardly, small and weaselly. Do it face to face.

Q. If a guest arriving for dinner brings a bottle, is it impolite not to serve it?
A. No. Guests understand that you've probably planned the wine beforehand and, anyway, one bottle isn't going to go far if you're having more than four people round.

Q. Is it ever all right to complain?
A. Of course. The key is to keep your voice beautifully soft and polite whilst you utter the killer complaint. Do not raise your voice, do not shout, just say in the most gracious tones, 'Please never treat me like that ever again.' Or whatever else it is you wish to complain about.

And Finally . . .

A Few Things I Wish I'd Known Long Ago

- I wish I'd known how wonderful it was to be twenty, thirty, forty . . .
- You can't please all of the people all of the time.
- Don't be too afraid of making an enemy – sometimes courage and honesty require it.
- Never take offence – only small people take offence.
- If it doesn't fit in the shop, it's not going to fit when you get it home.
- The things you worry about are almost never the things that happen.
- Never have anything to do with men who carry little purses.
- It's better to clean and tidy less and read more.
- Never go out with a man who doesn't make you laugh.
- You can't change most people. Don't expect them to give what they are unable to give.
- Don't do anything grudgingly. If you're going to do it, however much you hate it, you might as well do it well.

- Never be mean with tips. It always leaves one feeling lousy.
- You can't have too many sexy shoes.
- Sexiness is nothing to do with being size 8 or looking like Sienna Miller.
- It's never worth saving things for best. Use the things you love every day.
- It's always worth reading – and learning – poetry.
- A great haircut is worth any number of new dresses.
- Never buy anything because 'It's bound to come in useful.'
- Never buy anything that you don't love or that isn't absolutely right.

Acknowledgements

I would like to thank all those many editors on *The Sunday Times*, *Financial Times* and *The Times* who have encouraged me through the years, given me a platform, sent me off to weird and wonderful places and generally allowed me to have more fun than sometimes seemed decent. Also, huge thanks to Eleanor Birne and Nikki Barrow at John Murray, whose idea this book was in the first place.

The author and publisher would like to thank the estate of Elizabeth David for permission to reprint the orange soufflé recipe on page 358 from *A Book of Mediterranean Food*, Penguin Books, first published in 1950.

Index

Website addresses all omit the www. prefix